Captivating **Cappadocia:**

The Comprehensive Guidebook to the Heart of Turkey

By Duke Dillard

WWW.CAPTIVATINGCAPPADOCIA.COM

Updated Fall 2018

Published by: **Birds of a Feather Press**

Print ISBN: **978-1-944370-11-4**

First Print Edition: 2018

To Laurie Dillard

It is only appropriate that this travel guidebook be dedicated to the love of my life, my wife, the best travel companion possible. We have literally traveled around the world together, but more significantly we have traveled together through life in all its crazy ups and downs. In you God has truly given me more than I could have asked for or imagined.

I just wanted to marry a pretty woman. I had no idea what I was doing or what was needed for marriage. I said all the right things, but I was clueless. Thankfully God was looking out for me (probably due to my mom's prayers) and was abundantly generous. He gave me a beautiful woman who only grows more beautiful as time passes. But He did not stop there... You are also wise and loving, kind and caring, passionate and productive and disciplined; you pursue deep, intimate relationship, and you are constantly growing in grace. Your love for God challenges and inspires me.

Putting up with me and my immature selfishness for all these years while living in countless places around the world has been a herculean task which you have taken on with grace, perseverance, and even encouragement. You have stood with me when I did not deserve it and have not given up on us. I would not be nearly the man I am if not for you.

Parenting our seven children with you has been both our greatest joy and challenge. We are not perfect parents, but we are perfect for our kids. I thank God daily that I get to walk with you as we lead our babies.

Our life together has not been easy or boring. We have shed many tears and laughs. We brought our woundedness into our relationship and have caused more wounds still. Yet, we have been perfect for each other, and, as time goes, we are able to be healing balm for each other as God's grace works in us.

I write this on our 21st wedding anniversary. I would not trade these 21 years for anything in the world, and I eagerly look forward to many more.

This book has taken four years to write, and you have been beside me with encouragement the whole way. Thank you. I love you as much as I am capable of loving another person.

Duke Dillard, January 7, 2016

Table of Contents

FOREWORD xi

INTRODUCTION xiii

SECTION I: BEFORE YOU ARRIVE 1

CHAPTER 1: PLAN YOUR TRIP 3

CHAPTER 2: BEFORE YOU ARRIVE 5

CHAPTER 3: HOW DO I GET TO CAPPADOCIA? 9

CHAPTER 4: WHICH TOWN SHOULD WE STAY IN? 15

CHAPTER 5: CAPPADOCIA HOTELS 21

CHAPTER 6: CAMPING IN CAPPADOCIA 29

CHAPTER 7: CAPPADOCIA TOURS 35

CHAPTER 8: HOT AIR BALLOONING 51

CHAPTER 9: HOT AIR BALLOON RIDE QUESTIONS TO ASK BEFORE BOOKING 59

CHAPTER 10: ALL 25 HOT AIR BALLOON COMPANIES 65

CHAPTER 11: RECOMMENDED TRAVEL/TOUR AGENCIES 81

CHAPTER 12: WHAT TO DO AND SEE 83

SECTION II: ON THE GROUND IN CAPPADOCIA 101

CHAPTER 13: ON THE GROUND IN CAPPADOCIA INTRODUCTION 103

CHAPTER 14: CAPPADOCIA PUBLIC TRANSPORTATION GUIDE 105

CHAPTER 15: FEED ME! 107

CHAPTER 16: TURKISH FOOD & DRINKS 117

CHAPTER 17: SHOPPING 129

CHAPTER 18: IN CASE OF EMERGENCY 143

SECTION III: 1, 2, & 3 DAY ITINERARIES 145

CHAPTER 19: 1, 2, & 3 DAY ITINERARIES INTRODUCTION 147

CHAPTER 20: 24 HOUR PLAN 149

CHAPTER 21: TWO DAY PLAN 153

CHAPTER 22: THREE DAY PLAN 159

SECTION IV: CAPPADOCIA DETAILS **165**

CHAPTER 23: CAPPADOCIA DETAILS INTRODUCTION 167
CHAPTER 24: BRIEF HISTORY OF CAPPADOCIA 169
CHAPTER 25: GEOLOGY IN BRIEF 191
CHAPTER 26: 14 TOWNS IN CAPPADOCIA 193
CHAPTER 27: 40 RECOMMENDED BOOKS RELATED TO TURKEY 199
CHAPTER 28: MY FAVORITE CAPPADOCIA PHOTOGRAPHS 209
CHAPTER 29: HIKING CAPPADOCIA'S VALLEYS 221
CHAPTER 30: OFF THE BEATEN PATH 255
CHAPTER 31: MY EXPERIENCE AND A BRIEF HISTORY OF HOT AIR BALLOONING 269
CHAPTER 32: UNDERGROUND CITIES 273
CHAPTER 33: HORSEBACK RIDING TOUR OPTIONS 291
CHAPTER 34: JEEP SAFARI TOURS 297
CHAPTER 35: TURKISH NIGHT CULTURAL SHOW 301
CHAPTER 36: WHIRLING DERVISH SHOWS 303

SECTION V: APPENDICES **305**

CHAPTER 37: APPENDICES INTRODUCTION 307
APPENDIX 1: PRONUNCIATION GUIDE 309
APPENDIX 2: TURKISH LANGUAGE HELP 311
APPENDIX 3: PRICE LIST 313
APPENDIX 4: BOOK UPDATE WEBSITE 317
APPENDIX 5: CAPTIVATINGCAPPADOCIA.COM LOGO 319
APPENDIX 6: DISCOUNT OFFERS 321
APPENDIX 7: CAPPADOCIA MAPS 323

ACKNOWLEDGEMENTS 329
ABOUT THE AUTHOR 331
OTHER BOOKS BY DUKE DILLARD 333

FOREWORD

What do you hold in your hands?

This may seem like a strange question. You just bought a book, right? Wrong!

You just purchased the best time in Cappadocia that is possible for humans.

You get the following:

1. **TRAVEL GUIDE:** A complete guide to everything you need to know to plan your time in Cappadocia written by a foreigner who has lived here continuously since 2011.

2. **TRAVEL CONSULTANT:** Email me before your trip. I will answer questions that are not covered in the book as well as give advice/ details to help you make decisions about how to spend your time. I am happy to help with information for your trip at no extra charge. This alone is worth the price of the book.

3. **MONEY SAVING DISCOUNTS:** Many of the companies we recommend give discounts to people who have purchased the book. These more than pay for the book.

   Consider a hot air balloon ride. A 10% discount will save you up to $20. Add that to a hotel and restaurant discounts and this book could pay for itself many times over.

   Full Disclosure: I recommend only companies that I believe will serve you well. I receive nothing from these companies for including them in this book.

   > **NOTE**: To get the discount at the places listed in the book show them the Captivating Cappadocia LOGO at the back of the book.

4. **DONATION TO CHARITY:** We donate a percentage of the profits from this book to help the refugee crisis in Turkey and Europe. Each year we increase that percentage by one percent so in 2016 we gave 16%, in 2017 we gave 17%, in 2018 18% and so on.

5. **GUARANTEED SATISFACTION:** I was going to give a money back guarantee but realized it is too complicated since I'm not selling the book directly.

   However, if you are disappointed with the book and feel like you did not get your money's worth, please email me, explain the problem, and I will do my best to make it right. The same goes if you used one of the companies we recommend and did not have a good experience.

Here is my personal email: dukedillard@captivatingcappadocia.com

Go to Appendix 5 and Appendix 6 to learn more about the great discounts available through this book.

INTRODUCTION

Welcome to CaptivatingCappadocia.Com's No-Frills/ Discount/Everything-You-Need/All-Inclusive/Full-Service Cappadocia Travel Guide!

FIRST IMPRESSIONS

I first visited Cappadocia in 2009. We were living in Ankara and my dad visited Turkey for the first time. We booked a hotel, the Kismet Cave House in Göreme, at the recommendation of a friend and headed down for a couple of days. At the time I was driving a 1987 VW Minivan and was not sure if we would make it. On a side note, a great way to get your dad to help pay for a new car is to take him on a road trip in your 22-year-old clunker. Worked for me.

Back to our story... We went to the Open Air Museum, marveled at the fairy chimneys, visited a pottery shop, and tasted some wine. But the highlight of the trip was Faruk Keleş, the owner of the Kismet Hotel. Two years later when we decided to move to Cappadocia, I asked Faruk to help us find a home. We have been close friends ever since. In fact, when he visited America, he stayed with my in-laws.

PURPOSE

This experience encapsulates the purpose of CaptivatingCappadocia.com and this guide book. Cappadocia is unique in the world. But in the end the best memories come from a combination of amazing experiences and relational connections. If this guide book helps you to have a great time and connect with at least one Cappadocian, then we have done our job well.

All the major travel guide companies include Cappadocia in their books. Usually they hire someone to spend a couple of months in the area, check out the places they have listed in the past, include any new places, and generally maintain the status quo.

24/7/365

Our M.O. is a bit different. Actually, it is a lot different. We live here year-round and spend time every day in the places and with the residents that we introduce on our website and in this book. We eat at the restaurants and stay in the hotels and have personal relationships with the owners. The places listed are ones we think you will have the chance, if you wish, to meet someone that will make your time fuller, more memorable.

OUR PROMISE

Because we know these people personally, we do not like to write bad reviews. Perhaps you heard a phrase from your mother or a teacher when you were younger, "If you can't say anything nice, don't say anything at all." This is the approach we take in this guide. We only recommend hotels, restaurants, tour companies, and experiences that we know will serve you well. Our PROMISE to you is that if you have a bad experience at any of the places we recommend, let us know, and we will do our best to make it right.

There are hundreds of hotels and restaurants in Cappadocia. We cannot review all of them. Instead, we have chosen a few that cover the gamut of price points and tastes. If we do not mention a place, it does not mean that we do not like it. We just cannot make a promise about it. But any place we do review is one that we believe will please you and make your time in Cappadocia more memorable.

BOOK LAYOUT

In an attempt to best serve you, this book is laid out with your needs in mind. We have thought through the process of planning a trip to Cappadocia and have laid it out accordingly.

Section I covers the pre-trip steps including weather information, booking flights, buses, and hotels, tour information, information about hot air balloon rides, and recommended tour/travel agencies.

Section II puts you on the ground. We lay out the plethora of things to do and see in Cappadocia as well as give information about transportation within the region, restaurants and food, buying gifts and souvenirs, carpets, pottery, and tasting wine.

Section III goes a step further and helps you specifically plan your days. I break it down for you in a 1, 2, and 3 day itinerary.

Section IV gives you some basic details on the region including a brief history, geological tidbits, our favorite photographs, some recommended books to read while traveling in Turkey, and maps.

Section V includes 5 appendices offering Turkish pronunciation help, some helpful Turkish words and phrases, a Cappadocia price list for all the sights and activities, the website on which you can find any updates to this book in-between editions, and a list of the discount offers available to those who purchase this book.

HOW TO READ THIS GUIDE

You can read this book straight through, if you like, but most readers will want to jump around to the topics that interest them and the table of contents provides hyperlinks to make that easy (e-book). In the last part of the book we cover some of the extraneous topics that may or may not appeal to you as well as some of our favorite photos and books about Turkey that will complete your adventure.

ALMOST LAST NOTE

You may recognize much of the information from the blog; however, let me assure you that significant changes have been made. I did not simply copy, paste, publish. I went through each post and edited it to make it work for a book. In many sections I totally re-wrote the content. I also did the work of combing through all the information, organizing it, and putting it in one place. I hope you are pleased with the result.

RECOMMEND BUT DON'T GIVE

Warning: I am going to appeal to your integrity here. I spent literally thousands of hours and a lot of money writing this book. I am grateful that you purchased it. I have no doubt it will serve you well. I would appreciate it if you would recommend it to friends and let them purchase their own copy. With the discounts it pays for itself so they will not be losing money buying it, and it will help me to be able to continue to keep it updated. Thank you.

We are eager to make this the most helpful Cappadocia guidebook out there. If you have ideas, suggestions, critiques, or questions, please write me at dukedillard@captivatingcappadocia.com and even more importantly, please write a review on Amazon.

SECTION I:
BEFORE YOU ARRIVE

CHAPTER 1

PLAN YOUR TRIP

Cappadocia is an expansive region touching parts of 5 central Turkish provinces (Nevşehir, Aksaray, Kirşehir, Kayseri, and Niğde). You will not be able to see and do everything available which is probably part of the reason why you bought this book.

Well over 2 million people visit Cappadocia each year and each is unique. Some like package tours and some want to do their own thing. Some go full luxury and some spend as little as possible. Some want to hike and be in nature and some are happy to view the sights from comfortable car seats. Some want total control and some like to be blown about like a falling leaf. Some want to see everything and some are happy spending all their time in just a few places. Cappadocia has something for all of you.

I have tried to take this diversity into account in writing this book. You will have to be the judge. When it comes to planning your trip this guide should help you regardless of your preferences.

CHAPTER 2

BEFORE YOU ARRIVE

The purpose of this section is to help you make good decisions as you prepare to come to Cappadocia. The assumption is that you are early in the planning stages and have a lot of questions like the following…

* What is the weather like in Cappadocia? When is the best time of year to visit?
* How am I going to get to Cappadocia?
* How do I get from the airport to my hotel?
* Where am I going to stay?
* How do I see everything in Cappadocia? What tours are available?
* What do I need to know about Hot Air Balloon rides?
* Can you recommend any tour/travel agencies?

If any of these questions are on the tip of your tongue, then read on…

CAPPADOCIA WEATHER

Cappadocia weather is quite unpredictable, at least in regards to specific days. However, when observed from a distance, general patterns do emerge. Cappadocia experiences 4 distinct seasons, but from year to year they can vary considerably.

The following descriptions should help give you a picture for decision making, but you will need to be checking the weather reports immediately before your trip to know how to pack. Overall, I recommend layers when it comes to clothing since anytime of year can see a diversity of weather even within the same day.

Generally speaking Cappadocia's air is quite dry, even when it rains. By the next day you think that maybe the rain was a figment of your imagination. Expect to experience dry skin if that is your tendency.

WINTER

By late October the heat is on (coal in villages and natural gas in towns) and will continue often into April. The snow can fall as early as November but generally will not stick until late December. From there it can continue intermittently through April but will be rare after March 1.

Even without snow you should expect to wear a jacket starting in October and heavy coats from mid-November into March. The locals officially put there coal burning stoves away on May 1 so until then they expect that it may be cold enough to need heat, at least at night. This does not mean that every day is cold as there will be warm spells, but the temperature could still drop until that May date.

Also, for at least 2-3 weeks during this season the area can experience a dense fog that makes hot air ballooning difficult. In fact, during these months the most hot air balloon cancellations occur. Balloons still fly on most days (between 250-280 days per year), but be ready to be disappointed during these months. Be sure to book your balloon flight as early in your stay as possible so that you can reschedule if bad weather forces your flight to be cancelled.

Be aware that these months see far fewer tourists. This means that lines are shorter but also that some hotels and restaurants are closed and some valleys may be closed due to weather (snow, rain, mud). Also, the shorter days mean that less can be accomplished in a place in which the vast majority of sights and activities are outdoor.

SPRING

From May through late June and even into early July we expect spring weather which means warm days with cool nights. Rain is not uncommon. In my opinion this is the best time to visit as the trees are budding, life is stirring again, everything is available, and the temperatures are perfect for seeing all the attractions both indoor and outdoor. At the same time, the weather is still unpredictable and cancellations occur for the balloons.

SUMMER

Sometime in July the temps move into the officially hot range (40 celsius, 100+ fahrenheit) and stay that way for 2-4 weeks. For a couple of weeks even the nights are hot. By mid to late August this heat wave has passed, and everyone starts thinking of fall. During these two months it will rain once or twice at most. Longer days allow you to accomplish much more in less time even if you just want to relax and watch the grass grow.

FALL/AUTUMN

By mid-September fall has descended and again Cappadocia has entered the prime visiting time until mid to late October, and the year has come full circle. This is the time we sit on our balcony and marvel at how blessed we are to live here. Expect warm days and cool nights. Wear 3 layers.

DETAILED REPORTS OF PAST YEARS

On our website we track the weather each day and then at the end of each month we post the results. Click on the links below to see the weather details for past years. Of course, weather changes from one year to the next, but this should give you a good idea of what to expect for the month, if not for the actual days.

Here is the link:

www.captivatingcappadocia.com/monthly-cappadocia-weather-links/

CHAPTER 3

HOW DO I GET TO CAPPADOCIA?

If you are flying to Turkey, you will most likely not be able to fly directly to Cappadocia. I expect over 90% of flights to Turkey go through Istanbul. How you get to Turkey is beyond the scope of this book. But once you arrive you need to find a way to get to Cappadocia and this is where we can help.

You basically have three options to get to Cappadocia from Istanbul, Izmir, Ankara, or Antalya:

FROM ISTANBUL

Most people are coming to Cappadocia from Istanbul. If you are coming from Ankara, Izmir or Antalya, skip this section.

OPTION 1: FLY

At least 3 airlines currently fly from Istanbul to Cappadocia. The question you need to consider first is which airports to use?

Which Istanbul Airport?

Atatürk International Airport (IST) is on the European side of Istanbul while the smaller Sabiha Gökçen (SAW) is on the Asian side. They are a couple of hours apart with no easy way to transfer. This means that if you find a cheaper flight from one but need to get to the other, it will not be worth it.

Which Cappadocia Airport?

You have 2 airport options in Cappadocia. Kayseri Airport is about an hour away and Cappadocia (Nevşhir) Airport is a little closer (around 45 minutes depending on your destination).

Airlines

As in most countries the airlines differentiate themselves according to price and service. Turkish Airlines will usually be more expensive but offer better service. For instance, every Turkish Air flight includes a meal. The other three airlines would be considered budget airlines in every sense of the word. I have flown all of them and can say that you get what you pay for. Turkish Air owns Anadolu Jet. Prices change too often to quote them in a book so be sure to check each online.

Also, the airlines have shown a tendency to change regularly so be sure to double check the information below. Two other airlines operating in Turkey, Atlas Global and Onur Air, were flying to Kayseri but are not as of August 2018. Also, Sun Express flies direct from Izmir to Kayseri (round trip). They do have a Istanbul-Kayseri flight, but they do fly from Kayseri to/from multiple cities in Germany.

Airlines to/from Istanbul:

Turkish Airlines - www.turkishairlines.com/en-int/

Turkish Airlines (THY) only flies from Ataturk International Airport (IST). The flights to Kayseri go throughout the day (up to 7 flights in a day) whereas the flights to Nevşhir are only two to three times per day depending on the season. This is the ONLY airline with flights to Nevşhir.

Turkish Airlines does provide excellent service and serves a light meal on the 75 minute flight.

Pegasus Airlines - www.flypgs.com/en/

Pegasus flies out of Sabiha Gökçen (SAW) to Kayseri every day (up to 5 flights per day). They only allow one 15KG bag per person plus a carry-on.

Anadolu Jet - www.anadolujet.com/aj-en/

Anadolu also only flies from Sabiha Gökçen (SAW) to Kayseri. They have 2-3 flights per day.

AIRPORT TO HOTEL SHUTTLE - VERY IMPORTANT!!!

The shuttle should be around 30TL per person. You must arrange it before arriving because the shuttles only go according to reservations, not flights.

You have a couple of options for arranging the shuttle. The easiest way is to have your hotel set it up. Unfortunately, sometimes hotels try to take advantage of their guests by charging a much higher shuttle fee. If this happens to you, and you do not want to pay, you can make a reservation yourself at one of the following places:

Helios Transfer - Write them at info@heliostransfer.com

ATS Fly Transport - www.atsflytransport.com/

Argeus Travel Airport Shuttle - www.argeus.com/airport-transfers

Write one of these companies with your flight information and the number of people, and they should send you a confirmation.

OPTION 2: BUS

If money is an issue and time is not and you can sleep sitting on a bus, then Turkey's buses, some of the best in the world, are an attractive option. You do not have to travel by night but many people do so as not to lose an entire day of their trip. Expect to travel for 10-12 hours from Istanbul to Cappadocia. The bus stops in Nevşehir and you switch to a free shuttle that will take you to any of the towns.

You can be dropped off in whichever Cappadocia town you desire and then walk or taxi to your hotel. You can buy directly from the bus companies' sites (see below), but sometimes international English speakers get a little frustrated with the process. I recommend making a reservation on the bus company site (if you can figure it out) and then paying when you arrive for your bus trip.

Bus Companies

I have not made the trip from Istanbul by bus but have used these companies for other trips (to Ankara, Antalya, and Adana) and can happily recommend all of them.

Personally, I am not a big fan of buses, but these are as comfortable as any I have been on in the world. Four companies operate in Cappadocia.

Nevşehir Seyahat

> I have taken these buses a number of times going to Ankara and back and can vouch for their comfort. In my experience, each seat has a TV screen with a number of channels (all the shows are in Turkish) showing Turkish sitcoms and popular movies, including dubbed American movies.
>
> The buses generally leave Istanbul at 8:30pm and 9:00pm with a listed duration of 12 hours. The return trip also leaves at 8pm and 9pm. (Note: Times can change so check the websites to confirm times.)

Metro

> Metro goes from Istanbul at 8am (duration 11.5 hours), 9:15pm (11.5 hours), and 10pm (10 hours).

Süha

> Süha only has one bus a day going each way. From Istanbul their bus leaves at 8:30pm and takes 12 hours. The return trip leaves at 7pm.

Kamil Koç

> Kamil Koç is the newest line serving Cappadocia and has a 1pm and 10pm bus leaving Istanbul for Cappadocia.

There are too many rental companies to mention them individually. As of January 2019 most of the local companies will rent you a sedan for around 150-200TL per day (not including gas). The big chains (Avis, Hertz,...) will be more than that. Much depends on the season and what they think they can get from you (I will probably get in trouble for saying that). They should have a printed price list available from which you should be able to negotiate downwards.

Remember that everything in Turkey is based on relationship and act accordingly. Also, note that gasoline in Turkey is very expensive (close to the highest prices in the world) so try to get a slightly cheaper diesel and do not expect to get an automatic. Most of the cars in Turkey are manual.

Thus, in the end this is the most expensive option. At the same time it gives you the most freedom. Get a GPS and enjoy the trip through the Turkish countryside. Once you get out of Istanbul the traffic is light and the scenery is diverse and beautiful. On a side note, but an important one, after driving through Turkey many times, my family recommends OPET gas stations for bathroom stops.

OPTION 3: RENT A CAR

For a rental company in Cappadocia, I recommend Silk Road in Göreme or Enterprise in Ürgüp. Do not forget to mention CaptivatingCappadocia and get your 10% discount.

Here is their contact information:

Silk Road, Göreme

Office Telephone: 0384-271-2683 (from within Turkey; this is a landline number)

Cellphone: 0532-641-0629

Email: silkroad.scooters@hotmail.com

Enterprise Rent-a-Car

https://www.enterprise.co.uk/en/car-hire/locations/turkey/nevsehir-kapadokya-airport-lfds.html - be sure to put Urgup, TR for the location. Nevsehir Airport (NAV) is also available, but I know the guy in Urgup.

Urgup location: Huseyin Ivgen - Manager

+90 384 341 65 41

FROM ANKARA, IZMIR, ANTALYA, OR OTHER

The information is similar to what I wrote about Istanbul. If you have specific questions not answered here, please shoot me an email, and I will help you work out the details.

(dukedillard@captivatingcappadocia.com)

OPTION 1: FLY

IZMIR - Sun Express (http://www.sunexpress.com/en) offers a direct flight once per day from Izmir to Kayseri and back. Izmir is a 14 hour bus ride and flying through Istanbul adds another 4-5 hours to the trip so this is a great deal. Flights sell out fast so be sure to reserve in advance.

ANKARA - No company offers a direct flight from Ankara to Kayseri. Turkish Air and Anadolu Jet both go through Istanbul which makes it longer to fly than to take the 5 hour bus ride.

ANTALYA - This is another interesting quandary. A few days per week Pegasus offers a direct Kayseri - Antalya flight, but it only flies once per day. If it fits with your schedule, great. If not, you will have to go through Istanbul. This adds enough hours to the flight to make travel time almost as long as taking the 9 hour bus ride.

I flew to Antalya from Kayseri once, and there was a short delay so it took me 10 hours to get from door to door. I would have been better off taking the bus. The only issue is timing. If you have to leave at a certain time, then you may have to fly. In terms of budget, the bus is cheaper than flying. However, in the summer when tourism is high, Turkish Air has been known to offer a direct flight so be sure to check.

OPTION 2: BUS-see Istanbul section

I recommend taking the bus from Ankara and Antalya since it is cheaper and in many cases faster than flying (and just as comfortable if not more so). I would fly to Izmir since it is a direct flight unless money is very tight and time is not.

OPTION 3: RENT A CAR-see Istanbul section

Nothing to add from the Istanbul section above.

NOTE: If you are coming from other cities, then this information applies in regards to the companies to use. You can either write me or look at the company websites. At the time of this writing there is no other city in Turkey that has direct flights to Cappadocia.

CHAPTER 4

WHICH TOWN SHOULD WE STAY IN?

Before you can pick a hotel in Cappadocia (next section) you need to decide in which town you want to stay. Read the descriptions below and once you know, then go to the next section and pick the right hotel for you. (Towards the end of the book, I have included a more detailed section of the towns of Cappadocia that looks at what to see rather than focusing on whether to stay there or not.)

Many people do not understand that Cappadocia is a region, not a city. And although the region is quite vast touching 5 Turkish provinces, the central towns are mostly small and sit relatively close to each other.

We often get asked which town is best to stay in, but the answer can be different for each person. Thus, this section is written to help you answer the question for yourself.

Below I was going to list each Cappadocia town with some pros and cons. Then I realized that what is a pro for you may be a con for the next person. So, instead we are simply highlighting some features about each of 10 towns and letting you decide what will suit you best.

10 TOWNS (Listed alphabetically)

NOTE: See the Maps in Appendix 7 to locate each town in the region.

* Avanos	* Mustafapaş
* Çavuşn	* Ortahisar
* Göreme	* Uçhisar
* Guzelyurt/Ihlara	* Ürgüp
* Ibrahimpaş	* Nevşhir/Kayseri

NOTE: Recommended hotels are listed for each town. Details are given in the hotels section.

Do you prefer quiet or busy? Remote or center? Authentic or touristy? Walking or driving? Concrete or dirt? Few choices or many? Whatever your preference you will find it in one of these Cappadocia towns...

AVANOS (Pop: 14,000)

Features:

* Red River with jet boating and gondolas (not available in winter) as well as riverside cafes and parks
* Tens of pottery shops with masters allowing you to try making your own pot for free
* Best open air market (fresh fruits and vegetables and everything else under the sun) in Cappadocia every Friday
* Nice town square with lots of shops and restaurants and a good picture of local life
* No fairy chimneys and very few cave hotels
* Intercity Bus station
* Bus to Göreme/Nevşehir and Ürgüp every hour
* If I were staying in Avanos, I would want my own transportation, but it is possible to see Cappadocia using public transport and tours.
* Recommended hotels: Hikmet House (boutique), Double Tree (large), Duru (economy)

ÇAVUŞIN (Pop: <1000)

Features:

* Authentic Turkish village (although impacted by tourism)
* Oldest, biggest cave church in Cappadocia (but no paintings), and another beautifully restored cave church
* Relatively close to Paşabağ
* Nice fairy chimneys and cave hotels
* Smaller, not as many tourists, quieter than most of the other towns
* Touches Red/Rose Valleys making for wonderful hiking opportunities
* Public bus passes every hour for Avanos, Göreme, and Ürgüp
* If you like walking and are okay with the bus, then Çavuşin is a good option. Having your own transportation would be a bonus
* Restaurant selection is bare bones so you may need to go to another town some of your nights or eat at your hotel
* Recommended hotels: Azure Cave Suites

GÖREME (Pop: 3000)

Features:

* Most touristy town; generally quite busy with lots of hustle and bustle, especially for its size

* Amazing fairy chimneys throughout town
* Really nice carpet and gift shops
* Biggest selection of cave hotels at every price level
* Walking distance to a Pigeon, Red/Rose, Swords, Zemi, and Love Valleys and the Open Air Museum
* Great sunset and panoramic viewpoints
* Large selection of diverse restaurants
* Most of the scooter and ATV rental companies are based here as well as the horse ranches
* Does not feel as "Turkish" as some of the less touristy towns (maybe that is subjective)
* Listed by BudgetTravel and YahooTravel as one of the "World's 16 Most Picturesque Villages"
* Intercity Bus station
* Public bus towards Avanos and Ürgüp every hour and Uçhisar/Nevşehir every half hour.
* This is one of the few places in Cappadocia in which you can easily get by without your own transportation
* Very few large hotels which means very few, if any, large tour groups stay here
* Recommended hotels: Kismet Cave House, Kelebek Cave Hotel, Sultan Cave Suites, Aydinli Cave Hotel. Budget: Shoestring Cave Hotel, Nomad Cave Hotel, Rock Valley Pension

GUZELYURT/IHLARA (Pop: <1000)

Features:

* Good option if you are returning to Cappadocia and feel like you already have "done" the Avanos-Göreme-Ürgüp triangle.
* Much to see in this area that most tourists miss. This includes breathtaking valleys (Monstery and Ihlara), historical churches, and Gaziemir Underground City as well as Narligöl crater lake.
* Definitely need your own transportation to get to explore it well.
* Recommended hotels: Cappadocia Gelveri Cave Hotel

IBRAHIMPAŞA (Pop: <1000)

Features:

* Most authentic Turkish village in central Cappadocia; it is just a couple of clicks away but feels like another world
* Quiet

* Has almost no sense of being touristy, except for the very few hotels
* Many nice hikes from this location
* If you stay here, you will probably want to have a rental car unless you like taxis, tours, or really like to walk long distances
* Recommended hotels: Babayan Cave Evi

MUSTAFAPAŞA (Pop: 1500)

Features:

* Formerly a Greek town with much preserved (Former name: Sinasos)
* Less tourists stay here making it quieter but meaning there are only a few hotels and restaurants
* Unique historical buildings due to its Greek history
* 2 Cappadocia wineries based here and no lack of gift shops
* No fairy chimneys
* Probably need own or arranged transportation as it is 10 minutes (by car) from Ürgüp and at least 25 from Göreme
* Recommended hotels: Gul Konaklari- Sinasos

ORTAHISAR (Pop: 2000)

Features:

* Good mix of authentic local and tourist options
* Lots of good hiking originating from the town
* Great views from hisar (the rock fortress)
* A few restaurants and nice cave hotels
* Most of the tourists just visit by bus so evenings are more sparse
* Centrally located but probably need your own transportation; public transportation not as easily accessed
* Recommended hotels: Castle Inn, Hezen Cave Hotel

UÇHISAR (Pop: 3000)

Features:

* Incredible views
* On a clear day the hisar (rock fortress) gives the best view in Cappadocia
* Quiet
* Claims some of the nicest hotels in Cappadocia
* Borders Pigeon Valley meaning easy access to a nice hike
* Easy access to Göreme

* Quality carpet and souvenir shops
* A good although small selection of restaurants
* Relatively easy access to public transportation: every half hour to Göreme and Nevşehir, every hour to Avanos
* Recommended hotels: Taşkonaklar Cave Hotel, Argos in Cappadocia

ÜRGÜP (Pop: 20,000)

Features:

* Probably the most developed town (not city) in Cappadocia; usually busy
* The place to be if you want to sample different Cappadocia wines
* Large selection of hotels and restaurants including perhaps the nicest restaurants in the region
* Best town square with many unique shops
* Temenni Hill offers a nice, quiet place with a beautiful view
* Public transport to Göreme and Avanos every hour
* Helpful to have your own transportation or arranged transportation
* Recommended hotels: Kayakapi Premium Caves (ultra deluxe), Dinler Urgup (large), Selçuklu Evi (boutique)

NEVŞEHIR/KAYSERI (Pop: 100,000/1,000,000)

I have included these because they are technically in Cappadocia and have plenty to see even though relatively few tourists stay in them.

Nevşehir (population 100,000) has fascinating Ottoman historical buildings, but I do not think you need to stay there to see them.

Kayseri also has more to offer than most realize including beautiful Erciyes Volcano with its ski slopes. I would not encourage people to stay in these towns unless you have a specific interest in one of the sights and need to spend your whole time there. Otherwise, you can easily make a day trip. Kayseri has a population of over 1,000,000 and boasts some nice malls and even Starbucks, but neither Kayseri nor Nevşehir "feels" like Cappadocia.

DECISION TIME

As for me, I love living in Çavuşin, but when staying in a hotel and acting like a tourist, Uçhisar is my town of choice. I love the quiet, the view, and the access.

What about you?

Hopefully, with this information in hand you can scroll down or flip the page and choose a hotel that fits your preferences...

CHAPTER 5

CAPPADOCIA HOTELS

Hotels in Cappadocia are unique in the world. For many destinations you just want to see the sights. The hotel is nothing more than a bed. But in Cappadocia the boutique hotels are part of the attraction. This is why you want to pick your hotel with care. If this is your first visit, I recommend that you stay in a cave hotel. It is an interesting experience, definitely one you will not soon forget.

With so many hotels in Cappadocia, choosing one can be very difficult. I am not going to try to review every hotel. My guarantee to you is that I know the hotels I recommend. I know the owners, I have been in the hotel, and if you have any problems, just let me know, and I will do my best to make it right. None of these hotels give me anything for this recommendation, but some of them are giving you a DISCOUNT for buying this book.

Let me give you a little background on how things work in Cappadocia (and maybe everywhere?). The hotels make money by booking rooms but even more by booking tours, balloon rides, and other activities for their guests. Generally speaking, they do not charge more for these things than you would pay if you booked them directly and probably less than if you booked them through a travel/tour agent.

Through this book you can see the advertised prices for the different activities so you will know whether you are being overcharged. Booking the activities through your hotel is normal and legitimate and is probably the easiest way to do it as long as they do not try to take advantage of you.

And one more note about booking your rooms: whenever possible book directly with the hotel. This will usually get you the best price especially for locally-owned hotels. Going through a site like Booking.com or TripAdvisor can be helpful but will cost you. They offer a service, and they charge for it. The hotels pay them up to 30% for each room booked which means you pay more.

If you use one of those services to find your hotel, then it is fine to book a room through them. But if you choose a room from here or some other source, then I recommend going directly through the hotel's website. For this reason I have put the hotel websites with each hotel below. If you are reading this as an e-book, you can click on the hotel name or use the address given next to the name below.

NOTES ON PRICES: Most of the hotels have advertised prices, but since they offer lots of deals they asked me to not list specific prices. Instead I have put them into 4 categories as follows:

Budget = Under $25 per night
Reasonable = Between $25 and $75 per night
Comfortable = Between $75 and $200 per night
Luxury = Over $200 per night

(UNLESS OTHERWISE STATED EVERY HOTEL IN THIS SECTION WILL GIVE YOU A DISCOUNT OR SPECIAL GIFT IF YOU SHOW THEM YOU BOUGHT THIS BOOK. JUST SHOW THEM THE CAPTIVATING CAPPADOCIA LOGO AT THE FRONT OF THE BOOK.}

NOTE: See the Maps in Appendix 7 to locate each town in the region.

AVANOS HOTELS

Hikmet House
(www.hikmetshouse.com/)

Number Of Rooms: 5 (no caves)

Personal anecdote: *I have stayed here and greatly enjoyed it. The breakfast is delicious and it is a great place if you are seeking something more quiet and out of the center while still being close to everything.*

Amenities/Notes: Buffet breakfast, wifi, a bit off the beaten path on the backstreets of Avanos

Price Range: REASONABLE

Duru Hotel
(www.duruhotel.com/)

Number Of Rooms: 17 (no caves)

Personal anecdote: *We use this hotel for all of our tight-budgeted friends. It is comfortable, a great value, has a breathtaking view, and the family that owns/runs it are wonderful people. It is located on the hill overlooking the main square of Avanos.*

Amenities/Notes: This is a budget hotel so does not have a lot of extras but like all hotels, they do have free wifi. Their open buffet breakfast is delicious.

Price Range: BUDGET

ÇAVUŞIN HOTELS

Azure Cave Suites

(www.azurecavesuites.com/)

> **Personal anecdote:** *Azure is right up the hill from my house. I have eaten breakfast there and stop by every so often to have a chat with the owner, Ferhat. My wife and I stayed there and loved it. It is a definite Wow! experience. Most hotels try to meet your needs, but Azure tries to meet your wishes.*

Number Of Rooms: 14 rooms (all caves)

Amenities/Notes: Buffet breakfast, free wifi, free shuttle to Göreme, beautiful view

Price Range: COMFORTABLE - Instead of a discount you will receive a small gesture if you stay here and show that you bought the book. It is a bit of a mystery, but you will be happy with it.

GÖREME HOTELS

Kismet Cave House

(www.kismetcavehouse.com/)

> **Personal anecdote**: *Kismet is another favorite. The first time I stayed in Cappadocia in 2009 I stayed here and have been fast friends with Faruk, the owner, since those days. Faruk has traveled to Australia, New Zealand, and America and stayed with former guests who became friends, a common experience for his guests. There are nicer hotels in Cappadocia, but you won't find a better owner. If you are looking to see more than the sights, then Kismet is a good option.*

Number Of Rooms: 8 (4 caves)

Amenities/Notes: Be sure to make time for sitting in the entryway or office and drinking a cup of tea with Faruk. It may be the best time you spend in Cappadocia.

Price Range: COMFORTABLE

Kelebek Cave Hotel

(www.kelebekhotel.com/)

> **Personal anecdote:** *I have not stayed here, but it is perennially at the top of all traveler ratings and is a wonderful hotel by every standard. If I was visiting Cappadocia (and didn't live here), I would want to stay at Kelebek.*

Number Of Rooms: 45 (35 are caves)

Amenities/Notes: Organic breakfast served in a private valley if you wish, free wifi, swimming pool.

Price Range: COMFORTABLE **(No discount available)**

Sultan Cave Suites
(www.sultancavesuites.com/)

> **Personal anecdote:** *I have not stayed here, but it is owned by my friend, Mehmet Daşdeler, and I have visited with him at the hotel many times. The facilities are wonderful and the view is wonderful. A bonus is the hotel sits right next to Seten Anatolian Cuisine, also owned by Mehmet, which is one of the nicest restaurants in the region.*

Number Of Rooms: 30 (22 are cave)

Amenities/Notes: Buffet breakfast, free wifi, beautiful view

Price Range: COMFORTABLE **(No discount available)**

BUDGET OPTIONS IN GÖREME

These four places will make your wallet happy. Most have hostel type rooms in which you share a room with a bunch of strangers as well as private rooms. You get what you pay for and these are very inexpensive. Given these are already discount hotels, they will not give an extra discount for book owners.

* ***Nomad Cave Hotel*** (www.nomadcavehotel.com/)
* ***Rock Valley Pension*** (www.rockvalleycappadocia.com/)
* ***ShoeString Cave House*** (www.shoestringcave.com/en/index1.html

  NOTE: Shoestring renovated their rooms so their prices are a bit more, but they are still considered budget, especially for a couple.

GUZELYURT HOTELS

Cappadocia Gelveri Cave Hotel
(www.cappadociagelvericavehotel.com/en/index.php)

> **Personal anecdote:** *I have not actually stayed here. My favorite place in Guzelyurt closed. A good friend stayed here with his family and enjoyed it.*

Number Of Rooms: 35 (13 cave rooms)

Amenities/Notes: The rooftop terrace is perfectly situated for beautiful sunset views. The breakfast is decent, not amazing.

Price Range: ECONOMY **(No discount available)**

ORTAHISAR HOTELS

Hezen Cave Hotel
(www.hezenhotel.com/)

> **Personal anecdote:** *This is one of the first places I visited when we moved to Cappadocia. The view of the hisar and the extended valley region is gorgeous, and the rooms are exquisite.*

Number Of Rooms: 15

Amenities/Notes: They take good care of you here. You may want transportation if staying here.

Price Range: COMFORTABLE **(No discount available)**

UÇHISAR HOTELS

Taşkonaklar Boutique Cave Hotel
(www.taskonaklar.com/index.php)

> **Personal anecdote:** *This is my favorite place to stay when I am not at home. The owner is a friend and the hotel is top of the line. Their cave rooms are large and airy and the view of Pigeon Valley and Erciyes Mountain is breathtaking. Each room has an outdoor sitting area which is wonderful when the weather is nice.*

Number Of Rooms: 23 (6 caves and the rest are a mix of cave and stone)

Amenities/Notes: The open buffet breakfast is wonderful. They offer dinner as well which is nice after a day of touring, especially while sitting in their courtyard overlooking the valley.

Price Range: COMFORTABLE

ÜRGÜP HOTELS

Kayakapı Premium Caves
(www.kayakapi.com/)

> **Personal anecdote:** *I stayed here for my 20th wedding anniversary, and we had a great time. This is one of the nicest hotels in the world. They have taken a historical hillside in Ürgüp with ruined cave houses and konaks and transformed it into a hotel in which an Ottoman Sultan would feel at home.* The rooms are spacious and elegantly decorated yet still maintain a comfort and coziness that keeps you relaxed and not wanting to leave. *They have 7 categories of rooms so that they can accommodate many different visitors. If you can afford it, this will definitely put Cappadocia over the top as one of the most memorable vacations of your life.*

Number Of Rooms: 36 (35 caves)

Amenities/Notes: They serve perhaps the best breakfast in Cappadocia- Wow! The pool is great as is the hamam and fitness center. The restaurant serves the best steak I have ever eaten (they raise their own cattle) and there is a cafe and shops on site. The location provides a nice view but is a bit out of the way in terms of getting to the sights in Cappadocia. They provide a free shuttle into Ürgüp which is helpful but to get to Göreme you will need to take a taxi (or the public bus from Ürgüp).

Price Range: LUXURY (but their standard room is in the comfortable range)

Selçuklu Evi Cave Hotel
(www.selcukluevi.com/)

Personal anecdote: *I have not stayed here, but we wrote about it on CaptivatingCappadocia.com, and my partner stayed here with his family. He loved it. They have done a great job and have a great story.*

Number Of Rooms: 20

Amenities/Notes: Wonderful courtyard areas, beautiful views, great breakfast. It is like a little paradise garden tucked away in the town.

Price Range: COMFORTABLE

OTHER RECOMMENDATIONS

I do not have the same relationship with the following hotels, but I think they are special, and I just could not write a book on Cappadocia without mentioning them. So, I CANNOT guarantee you a discount at these places, but they are still worth a look-see if you do not find what you are looking for above.

Double Tree Hotel
(www.doubletree3.hilton.com/en/hotels/turkey/doubletree-by-hilton-hotel-avanos-cappadocia-NAVDTDI/index.html)

Personal anecdote: I have stayed here and often use their lobby as my office. This is easily the nicest big hotel in the region. The staff is friendly, the facility is comfortable, the view is beautiful, and it fits what you would expect from Hilton.

Cappadocia does not have many big chain hotels. The draw is the unique boutique cave hotels. This means that big hotels like Double

Tree serve mostly tour groups. However, if you feel claustrophobic in a cave or have a rewards program with Hilton, then the Double Tree is a good option. They are located outside of Avanos.

Amenities/Notes: They have a restaurant, hamam/spa, fitness center, and pool.

Price Range: COMFORTABLE

Argos
(www.argosincappadocia.com/EN/)

> **Personal anecdote:** *I have not stayed here but have toured it, and it is amazing. They have cave rooms with swimming pools in the room! The view is beautiful, the grounds are refined, the food is wonderful, and the rooms are luxurious. These people know what they are doing, and you realize it as soon as you arrive.*

Price Range: LUXURY

Gamirasu Cave Hotel
(www.gamirasu.com/)

I have not been here, but it is definitely one of the top few hotels in the region. It is way off the beaten path so be prepared to ride a bit to get to the main attractions.

Price Range: LUXURY

CHAPTER 6

CAMPING IN CAPPADOCIA

Each alternative provides a unique selling point so you will want to think about what is most important to you. Note that some of these are hotels as well as campgrounds and their websites do not always make that clear. I cover the following features for each camping option to help you make your decision.

PRICE

The price range is not large between the different locations, but other features vary considerably.

FACILITIES

A couple of places have grass (Ada & Green) while the rest are quite dusty.

SWIMMING POOL

All four have swimming pools but only one has water slides (Göreme). Most of them allow "outsiders" to use the pool for around 20TL per person per day.

INTERNET & LAUNDRY

They all provide free internet and all charge for laundry.

RESTAURANT & KITCHEN & MARKET

They all have a restaurant and provide kitchen facilities. Four have mini-markets on site.

ELECTRICITY HOOKUPS

Five of the six provide electricity but one (Kaya) is nicer than the rest.

SEASON & MANAGEMENT

All are family-run (no big corporations) and most are open year-round with reservations although camping in the winter (December-mid February) in Cappadocia is generally not going to be that fun unless you like the cold and rain/snow.

TENTS & RVs

All of them accept tents and RVs (Karavan in Turkish).

Turn the page to see the Campgrounds or go directly to the one you want.

Göreme Camping

(www.Göremecamping.com/)

TENT = 12TL/Person

RV = 5-6 Euro depending on different variables like size, # of people, and length of stay

LAUNDRY = 5kg load for 5 Euro

KITCHEN FACILITIES = free use with your own stove but if you use their stove it is 2 Euro per day

RESTAURANT & MARKET = prices vary depending on what you order/buy

INCLUDED = Pool, toilets, shower, electricity, internet

Opened in 1992 Göreme Camping offers Cappadocia visitors a unique experience with the only pool in the region that has two water slides.

The campground is located outside of Göreme, a few hundred meters off the road to the Open-Air Museum (first left after the Tourist Hotel). The facilities are clean and run by a wonderful local family.

FACILITIES

Both individual sites and open spaces for multiple tents are available. Plenty of trees but no grass.

SWIMMING POOL

25 meter pool with two water slides.

INTERNET & LAUNDRY

Internet is free and a 5kg washing machine is available but the guests cannot use it on their own. You give your dirty clothes to them and pay 5 Euro per load. They will return your washed clothes to you. (This is the case with every facility.)

RESTAURANT & KITCHEN & MARKET

They make basic dishes like grilled-cheese sandwiches (Turkish: Tost). The kitchen facilities are clean and adequate. To use their stove is 2 Euro per day. The market has basic items.

ELECTRICITY HOOKUPS

Each site has an electric box with at least two plugs.

SEASON & MANAGEMENT

They are open from March 1st to October 30 and the week around New Years. They live here so if you want to camp in February, just write them and make a reservation. They will open for you.

TENTS & RVs

Both are welcome.

CONTACT TELEPHONE #: +90 384 271 25 23

EMAIL: camping@Göremecamping.com

Kaya Camping

(No website but this site gives helpful information: www.eurocampings.co.uk/turkey/Nevşehir/ortahisar/kaya-camping-caravaning-101075/)

Outside of Göreme above Open Air Museum.

TENT/RV = 16.5 Euro for 2 people with 3.5 Euro per kid.

LAUNDRY = 10TL per load.

KITCHEN FACILITIES = free

RESTAURANT & MARKET = prices vary depending on what you order/buy

INCLUDED = Pool, toilets, shower, electricity, internet

Opened in 1978 this may be the nicest campground in terms of facilities and had the most guests when I visited. They are highly rated in most European camping club magazines and deserve it.

The only issue is no grass but the sites are nicely separated with plenty of shade and brand new electrical outlets sporting the new European plugs. The location is probably the farthest from stores and such, but their market is well stocked and the view is wonderful, overlooking the valley between Göreme and Çavuşin.

FACILITIES

As I said above these are probably the nicest facilities taken altogether. No grass but everything else is top of the line. The sites are clearly delineated with plenty of shade and the bathrooms and shower facilities are clean with the hot water always set at 80 degrees.

SWIMMING POOL

Nice swimming pool- probably the fourth largest.

INTERNET & LAUNDRY

Internet is free and laundry is 10TL per load.

RESTAURANT & KITCHEN & MARKET

Order what you wish from the cafe, use the kitchen facilities, and shop in the best market among the campgrounds.

ELECTRICITY HOOKUPS

State of the art including a plug for three-pronged European machines available in every site.

SEASON & MANAGEMENT

Open year-round and run by the same company that runs Kaya Balloons and at least one hotel in Ürgüp.

TENTS & RVs

All are welcome.

CONTACT TELEPHONE #: +90 384 343 3100

E-MAIL: kayacamping@gmail.com

Panorama Camping

(www.Göremepanoramacamping.com/)

TENT/RV = *see note*[1]

LAUNDRY = 5 Euro per load

KITCHEN FACILITIES = free use

RESTAURANT & MARKET = prices vary depending on what you order/buy

INCLUDED = Pool, toilets, shower, electricity, internet

Outside of Göreme off the road to Uçhisar

The Demerci family opened this campground in 1979 working hard to turn their land overlooking Göreme into the site with the nicest view among the different camping alternatives. The upkeep is a bit lacking but the facilities have clearly been well-used over the years.

FACILITIES

The sites are nicely separated with plenty of shade and a beautiful view but no grass.

SWIMMING POOL

The pool is small.

INTERNET & LAUNDRY

Internet is included and laundry is 5 Euro per load

RESTAURANT & KITCHEN & MARKET

Market has a few basic items, kitchen is available to use and restaurant will make what you order. The family also owns a cafe in Göreme which is a just a few minutes walk down the hill (this means the walk back up is quite strenuous).

ELECTRICITY HOOKUPS

Every site has electricity readily available.

SEASON & MANAGEMENT

They are open year-round.

TENTS & RVs

All are welcome.

Tent/RV Note[1] = They would not give me a price as they did not want something printed that would soon be out of date. I assume the price is similar to the other campgrounds.

CONTACT TELEPHONE #: +90 384 271 2352

EMAIL: panoramacamping@hotmail.com

Dilek Camping

(www.dilekcamping.com)

TENT/RV = *see note*[1]
LAUNDRY = Available but didn't give a price
KITCHEN FACILITIES = free use
RESTAURANT & = prices vary depending on what you order/buy
MARKET = None
INCLUDED = Pool, toilets, shower, electricity, internet

Located right outside of the center of Göreme on the road to the Open Air Museum. Stay in your own tent or RV/Caravan or choose a bungalow for more protection.

Enjoy a meal in their cafe, cook your own food, do your laundry, and even go for a swim if you so desire and take a hot shower. The grounds are a little run-down and there is no view like some of the other campgrounds have, but the location is central and the people are friendly.

FACILITIES

There is grass in some parts. Enough room for 60 tents. The sites are not well-defined so you can end up quite close to others.

SWIMMING POOL

The pool looks fun.

INTERNET & LAUNDRY

Internet is included and laundry is available for pay.

RESTAURANT & KITCHEN & MARKET

Kitchen is available to use and restaurant will make what you order.

ELECTRICITY HOOKUPS

Electricity is readily available but you may need an extension cord.

SEASON & MANAGEMENT

They are open year-round.

TENTS & RVs

All are welcome.

CONTACT TELEPHONE #: +90 384 271 2395

CELL PHONE: +90 543 693 0101

EMAIL: info@dilekcamping.comotels

CHAPTER 7

CAPPADOCIA TOURS

NOTE: See the Maps in Appendix 7 to better understand the tour routes.

I spent a week with my family in Antalya the first year after we moved to Turkey. The week consisted of going from our hotel room to breakfast to the pool to lunch to the beach to nap time to dinner to the hotel entertainment and then to bed. We repeated that for 6 days.

That schedule has NEVER happened in Cappadocia. As has been mentioned, this region touches 5 Turkish provinces and takes 2+ hours to drive from one end to the other in almost any direction. Visiting Cappadocia means getting out and seeing the sights, and enjoying different experiences each day, even each hour.

HOW TO DECIDE WHICH TOURS TO DO?

For this reason tours are very popular among visitors. But what do you want to include and which tours will allow you to see everything on your list in your allotted time? This section will guide you through the tour maze, but first you need to know your answer to two key questions.

2 QUESTIONS TO ANSWER BEFORE TOURING CAPPADOCIA

1. What is your budget, i.e. how much money are you willing to part with?
2. How much time do you have?

Do you have the answers in mind?

Great! Now you are ready to plan your time. Here are your options:

PACKAGED TOURS

The first and easiest option is a "packaged" Cappadocia tour. These are set group tours that last from around 9:30am until 5:30pm. The price is reasonable, the day is full, and you will be with around 10-15 people.

Lunch, an English speaking guide, and transportation are included. You can sign up through your hotel or any local travel agent. The two most popular are the Green and Red Tours. Other options include the Blue Tour or the

Undiscovered Cappadocia Tour which is similar to the Blue but offered only by Heritage Travel.

For most people this is the best value recommendation. The balance between money spent and sights seen is optimized on these tours, and they include most of the main attractions of the region.

CUSTOM/PRIVATE TOURS

For some of you, however, time, money, and preferences will conspire to move you away from the packaged tours and towards the private tour. Money is not an issue, none of the tours have the combination of sights you want to see, and you do not have time to do multiple tours.

For you this is the best option. You can arrange a car and driver through your hotel or local travel agent (guide is optional). Tell them what you want to see and that is what you will see; no more, no less. You will not have to spend time shopping if you do not want to (each packaged tour includes time shopping but no requirement to buy). You will not have to listen to questions from strangers in the group since you will be alone.

Start when you like and finish when you like. Have it your way! For this expect to spend up to 700-1000TL for 2 people for a day tour and then another 75-100TL per person above 2 people (assumes using a van and a guide and includes lunch and entrance fees).

DIY TOURS

And then there is the group that shops at Home Depot. You do not want somebody else telling you what to do or determining what is important to you. No. Rent a car, grab a map, pick your places, and head out. Getting lost will be part of the adventure. Maybe you will go to the first place, fall in love, and stay all day. No guilt that you made the driver sit there waiting for you.

If this is you, go for it. Tour Cappadocia your way. Renting an economy car should be no more than 150-200TL per day. Remember that gasoline is expensive (around 5TL per liter) and be sure to check on entrance fees when setting your budget (most are 25-30TL).

The best place to check entrance fees is the Turkish government's site.

SEASONS

With that said I probably should say a word about seasons. Winter (late November - end of March) is generally cold and often wet, sometimes with snow. You can expect it to be dark by 5pm. This means hiking is more of a slog, often clouds obscure beautiful views, and you have to move quickly to see everything before the sun sets.

In spring and fall do not be surprised by some rain and strong winds. Summer is hot and dry so plan on packing water. For a fuller view see the Weather Section of this book.

WHAT TO INCLUDE

This has been mentioned in the What to Do & See Section, but you will probably find it helpful for me to give a quick recap of the key attractions and activities to include. You definitely need to include an underground city, the Göreme Open Air Museum, and a valley hike when you tour Cappadocia.

Other popular attractions are the various panoramic views, the rock towers in Uçhisar and Ortahisar, Mustafapaşa (old Greek town), Çavuşin village, Pasabag's fairy chimneys.

If you are interested in local craftsmanship, then the winery, the pottery shops, and the carpet shops are good stops that include demonstrations. Honestly, there is so much to see in Cappadocia that you could spend days here and not see it all, but if you see some combination of these places, you will have done well.

GREEN TOUR

WHAT YOU NEED TO KNOW

* **Price**: 33 Euros (as of fall 2018)
* **Time**: 9:30 am – 6 pm (available every day, year-round although may vary in the winter depending on weather)
* **Attractions**: Derinkuyu Underground City, Ihlara Valley hike, Selime Monastery
* **Photo Opps**: Pigeon Valley Overlook, Göreme Panorama
* **Shopping**: Onyx Jewelry Factory, many tourist stalls at each stop (no obligation to buy anything anywhere)
* **Price includes**: Transportation, tour guide, lunch (drinks extra), entry fees
* **Price does not include**: Souvenirs, snacks, drinks at lunch
* **Hidden costs**: None unless you include lunch drinks as hidden
* **How to sign up**: Ask at your hotel or any local travel agency. The price

should be the same regardless. You can try to bargain if you like to. This tour generally does not sell out.

WHAT I LOVE MOST ABOUT THIS TOUR

Living here I did not need to go, but I wanted to know if I could recommend the Cappadocia Green Tour to people, so when a visiting friend wanted to go, I jumped at the chance. Often in tourism situations the system is set up to take advantage of the ignorant tourist. However, in this case, I am happy to report that everybody wins.

You could not do this tour on your own for the advertised price; the guide alone would cost more than the whole tour. The companies are not competing here. There is one Green Tour and everyone who signs up goes on that tour. Once they get 15 people they start another van. The tourist saves money and the companies make money: a real win-win.

MY EXPERIENCE

The 16-seat van picked us up at the hotel around 9:30. We went around Göreme, stopping at a few hotels to fill up the van. Finally the tour guide hopped on, and we set off close to 10am. Our tour guide was a year out of the tourism faculty of Nevşehir University. She was energetic and knowledgeable, but her English accent was sometimes difficult to understand, the result of learning English from non-native English speakers.

Regardless, I understood most of what she said. (I am not criticizing but rather critiquing. Her English was much better than my Turkish, and she shared much valuable information. My purpose is to prepare you for what you may encounter.)

Our group consisted of me and my British friend, two Asian-American women, six Koreans, a young couple from Australia, a Filipino photographer living in Dubai, and two other people whose country of origin I cannot remember.

15 was a good number in that we did not have to strain to hear the guide. At the same time we had the opportunity to meet a few new people from all over the world.

DERINKUYU UNDERGROUND CITY

The first stop was 35 minutes away in Derinkuyu where we descended into the underground city. Our guide took time in the van to explain some of the history of Cappadocia, asked everyone their names and countries of origin, and prepared us for what to expect in Derinkuyu.

She started at the ventilation shaft above ground and then took us into the climate controlled underground tunnels. Only 25% of the troglodytic city is open to the public and excavations are ongoing.

What we saw went 8 stories (100 meters) underground and included a winery, a baptismal, meeting rooms, a church, a well, a grave, and a kitchen, but no toilets. Hmmm? Historians guess that up to 2000 people could have lived in the city at one time. The stank must have been excruciating!

The guess is that it was used only during invasions to hide from enemies and only for a couple of months at a time. The structure dates back thousands of years. Apparently, the Hittites used the first two floors for their animals. Over time the different local inhabitants dug deeper and deeper.

They say that every house in the town has a basement that connects to the subterranean metropolis. The above ground invaders must have wondered if they had entered a ghost town or magical land with disappearing people! We wondered if we were going to encounter the Balrog around the next corner and kept listening for drums (forgive the LOTR reference).

Given that Cappadocian winters are quite harsh (this region was once called the "Land of Snow"), wood is scarce, and the temperature underground is steady throughout the year, I wonder if the locals used the underground areas in the winter as an easy way to stay warm?

IHLARA VALLEY HIKE

We had a few minutes to look around the tourist stands after returning to sunlight and then were off for the 30 minute ride to Ihlara Valley, a lush, green river canyon that is my family's favorite place in Cappadocia.

The valley is 14 km long, and we were dropped off at about the 3km point. After descending a couple of hundred stairs to the canyon floor, our guide showed us the Ağaçaltı cave church dating to the 4th century with paintings from the 10th century.

After that we freely followed the flat, winding path along the river surrounded by towering cliffs bejeweled with caves and echoing 1500 years of secrets.

3-4 kilometers later we stopped at a riverside restaurant for lunch which included soup, salad, and a choice between trout, chicken, vegetarian, or meatballs. Most of the dishes were baked/broiled except for the grilled chicken and Adana şiş. Drinks were extra (a can of juice cost 4TL and a half-liter bottle of water was 1TL). The food was very tasty after the hike.

SELIME MONASTERY

Back in the van and 15 minutes later we arrived at the base of a pockmarked cliff towering over an old Greek village and some freaky cone-shaped rocks. Little could we have suspected what awaited us.

We ascended the steep lower section of the mount past the first couple of fairy chimney formations from whence our guide gave us the general layout of the monastery before turning us loose for half an hour to explore.

The monastery dates from the 8th-10th centuries and included a missionary school, a living area, and at least one church. Across the valley the opposite cliff housed a twin female monastery.

For the brave there are footholds carved in the rock leading all the way up the cliff. We were forbidden from attempting this route and nobody tested fate. We did not need to as the available complex was awe-inspiring and kept us busy for the allotted time.

Clearly the different rooms were all covered and connected at one point but are now partially exposed due to erosion and falling rocks. The rooms are massive with carved second floors and balcony levels. Our group walked around with exclamations of "Wow!", "Amazing!", "Can you believe this?", and "How did they do this?" regularly flowing off our tongues. The 30 foot ceilings were hard to explain.

PIGEON VALLEY PHOTO OPP

After descending back to the parking lot we began the hour long drive to Pigeon Valley during which everyone enjoyed a bouncy nap.

We were given 10 minutes to take pictures of the valley and Uçhısar rock tower/castle, feed the pigeons, look at the evil eye tree, and shop for more of the souvenirs we had seen at every other stand along the way.

ONYX JEWELRY FACTORY & DEMONSTRATION

Our guide gathered us again, and we crossed the street to the Onyx jewelry factory. We began with a demonstration of carving a piece of white onyx on a lathe into the shape of an egg. Once it was done the craftsman gave it to one of our group as a gift. Afterwards we were free to tour the sales room and look at beautiful, overpriced jewelry.

GÖREME PANORAMA

10 minutes later we were at our last stop overlooking the town of Göreme. Honestly at this point everyone was ready to be done. The view is breathtaking

making it clear why Göreme is unique in the world and the most popular place for overnight accommodation in Cappadocia.

HOME & SUMMARY

Down the hill, and we were back in Göreme being dropped off at the hotel. I looked at my watch and it read 5:53pm. My friend and I agreed that the tour could not have gone better; it included the perfect number of attractions, we never felt rushed or bored, and by the end we were ready to be done.

RED TOUR

WHAT YOU NEED TO KNOW

* **Price**: 30 euros (as of fall 2018)
* **Duration**: 9:30am to 4-5pm
* **Attractions**: Göreme Open Air Museum, Çavuşin Old Cave Village, & Pasabag
* **Photo Opps**: Uçhisar Castle, Devrent Valley, Ürgüp 3 Beauties Fairy Chimneys
* **Shopping**: Avanos Pottery Shop (Includes demonstration)
* **Optional**: Carpet Shop (includes demonstration) or Winery tour (includes extra charge and tasting)
* **Price Includes**: Transportation, lunch, entrance fees, English-speaking guide, pickup and drop off at hotel
* **Price does not include**: Souvenirs, Snacks, Drinks at lunch
* **Hidden costs**: None
* **How to sign up**: Ask at your hotel or any local travel agency. The price should be the same regardless. You can try to bargain if you like to. This tour generally does not sell out.

MY EXPERIENCE

I did the tour in the spring, and we began at 9:30 after picking the rest of the group up at their hotels. The tour starting times are dependent on everyone returning from their hot air balloon flights. This means that Cappadocia tours will generally start between 9 and 9:30.

UÇHISAR CASTLE PHOTO OP

Our first stop was below the Uçhisar Castle. On the way our guide, Efe, introduced the tour and gave us key information to know in case we got lost or separated from the group.

After a brief introduction of the history surrounding the rock tower, we had 10-15 minutes to explore and take pictures.

Those who wanted to do some shopping had no lack of opportunities at the many shops lining the street. After the allotted time we met back at our van and headed to the...

GÖREME OPEN AIR MUSEUM

Again we followed the same pattern. Our guide told us about the history of the churches as well as the early Christian community in Cappadocia and then gave us an hour to explore the area (this was plenty of time for our group).

The Open Air Museum has changed since 2012. When I first arrived in Cappadocia, visitors could take pictures of the paintings and spend as much time as they wished in the cave churches. However, today, no photography is allowed inside the caves and, especially in the busy season, time limits are enforced.

On the day we were there the crowds were moderate, and I did not feel rushed. Another change is that guides are not allowed to give their spiels inside the churches so you will see groups standing in front of the entrances listening to their guides before entering, and in many cases the guides do not even accompany their groups through the complex but just give them all the needed time to roam and either listen to the rented audio tours or read the signs in front of each church.

DARK CHURCH: EXTRA FEE IS WORTH IT

The Dark Church has been renovated and carries an extra 8TL charge (not included in the tour cost). I recommend paying the extra amount. The paintings are stunning.

At the end of our hour, we gathered at the entrance and walked down to the expansive Buckle Church, which is the highlight if you did not see the Dark Church. Then it was back in the van and off to...

ÇAVUŞIN OLD CAVE VILLAGE

I waved to all my neighbors as we drove up to the old village and started climbing the hill. Efe gave us the background of the Greek-Turkish people swap of the 1920s. Until that time many Greeks inhabited Cappadocia including Çavuşin village.

In Çavuşin we entered a rare cave mosque which had formerly been a church. We also explored some old caves and climbed to the top of the hill to view Red Valley.

At that point we stopped to buy some fresh squeezed orange-pomegranate juice and ended up getting a tour of the seller's childhood cave home. She told us she would love to do repairs and move back. Seeing the cave rooms and hearing the stories about how they heated and made carpets was a real treat for our group.

Once we arrived back down the hill and got in the van, it was time for...

LUNCH

We went to a local Göreme restaurant, Ay Dede, and enjoyed a feast including humus, spiced yogurt, salsa, and potato croquette appetizers, Testi Kebab over rice, and then a semolina dessert. Everything was included in the tour price except drinks which were available for an extra charge. (Different groups go to different restaurants which is why I have not put more information about this place.)

Lunch was our first opportunity as a group to get acquainted, and I enjoyed learning about each member of our new community. I was fortunate to be with a small group, and we really enjoyed each other in all of our diversity.

This is a bonus of the package tours: an opportunity to spend a day with a diverse group of people. Our small pack included a retired Korean couple, and two just-out-of-medical-school American women, one of Egyptian and the other of Palestinian descent, traveling from New York city.

With full stomachs and a feeling a bit more bonded, we found our seats in the van, and got back on the road to an...

AVANOS POTTERY SHOP/DEMONSTRATION

Our guide gave us a bit of introduction to the history of pottery making in Avanos which apparently dates back 3000 years to the Hittites. This craft is maintained today, and we watched a pot being "thrown". Then one of the ladies from our group donned the potter's coveralls and tried her hand on the wheel. With a little help from the master, she was able to make a nice bowl.

With that done we were given some time to explore the shop and see their collection of items for sale. The prices were a bit steep for our group and with no bags in hand we got back in the van and went to our next stop.

PAŞABAĞ

Same song, next verse here. Our guide gave us an introduction to the area and then let us roam free for half an hour. Pasabag, translated General's Vineyard, has some of the best formed Fairy Chimneys in the whole region. And if you are getting bored you can ignore the chimneys and ride a camel (also available at Uçhisar and the Open Air Museum).

Not far down the road we were asked to use our imagination in...

DEVRENT (IMAGINATION) VALLEY

Camel Rock dominates this area but there are many other freaky looking rock formations just begging for someone to name them. Our guide pointed out Napoleon's hat, the turtle, the seals, the dancing couple and more. After a few minutes for taking pictures and exploring, we were back in the van and on the road towards Ürgüp.

3 BEAUTIES

We did not actually enter Ürgüp but went above it to the so-called symbol of Cappadocia, a family of fairy chimneys. This three generation set of formations majestically overlooks the valley but at this point of the day the sun is creating harsh shadows making picture taking difficult. We had a few minutes to look around and take pictures before finishing out trip.

OPTIONAL: CARPET SHOP OR WINERY

After leaving the three Beauties our guide gave us a choice of finishing the tour or seeing a carpet workshop. One couple was ready to be done so we took them back to their hotel. The rest of us wanted to see the carpet shop so we headed up to a shop in Uçhisar.

We were greeted and welcomed into a demonstration room in which the hostess explained the carpet making process while two Turkish women worked away on a loom. Next we observed the fascinating process for extracting silk from a silk worm cocoon. With that done we were ushered into a showroom and had countless handmade carpets and rugs spread out before us.

My co-tourists wisely left their credit cards at home fearing they would break the bank. However, they did find some pieces they liked and worked out how to have the carpets shipped to America. I happily watched but did not buy anything and felt no pressure to do so.

CONCLUSION

As the clock read 5pm, the two ladies were dropped off at their hotel, and I was taken back to my car.

Overall I had a good day and have no problem recommending the Cappadocia Red Tour. Personally, I like the Green Tour better. The sights on the Red Tour are all in this area making them easily accessible without needing a tour. At the same time having a guide adds a lot of information that is otherwise difficult to find and having transportation takes the hassle out of getting around.

BLUE OR UNDISCOVERED CAPPADOCIA TOUR

WHAT YOU NEED TO KNOW

* **Price**: 55 euros (credit card) or 45 euros (cash). [as of fall 2018]
* **Note**: This tour requires a minimum of four people so you will need to pay extra if nobody else signs up.
* **Duration**: 9:50am to 5:00pm
* **Attractions**: Mustafapaşa old Greek town, Keslik Monastery, Sobesos ancient Roman ruins, Soğanlı Valley hike, Derinkuyu Underground City
* **Photo Opps**: There are no stops just for photographs although there are many opportunities to take photographs at the main attractions.
* **Shopping**: None except for the souvenir stands near the main sites. This is a wonderful feature of Heritage's tours.
* **Price Includes**: Transportation, lunch, entrance fees, English-speaking guide, pickup and dropoff at hotel, water bottles in the van
* **Price does not include**: Souvenirs, snacks, drinks at lunch
* **Hidden costs**: None
* **How to sign up**: Through Heritage Travel. I expect your hotel can also make the arrangements for you.

MY EXPERIENCE

This may be the most aptly named tour in Cappadocia!

I have tried to go on the Blue Tour since shortly after arriving in Cappadocia in 2011 but found that it rarely happened. I talked to one guide who leads it, and he told me that he goes maybe 2-3 times per month, which explains why I had so much trouble.

Finally, I discovered that Heritage Travel offers their Undiscovered Cappadocia Tour almost daily, and it follows the same route as the Blue Tour without any "forced shopping" included. So, I signed up and spent a wonderful day with Serdar, the guide, and six tourists from China and Canada.

Most of the sites on this tour are rarely visited by tourists which gave us plenty of room and time at each stop. Some of the sites are unique to Cappadocia as well, making this perhaps my favorite tour offered.

Choosing this over the Green Tour is a difficult choice. They both go to Derinkuyu Underground City but the Green goes to Ihlara and Selime while this Undiscovered Tour goes to Soğanlı Valley, Sobesos Roman city, Mustafapaşa Greek town, and Keslik Monastery. Although I love Ihlara, I would now recommend this tour over the Green Tour.

But most local travel agents seem to prefer the Green Tour, and to do both tours is repetitive given that they both go to Derinkuyu. If I were in charge, things would be different.

If you want to do this tour, I recommend connecting with Heritage Travel and setting it up (your hotel can do this for you).

ON THE ROAD

The van left the Heritage offices in Göreme and picked up guests from their hotels at 9:45 am. I really enjoyed the slow pace of this tour. We started later, meaning nobody coming from a balloon ride would be rushed. Also, we had plenty of time at each stop, never feeling herded around.

Heritage charges more, but we made no stops at shops which meant spending a day with no pressure to buy anything.

Serdar, our tour guide from Ordu, spent the first part of the trip on the winding road to Mustafapaşa, describing the day and giving us a history lesson. Serdar studied to be a guide at university in Cesme on the Aegean Sea, and on a trip around Turkey he fell in love with Cappadocia. He worked as a freelance guide for a while but has been with Heritage for 3 years.

The 15 seat van, driven by Tayfun, was comfortable. We had plenty of room with only 7 guests on the tour. We were offered complementary bottles of water from the cooler up front.

Besides the water, the tour price includes transportation, the English-speaking guide (and his English was excellent), lunch (drinks are extra), and entrance fees to the different sites that required such.

MUSTAFAPAŞA

Serdar also gave us a geology lesson, finishing his talk as we entered Mustafapaşa at 10:15am. We exited the van at the top of the hill and walked down together to the center of the town, stopping once to look at Greek houses from the street. After a short, informative talk about the architecture of the town, we continued to the Constantine and Helen Church which is really the highlight of the visit.

Serdar gave us a bit of the backstory of the church which serves as a museum today since the Christians left town in 1923-24. Upon completing his spiel at 10:30am, Serdar gave us 20 minutes to walk around and take pictures. We had the option of paying a fee to enter the church, but none of us chose to as we understood that there was not much to see.

I walked around a bit before sitting down for a cup of tea with Serdar and Tayfun. The others in our group walked through the small town before heeding Serdar's advice and going to the bathroom since it was the last clean bathroom for a few stops.

At 10:50 we were back in the van and on the way to Keslik Monastery. Serdar explained more details about the people swap between the Turks (Muslims) and Greeks (Christians) after Turkey won its independence.

KESLIK MONASTERY

Around 11:05 we arrived at Keslik Monastery which dates to the 8th century. Serdar toured us through a few different caves, explaining the paintings of the Biblical stories and how the people probably lived. We saw the Archangel Michael Church from the 13th century, the dining hall/classroom, the winery, and St. Stephanos Church which dated from the 9th century. He finished the guided part around 11:30 and gave 20 minutes to wonder around and stop in the tea garden for a glass of Turkish black tea or apple tea of which we all partook.

SOBESOS

By 11:50 we were back in the van heading to the ancient Roman town of Sobesos. Serdar regaled us with more stories and history during the 10 minute ride and at noon we began walking through the ruins that date to the 4th century.

Apparently, by the 9th century the town was gone. The ruins are small but only 10% of the city has been uncovered. Due to a lack of funding no more digging is taking place. We were able to learn about the bath house, the agora, and a large meeting hall which became a church once Christianity took over. The perfect mosaics are unique in the region, highlighting why this tour is worth considering.

Serdar finished by 12:20 and gave us a few minutes to take pictures as we returned to the van. By 12:25 we were on the road to Soğanlı. Serdar let us rest and ponder what we had seen on this 30 minute ride. As we entered the area we passed some really cool cliffs full of caves and pigeon houses.

SOĞANLI VALLEY & LUNCH

At 10 minutes to one we watched the van drive away and began hiking through the valley towards the village. The trail dug into a steep hillside and passed a couple of very interesting cave churches, one of which is unique in Cappadocia having been sculpted on the outside as well as the inside.

You do not see this in Cappadocia and shows that it was done at a time when Christians did not fear being raided or persecuted. After passing these two churches we continued on across the hillside and down to lunch in the village, arriving by 1:20pm.

Sitting in the shade was quite nice after the sun-drenched hike, and we were treated to mezes (appetizers) of pide bread, butter, honey, salsa, cheese, and gözleme (Turkish quesadilla). As soon as we had enjoyed this for a while we were served a tomato, cucumber, onion salad and our entree.

For the main dish we were given a choice of beef guveç (cooked in a clay pot with peppers, tomatoes, and onions), chicken guveç, vegetable guveç or grilled meatballs all of which were served with bulgur wheat. I had the beef and it was tasty. Lastly, they brought fresh fruit which was a refreshing treat on a hot day.

At 2:20pm we were back in the van on the way to Derinkuyu Underground City. During the half hour ride Serdar gave us historical information on the underground cities starting with the Hittites. There are over 160 underground cities in Cappadocia but only a few are open to the public. Of them Derinkuyu is the largest.

DERINKUYU UNDERGROUND CITY

At 10 minutes to three we parked near the entrance to the underground city and made our way in. It was crowded so we spent a chunk of time waiting for other groups. However, we were not rushed and had plenty of time to see the vast caverns and learn about the history.

Without written documents, historians (and guides) can only make educated guesses about how these areas were used. The part of Derinkuyu that is open to the public goes 50 meters down (7 stories) with another 50 meters visible through airshafts and wells.

An hour later we were blinking rapidly, trying to get our eyes to adjust to the sunlight. Serdar gave us a few minutes to return to the van while avoiding the souvenir hawkers. Once back in the van the tour was done, and we were on the road back to Göreme and the Heritage office.

CONCLUSION

At 4:30 we exited the van for the last time (except for those who were taken back to their hotels). We sat in the shade and were offered a glass of local wine or fruit juice.

I said my goodbyes, hopped in my car, and headed home thinking this was maybe the best tour I had been on in Cappadocia.

CHAPTER 8

HOT AIR BALLOONING

Hot air ballooning is the most popular activity in Cappadocia. More people fly in balloons here than anywhere else in the world and for good reason. The landscape is unique and the conditions are perfect. Even the price, which seems expensive at first glance, is quite reasonable when compared with other hot air balloon rides around the world.

This may be the only reason you bought this book. With the discount on your flight, the cost of the book is more than covered.

In this section I will cover what you need to know to make the most of your hot-air balloon experience. I have broken it up into four sub-topics:

* **What to Expect**: A description of the experience giving you a good idea of what to bring with you and what will happen
* **Safety**: Is this a safe activity? Many people ask this question. I answer it in this section.
* **Questions to Answer Before Booking**: I walk you through the most important questions you need to answer when booking your flight. Answering these will eliminate surprises and set you up to maximize your experience.
* **Information on Each and Every Hot Air Balloon Company**: Which company should you choose? I'll give information on each company to help you decide.

Following you will find Companies that Give a Discount to You for Buying this Book. Just show them the LOGO.

* Royal Balloons (www.royalballoon.com/#)
* Turkiye Balloons (www.turkiyeballoons.com/)

There are 25 hot air balloon companies in Cappadocia. I have visited every one of them, spoken with their management and flown with a few of them.

I have chosen these 3 that I happily recommend. I get nothing for recommending them. You get a discount if you fly with them that will more than pay for this book. These are not the cheapest, but I have a good relationship with their management and am confident you will have a good experience with any of these five companies.

MAJOR CHANGE TO NOTE:

In 2018 17 of the 25 balloon companies formed a loose Cooperative. Eight companies remained independent. Below I separate them accordingly. As of fall 2018 the price for a one-hour flight is around 150-175 euros. The three companies above will give a discount with the purchase of this book.

With these changes I have decided not to list individual company's prices since they change regularly and offer special deals that I do not want you to miss because you were looking at a false price. You can expect that the vast majority of companies will have similar prices due to the new cooperative structure.

RESERVATIONS

One note on the timing of making reservations- Some seasons in Cappadocia are booked solid while others are slow. Regardless, I recommend booking your flight as soon as you know your dates. Be sure to book for the first possible morning you can so that if the weather is bad you will have a chance to book for the following mornings.

CHILDREN

Children under 6 are not allowed to fly. Children from 6-11 fly for half-price with most companies.

WHAT TO EXPECT ON YOUR FLIGHT

For most people a Cappadocia hot air balloon ride is a once-in-a-lifetime experience. For this reason everyone wants this opportunity to be as good as possible.

In this section I want to give you a notion of what to expect without spoiling anything. My assumption is that knowing what to expect will help you enjoy it more. If you prefer to be totally surprised, then I recommend you skip this section. I am just giving the bare-bones facts here.

If you want a more detailed description of my experience, I have included the story of my first flight along with a brief history of hot air ballooning towards the end of this book.

GET TO BED EARLY!

The goal is take off right before sunrise which provides for the best photo opportunities and gives the participants a glorious view of Cappadocia as the light slowly reveals more and more of the landscape. This means the van will be picking you up from the hotel around 5am depending on the time of year.

BREAKFAST

Some companies like Royal and Türkiye provide a full open buffet breakfast. For these companies you will be taken to their breakfast room where you can eat while you await the trip to the balloon.

Other companies provide a simple breakfast consisting of a roll and fruit with tea or coffee also served at the waiting area near their offices.

And still other companies take their guests straight to the balloon take-off point and serve them a simple breakfast (rolls and tea/coffee).

Once the time has come you will be taken to the take-off point. Ideally, you will get there a bit before the balloons are inflated so you can watch the process and snap a few photos in the near dark. In most cases a number of companies are inflating their balloons in the same vicinity increasing the excitement and carnival-like atmosphere.

Some companies have pre-set take off points but most of them vary the spots based on the wind. However, the vast majority of flights take off in the open areas between Göreme and Çavuşin and fly through those valleys towards Çavuşin and/or Love Valley. The main reason for this is that this area has the most fairy chimneys and open space for landing.

FLIGHT

Once your balloon is fully inflated and raring to go the crew will help you into the basket along with your fellow passengers. You want to get a space on the edge of the basket so you can see as much as possible. I recommend going on a flight with no more than 16 people; 12 is better.

The pilot will give you important safety instructions while continuing to shoot fiery blasts of gas into the envelope. Next thing you know you will be floating. One second you are on the ground, then you aren't.

The flames that fill the balloon with hot air can be quite hot (it is fire!) but nothing dangerous. Being bald I found it helpful to wear a hat. In the winter it is a weird mix of hot blasts and freezing cold air. Dress warmly as it is definitely colder at high altitudes.

In Cappadocia your flight will be an up and down adventure as your pilot takes you up high for a full view of the area and then will spend most of the flight going in and out of the different valleys. Once the sun fully rises the photo opportunities are severely diminished as the bright light washes out the colors.

The pilot determines the altitude and spin of the balloon but has no control over direction. However, pilots have a good idea of what the wind is doing at different altitudes. In Cappadocia the wind changes significantly in different areas and altitudes. I have seen balloons going one direction and then go a little higher or lower and start going the opposite direction.

On one of the flights I was on we were in the Red Valley area going toward Çavuşin. Our pilot took us up higher, and we suddenly shot left over to Love Valley. He clearly knew that would happen showing that though the pilots are at the mercy of the wind, they have a good grasp of wind conditions.

LANDING

Around the 50 minute mark (on one hour flights), the pilot, who had been communicating with the ground crew by two-way radio throughout the flight, started preparing for landing. He found a good spot, the crew arrived first, and they worked together to bring us down for a safe landing while we braced ourselves in the landing position.

On most flights the only way people get hurt is by not following the pilot's instructions during the landing. Instead of bracing themselves in the landing position, they try to take more pictures and end up getting hurt by the jolting experience (the landings are usually pretty gentle but can be jolting if the ground wind has picked up over the course of the flight).

Once on the ground you can expect to wait in the basket a bit. If everyone jumps out of the basket the balloon will take off again. The crew will secure the basket as the pilot lets the balloon deflate. When it is safe the crew will help you climb up and over the basket wall and back onto solid ground.

They throw together a makeshift ceremony and give you either a certificate or medal and a glass of some kind of celebratory drink in a champagne glass (it will be non-alcoholic).

BACK TO HOTEL

Take your last photos and then jump in the van for the trip back to your hotel. Depending on the season you will be back by 8:30am at the latest and can enjoy a second breakfast and prepare for the day's itinerary.

HOT AIR BALLOON SAFETY

Since people began flying hot air balloons in Cappadocia in the late 1990s there have been five crashes in which passengers died. Early on there was very little regulation and the companies took freedoms or risks they should not have taken. Usually everything was fine which encouraged more risk. With the amount of money to be made anyone could foresee changes coming. After the two accidents in 2013 and 2014, regulations were instituted making what was a safe experience even more safe.

ANALYSIS

Literally millions of people have taken a hot air balloon flight in Cappadocia and of those a handful have died from crashes. Let me be clear that one is too many. However, we live in a broken world and accidents happen.

Let's analyze the situation. A Cappadocia hot air balloon ride is in reality one of the safest activities you can do.

They had five crashes in which passengers died between 2009-2018 (for the 10+ years before that they had no fatal accidents but there were far less balloons in the sky). Being conservative we can say they average 50 flights a day (this is a very conservative estimate). Again a conservative estimate has them flying 250 days per year.

This means that in a 10 year span there were at least 125,000 flights. Of those there were five fatal crashes. I would say those are pretty good odds that your hot air balloon flight will be without major incident. Note, that sometimes people have been injured from rough landings, but that is usually due to the passengers not following the safety instructions.

How about in terms of number of people? Let us guess that the flights average 10 people (I expect it is much higher than this but I am trying to guess low). This means that between 2009 and 2018 at least 1,250,000 people flew and 7 died. Again, these are pretty good odds.

I have flown seven times and had great times on all my hot air balloon flights. My whole family has flown and felt perfectly safe the whole time. I mention this to make it clear that I feel secure enough to fly and let my children fly.

Also, I have personally spoken with leaders from every Cappadocia hot air balloon company, and they all stressed the importance of safety. They value human life, and they value the job they love. They do not want to risk their livelihood. They recognize how much mistakes hurt their business.

Even if they are acting in a totally selfish, greedy way, it is in their best interest to be safe. They lose much more from a crash than they gain from a risky flight. Plus, now that the aviation authority is in charge, they are not taking chances.

Does this mean no more crashes will happen? We all hope so, but realistically, we have to expect that they will. You are taking a risk when you fly in a hot air balloon. Granted it is a very low risk, much safer than many other things you do each day, but you are taking a chance.

PILOT TRAINING

To pilot a hot air balloon in Cappadocia you need two licenses. The first is the Private Pilot's License (PPL). To get this, one must take a three month class in which the first month is in a classroom and the second and third months involve time in a balloon.

After the three months the budding pilot has 6 months to fly 100 hours. These hours are done in small balloons (1-2 people) as I understand it. This gets the student a license to fly themselves, no passengers, thus the "private" in the title.

The next step is to get a Commercial Pilot's License (CPL). They have finished the 3 month class and the 100 hours. Next they take a 2 month course and complete another 100 hours in bigger balloons. Once they finish this second 100 hours they have to pass a test.

In total the process takes around 15 months and the pilot has flown well over 200 hours. At this point they can be hired by one of the hot air balloon companies. Generally companies will take on these neophytes and put them under another pilot in a mentoring system.

If you are uncomfortable flying with a new pilot, just tell the company, and they will make sure to put you with one of their more experienced pilots or you can pick a company that only has experienced pilots.

HELP YOURSELF - AVOID INJURIES

But even with the best pilots and the safest conditions, accidents still happen. The reality is that death is rare but injuries do happen on balloon flights. The vast majority of harm happens because the passengers do not listen to their pilot as I mentioned above.

If something is going to go wrong, it usually happens at the landing. The pilots give instructions for the landing position that each guest should assume when the time comes. However, some passengers decide they would rather take a picture of the landing which cannot be done from the landing position. Thus, when the balloon hits the ground they are standing up and get jostled about.

It is no surprise that these passengers get injured at times. The moral of the story is to obey your pilot and have a safe and wonderful flight.

NEW REGULATIONS

But if all of this is still not enough to convince you that ballooning in Cappadocia is a good bet, then maybe the new regulations will help. Following is an incomplete list of the regulations governing Cappadocia ballooning:

1. **Number of Balloons:** In the past every company could fly as many balloons as they could fill. No more is that the case. Never more than 100 hot air balloons can be in the air.
2. **Language Proficiency:** Pilots must be at an A2 level in English and Turkish. This is not a high level, but it will mean that some pilots have to improve their English.
3. **GPS:** Each balloon is now required to have the latest GPS devices on board.
4. **Wind Speed::** Balloons can only take off if the wind is below a designated "safe" maximum wind speed.

On top of this, the companies are required to do a Grab or Tear or Rip Test every 3 months. This involves checking the envelope (balloon material) to see if it is becoming brittle due to the heat. They also should replace the balloons after 1000 hours of use. In Cappadocia this translates to every 4-5 years.

CONCLUSION

First, I must say again that one person dying is too many. It is horrible. I am sure it was not worth the risk for those families who lost loved ones. They are surely still feeling pain and grief no matter how long it has been.

But with this said, only you know what you are willing to risk your life doing. Does a 1 in 170,000 chance work for you? Only you can say. I am okay with it. Clearly I am not alone as I see the sky full of hot air balloons every morning around my house. I think they are doing everything they can to ensure safety, but as I said, it is a decision each person has to make, and no judgment is put on those who decide to forego this luxury.

CHAPTER 9

HOT AIR BALLOON RIDE QUESTIONS TO ASK BEFORE BOOKING

1. Pilot: Experience? & Language? & Personality? This may be one of the most important factors affecting your floating adventure. Of course, experienced pilots demand higher salaries. One way companies save money is by using newer pilots.

Generally speaking, experience matters for Cappadocia balloon rides. In many areas of the world a balloon ride consists of reaching a high altitude and getting a wonderful panoramic view of the region. In Cappadocia, however, the heights should only make up a small portion of your flight. The best pilots will go high and then spend most of the ride dipping in and out of the canyons.

If you are an English speaker, is it important that your pilot speaks fluent English? All pilots have to speak English, but the required level is not high. The difference is a pilot who acts as a guide to what you are seeing versus someone who can give the basic instructions you will need to stay safe.

Of course, this affects answers to questions you may have, information about the area, and your general ability to connect relationally with your pilot. If this is important to you, ask about the English level of the pilot with whom you will be flying. You can ask which pilot speaks the best English (or whichever language) and request to fly with that pilot.

Also, if you are a people person, i.e. you like people, a gregarious pilot makes for a more enjoyable ride. I had two different experiences. On my first flight with Royal Balloons, chief pilot, Suat Ulusoy, regaled us with stories from his many years of experience and kept the mood calm and upbeat with helpful information about the area we were traversing on our flight. He then continued to entertain us while we were drinking champagne after landing.

On my second flight our pilot barely spoke the entire flight. And on my third flight with Istanbul Balloons the pilot was friendly and had excellent English but did not offer much information unless asked.

All three flights were enjoyable but the experience was different. Think about what you want and then ask for the appropriate pilot.

Related to this is the pilot's knowledge of the area. "How long has the pilot lived in Cappadocia?" is a question that may give a clue to this. Be sure to ask specifically about the pilot you will have as the different pilots in a company may be quite different.

2. Size of Basket? How many people you travel with impacts the price. My understanding is that the small baskets hold 8-12 people and the large baskets have a capacity of 16-20. You can imagine that standing in a corner of a basket with 3 people is better than being crowded next to 5. How much would you pay for this advantage? Is it worth 20-30 Euro? Only you can answer that for you.

The more expensive balloon companies ask you what a once-in-a-lifetime experience is worth. This is not a dinner at McDonald's. If you are only going to do this once, is it worth spending more to have the best experience possible? How much more? Again, only you know your budget and taste for adventure/comfort.

3. Length of Flight? 60 minutes or 90 minutes? The 90 minute flight is going to run you around 250 euros. Do you have to have the newest gadget? Do you only drive late-model cars? Are you competitive? Do you want to separate yourself from the masses? If the answer is yes, you will probably want to do the 90 minute flight.

I have only done 60 minute flights, but on my second flight we had to go farther afield to find a place to land and ended up being in the air for 90 minutes. The extra 30 minutes had a significant impact on the experience, but given my budget limitations, I would not have paid for it; i.e. it was not worth it to me, but it may be to you.

4. Navigation: High or Low? I mentioned this before, but it needs its own consideration. The more experienced pilots mix it up, but they will spend more time in the valleys giving great views of the fairy chimneys and rainbow-colored tufa hills.

As I watch balloons fly by our house every morning I notice that some stay high while others are going up and down. Ask the company what its practice is on this feature.

The reality is that most companies understand this reality and encourage their pilots to mix it up. You may want to ask this question just to see how they answer and try to read between the lines.

5. Breakfast? I flew with Royal Balloon and enjoyed a delicious full buffet Turkish breakfast in their comfortable headquarters before our flight. When I flew with Istanbul Balloons, on the other hand, we had a basic breakfast of tea or coffee and a breakfast roll in their waiting room.

Also my cousin flew a different company right after we moved to Cappadocia in 2011 and was offered breakfast rolls in a field while awaiting his flight. And yet another friend flew with a company that took their guests to a local restaurant for a buffet breakfast.

Is this important to you? How much is it worth? Asking these questions will give you an idea of how much the companies think their guests value these things.

Some say that a big breakfast that early in the morning right before getting on a balloon where bathrooms are not an option does not make sense. Others say that guests should have the option of choosing what they want for breakfast. Personally, I really enjoyed the big breakfast. You will have to decide what you prefer.

6. Take-off flexibility? The winds in Cappadocia change regularly. The different companies have more or less flexibility as to where they begin their flights depending on the size of their fleets (more balloons equals less flexibility). This may or may not affect your experience.

If the wind is "normal" (south to north) then take-off flexibility is not as important; but if, as is often the case, the wind direction changes, flexibility could mean seeing valleys and fairy chimneys versus plain open fields.

Most of the companies have a good bit of flexibility although some of the bigger ones are a bit limited. You can ask about this and see what they say. I have found that some companies use their flexibility to distance themselves from the other balloons in the area. You can ask about this as well. Often times you learn more from what they do not say then what they do say.

7. Transport Vans? All of the companies will pick you up and drop you off at your hotel. I have found that most of the companies use comfortable vans but only a few use "branded" vans; i.e., the company name is prominently shown on the van. Why is this important, you may ask?

It probably does not seem important until it is 5am and a few different vans show up at your hotel to pick up different people and you are not sure which is yours. That may be stress you do not want to deal with. I have heard of a few people who got in the wrong van and ended up at the wrong company. You do not want this to happen.

Another issue here to ask about is whether the van drivers speak English and whether they have a list of names of the people going with their company. This is rarely an issue but can give an added bit of comfort as the time for your flight approaches.

If this is important to you, ask about it. It is another feature that can affect the price.

8. Waiting area? Where will you wait for your balloon to be made ready in the morning? This is more important if you are here during the colder months. Most companies allow you to wait in their facilities and then transport you to the balloons right as they are ready.

Other companies will take you to the balloon, and you will wait there while they are filling it with the hot-air. You may enjoy watching the whole experience of filling the balloons or you may prefer a more comfortable waiting experience. Again, only you know you.

9. Balloon material: Nylon, Hyperlast, Silver-Coated Hyperlast? This is an invisible feature that most likely will not be important for your flight. Which material a balloon is made of has no bearing on the ride. However, if there is a problem, the stronger material is less likely to tear. A company that spends more for better material will most likely charge more for your flight. Is the latest, safest technology important to you? If so, you should ask about this.

The companies are supposed to carry out regular "grab tests" on their balloons. They all say they do, but you may feel better asking about it to show that safety is important to you. They all should also have the latest GPS technology. Also, how often do they replace their balloons? They should say no more than 1000 hours. All of these things cost money which means the price is affected.

10. Insurance? This is a hard one to gauge because you cannot know if insurance is necessary until something happens and 99.99% of the time nothing happens. Regardless, it is worth checking to see what insurance the company has. If this concerns you, ask them what happens if an accident occurs.

Of course, this does not have to mean a fatal crash. What happens if you get hurt climbing out of the balloon or if the transport van crashes on the way to or from the balloon? If they are wary of answering your questions, you may want to choose another company. This is another factor in the price of your hot-air balloon ride. Insurance is not cheap.

If your flight is cheap, this may be an area in which the company is skimping. What is your personality type? Are you a regular in Las Vegas? If so, no worries here.

11. How do they get their customers? There are four ways to get customers: travel agents, direct phone/internet, hotels, and tour guides. How they get their customers determines a lot about how they view their guests. The reality is that most people do not even know with which company they are flying until they arrive at the balloon. The choice was made for them. The real customer for the balloon company is the middleman.

Of course, if the passengers are not happy, they will complain to the middleman and that company will change if they get enough complaints. However, the companies that get a big chunk of their guests through direct reservations (this is most of my readers) will be more sensitive to the opinions of their passengers. By asking and finding an answer to the question of how they get reservations, you will learn a lot about how the company targets their business.

Let me say that all the companies want their passengers to have a good experience. I am just pointing out that some companies are focused on individuals and some are not.

Also, within this, your hotel will be willing to make a reservation with any company you choose. They usually have a company they prefer, but, if you give a certain company, they will honor your wishes. This generally does not change the price for you.

12. Unique Selling Proposition? Ask what sets the company apart from all the other companies. I asked this to each company and was surprised to hear their answers. Some of them have a clear vision and are able to articulate it well. Others do not.

Beware of companies that answer this question by disparaging the other companies. I found that companies sometimes do this but rarely were they telling the truth about other companies. I am not saying they were lying but that the information they gave was usually not correct.

For example, they would say how their pilots spoke English but the other companies' pilots did not. This is not true. When I say they were not lying, I mean that I think they thought they were telling the truth, but they just did not know.

Each one of these features costs something. The high-quality companies charge more because they have spent more on each of these features. Maybe that is important to you, maybe not. But now you can make an informed decision.

CHAPTER 10

ALL 25 HOT AIR BALLOON COMPANIES

How do you choose between the 25 Cappadocia hot air balloon companies?

For most people the choice is made for them. Either their travel agent, hotel, or tour guide sets it up. However, a good percentage of travelers still decide for themselves, and you are probably one of them.

I personally visited and interviewed every company. I asked them the 12 questions I recommend that you ask. Below I have given the answers.

12 QUESTIONS?

One way to make this fair was to ask each Cappadocia hot air balloon company the same questions. I printed out the questions and took them to each office. Everyone was happy to talk with me. Each company is clearly proud of what it does and very concerned about safety.

Some of the questions were impossible to verify and each company gave the same answer. For example, everyone says they have insurance. I have no reason to doubt them. Also, they all have varying degrees of flexibility as to where they can take off depending on the wind. And they all understand the importance of being able to navigate up and down, in and out of Cappadocia's wonderful valleys.

The other questions I asked were the following:

* When did they open?
* How many slots do they have and what size baskets[2]?
* How long are the flights and what is the advertised price[3] (some companies will negotiate if you call)?

[2] Slot? and Basket size? There are 2 flights or "slots" each morning. The first is at sunrise and the second is an hour later. The maximum is 100 balloons in the air so the companies have been given a certain number of "slots" they can use. The numbers given represent the number of balloons they get for the first and second slot respectively.Smaller basket capacity means more room and a better viewing position for each passenger.

[3] Length of flight and price? The companies cannot guarantee the length. 60 minutes usually means between 50 and 70 minutes. I have been a number of times, and we always went over the time. Also, the quoted price may not be up to date as the companies do not inform me when they change their prices. You will need to check with their website to verify the price. And most of the companies offer a cash discount.

* Do they serve basic[4] breakfast or open buffet[5] and where do their guests wait before flying?
* How many pilots and how much experience do they have as well as what languages do they speak?
* Are their guest transport vans branded[6]?
* What are their balloons made[6] of?

With the answers to these questions you should be able to get a good picture of what a company offers as well as how it differs from its competitors.

What this cannot capture is the personal touch that each company brings to the table. For that you will need to call and talk to someone or, even better, go by and meet the people at your company of choice. They will be happy to answer your questions and reserve a place for you on whichever day you are visiting.

[4] Breakfast? Some say a simple breakfast is better since the balloons have no bathroom. I have done it twice with companies that offered open buffet breakfast and everyone ate and nobody had problems in the balloon. Personally I preferred the bigger breakfast but I know not everyone does. You will be done in time to still enjoy your hotel breakfast. Also, some of the companies offer breakfast in their own places and some serve it at the take-off point. They say guests want to see the whole process. I personally like being in a breakfast room and going to watch the last part of the inflation process. If you want to see more of the process, you should choose a company who serves breakfast near the balloon. Be aware of the morning temperatures when you are making this decision.

[5] Open Buffet breakfast consists of a variety of hot drinks and juice as well as eggs, rolls/bread, meat, cereal, and fruit.

[6] Branded vans? This helps when a few vans show up to your hotel and you are trying to figure out which one is yours. I have heard of people getting in the wrong van. Make sure you know which company you are going with.

[6] Balloon envelope material? Different balloon manufacturers have different names for similar materials. In this post I have used the name Hyperlast to refer to a strong, safe, coated nylon material that most of the balloon companies use. Cameron calls it Hyperlast, Lindstrand calls it Hyperlife, Ultramagic goes with Ultralast, and Kubicek uses a polyester-based fabric that is different from Hyperlast but they claim just as good, if not better. I have no idea how to verify their claims except to say that they are not rated as high as the other companies among those with whom I spoke.

CAPPADOCIA HOT AIR BALLOON COMPANY DESCRIPTIONS

INDEPENDENT COMPANIES:

- Air Kapadokya
- Assiana Balloons
- Atlas Balloons
- Butterfly Balloons
- Royal Balloons
- THK Balloons
- Urgup Balloons
- Voyager Balloons

COOPERATIVE COMPANIES

- Anatolian Balloons
- Atmosfer Balloons
- Balloon Turca
- Cihangiroglu Balloons
- Comfort Balloons
- Deluxe Balloons
- Discovery Balloons
- EZ Air Balloons
- Goreme Balloons
- Istanbul Balloons
- Kapadokya Balloons
- Kapadokya Kaya Balloons
- Rainbow Balloons
- Skyway Balloons
- Sultan Balloons
- Turkiye Balloons
- Universal Balloons

AIR KAPADOKYA (www.airkapadokya.com)

WHEN DID THEY OPEN?	2012 but began flying in 2013
HOW MANY SLOTS?	3/2
WHAT SIZE BASKETS?	4, 12, 18, 20, 24 passengers
HOW MANY PILOTS?	5
PILOT EXPERIENCE?	Between 500-3000 hours
FLIGHT LENGHTS OFFERED?	60 minute, 90 minute (4 people)
PILOT LANGUAGES?	Turkish, English
TYPE OF BREAKFAST	Basic
WAITING AREA BEFORE FLIGHT	In the breakfast hall in their main offices in Göreme
BRANDED GUEST TRANSPORT?	No
BALLOON MAKER/MATERIAL	Hyperlast by Cameron, Ultra Magic, & Lindstand

* Air Kapadokya's guests mostly come from tour groups.
* Office in Göreme
* Contact Information: Email - info@airkapadokya.com
* Telephone - +90 384 271 31 66
* Website: http://www.airkapadokya.com

ANATOLIAN BALLOONS (www.anatolianballoons.com)

WHEN DID THEY OPEN?	2006
HOW MANY SLOTS?	5/2
WHAT SIZE BASKETS?	2, 12, 20 passengers
HOW MANY PILOTS?	7
PILOT EXPERIENCE?	Minimum 5 years
FLIGHT LENGHTS OFFERED?	60 minute (standard & comfort), 90 minute
PILOT LANGUAGES?	Turkish, English, Russian
TYPE OF BREAKFAST	Basic
WAITING AREA BEFORE FLIGHT	Tourist Hotel in Göreme
BRANDED GUEST TRANSPORT?	Yes
BALLOON MAKER/MATERIAL	Hyperlast from Lindstrand and Ultra Magic

* 80% of Anatolian Balloons' guests are from tour groups. They are owned by the same company as Discovery Balloons.
* Office outside of Göreme (on the road to Uçhisar)
* Contact Information: Email - info@anatolianballoons.com
* Telephone - +90 384 271 23 00, +90 533 739 44 44

ASSIANA BALLOONS (www.assianaballoons.com)

WHEN DID THEY OPEN?	2012
HOW MANY SLOTS?	3/1
WHAT SIZE BASKETS?	18, 20 passengers
HOW MANY PILOTS?	5
PILOT EXPERIENCE?	From 3 to many years
FLIGHT LENGHTS OFFERED?	40-50 minutes (short), 50-60 minutes (standard), special 2 person flight
PILOT LANGUAGES?	English, Arabic, Turkish
TYPE OF BREAKFAST	Basic
WAITING AREA BEFORE FLIGHT	Take-off point
BRANDED GUEST TRANSPORT?	No
BALLOON MAKER/MATERIAL	Hyperlast made by Cameron & Kubicek

* Assiana Balloons was formerly Mavi Ay Balloons but changed the name when ownership changed in 2012. It is owned by the same family that owns Perissia Hotel in Urgup. Most of their customers come from hotel and tour guide recommendations.
* Office in Ürgüp (Perissia Hotel)
* Contact Information: Email - info@assianaballoons.com
* Telephone - +90 549 650 4950, +90 384 341 2560

ATLAS BALLOONS (www.atlasbalon.com)

WHEN DID THEY OPEN?	2012
HOW MANY SLOTS?	2/1
WHAT SIZE BASKETS?	2, 6, 16, 20, 24 passengers
HOW MANY PILOTS?	2
PILOT EXPERIENCE?	Between 1000+ hours
FLIGHT LENGHTS OFFERED?	60 minutes
PILOT LANGUAGES?	English, Turkish
TYPE OF BREAKFAST	Basic
WAITING AREA BEFORE FLIGHT	At the Voyager Balloons office outside Avanos
BRANDED GUEST TRANSPORT?	No
BALLOON MAKER/MATERIAL	Hyperlast by Cameron and Ultra Magic

* Most of their customers come through agencies.
* Office in Avanos. They are now owned by the same people who own Voyager Balloons so offices in same place.
* Contact Information: Email - info@atlasbalon.com
* Telephone - +90 532 347 1514

ATMOSFER BALLOONS (www.atmosferballoons.com)

WHEN DID THEY OPEN?	2009
HOW MANY SLOTS?	7/3
WHAT SIZE BASKETS?	12, 20 passengers
HOW MANY PILOTS?	1
PILOT EXPERIENCE?	Average 5 years
FLIGHT LENGHTS OFFERED?	60 minute, 90 minute (4 people)
PILOT LANGUAGES?	English, Turkish
TYPE OF BREAKFAST	Basic + fruit
WAITING AREA BEFORE FLIGHT	Office in Avanos
BRANDED GUEST TRANSPORT?	Yes
BALLOON MAKER/MATERIAL	Hyperlast from Ultra Magic

* Atmosfer Balloons mostly serves tour groups and charges half price for children. They are owned by Dorak Holding which also owns Kapadokya, Sultan, and Rainbow Balloons.
* Office in Avanos
* Contact Information: Email - fly@atmosferballoons.com
* Telephone - +90 384 219 2643

BALLOON TURCA (www.balloonturca.com)

WHEN DID THEY OPEN?	2009
HOW MANY SLOTS?	3/2
WHAT SIZE BASKETS?	12, 20, 28 passengers
HOW MANY PILOTS?	6
PILOT EXPERIENCE?	Minimum 7 years
FLIGHT LENGHTS OFFERED?	60 minutes, 90 minutes
PILOT LANGUAGES?	Turkish, English
TYPE OF BREAKFAST	Basic
WAITING AREA BEFORE FLIGHT	Large room in their main office building in Göreme
BRANDED GUEST TRANSPORT?	Yes
BALLOON MAKER/MATERIAL	Hyperlast in Ultra Magic

* Most of Balloon Turca's guests come through tour agents and hotel recommendations. I found them to be the least helpful of all the companies I visited which is probably a sign that they do not want/need any customers from me.
* Office in Göreme
* Contact Information: Email - info@balloonturca.com
* Telephone - +90 384 271 30 00, +90 541 276 00 00

BUTTERFLY BALLOONS (www.butterflyballoons.com)

WHEN DID THEY OPEN?	2010
HOW MANY SLOTS?	4/2
WHAT SIZE BASKETS?	6-16 passengers
HOW MANY PILOTS?	7
PILOT EXPERIENCE?	From 3-30 years
FLIGHT LENGHTS OFFERED?	60 minutes, 90 minutes
PILOT LANGUAGES?	Turkish, English, and Spanish in the summer
TYPE OF BREAKFAST	Basic + Fruit
WAITING AREA BEFORE FLIGHT	At the main offices in Göreme
BRANDED GUEST TRANSPORT?	No
BALLOON MAKER/MATERIAL	Hyperlast from Ultra Magic, Cameron, and Kubicek

* Butterfly Balloons does not take groups. They are connected with Kelebek Hotel in Göreme and most of their guests reserve through the internet or hotel recommendations. Their baskets fit 20 but they take a maximum of 16 passengers. They are one of only a couple of companies that serve real champagne after the flight.
* Office in Göreme (Kelebek Hotel)
* Contact Information: Email - fly@butterflyballoons.com
* Telephone - +90 384 271 3010

CIHANGIROĞLU BALLOONS (www.cihangirogluballoons.com/)

WHEN DID THEY OPEN?	2002
HOW MANY SLOTS?	3/1
WHAT SIZE BASKETS?	10, 16, 20, 28 passengers
HOW MANY PILOTS?	3
PILOT EXPERIENCE?	Minimum 7 years
FLIGHT LENGHTS OFFERED?	60 minutes (standard), 60 minutes (comfort), 90 minutes (deluxe)
PILOT LANGUAGES?	English, Turkish
TYPE OF BREAKFAST	Basic served at take-off point but inside
WAITING AREA BEFORE FLIGHT	At take-off point
BRANDED GUEST TRANSPORT?	No
BALLOON MAKER/MATERIAL	Hyperlast from Cameron

* Cihangiroğlu Balloons' guests mostly come through travel agent bookings.
* Office in Uçhisar
* Contact Information: Email - info@cihangirogluballoons.com
* Telephone - +90 384 219 26 65, +90 536 416 80 88, +90 532 742 54 25

COMFORT BALLOONS (www.comfortballoon.com)

WHEN DID THEY OPEN?	2014
HOW MANY SLOTS?	2/1
WHAT SIZE BASKETS?	4, 8, 16, & 20 passengers
HOW MANY PILOTS?	5
PILOT EXPERIENCE?	Minimum 4 years
FLIGHT LENGHTS OFFERED?	60 minutes, 90 minutes
PILOT LANGUAGES?	Turkish, English,
TYPE OF BREAKFAST	Open Buffet
WAITING AREA BEFORE FLIGHT	Aydede Restaurant in Göreme
BRANDED GUEST TRANSPORT?	Yes
BALLOON MAKER/MATERIAL	Hyperlast by Lindstrand

* Comfort Baloons was formerly Maccan Balloons. They are owned by the same company that also owns Istanbul Balloons and Universal Balloons. Comfort Balloons' customers are a mix of agents, hotels, and internet.
* Office in Göreme
* Contact Information: Email - fly@comfortballoons.com
* Telephone - +90 384 290 1290

DELUXE BALLOONS (www.deluxeballoons.com)

WHEN DID THEY OPEN?	2009
HOW MANY SLOTS?	3/2
WHAT SIZE BASKETS?	12, 20, 28 passengers
HOW MANY PILOTS?	6
PILOT EXPERIENCE?	Minimum 7 years
FLIGHT LENGHTS OFFERED?	60 minutes, 90 minutes
PILOT LANGUAGES?	Turkish, English
TYPE OF BREAKFAST	Basic
WAITING AREA BEFORE FLIGHT	Large room in their main office building in Göreme
BRANDED GUEST TRANSPORT?	Yes
BALLOON MAKER/MATERIAL	Hyperlast in Ultra Magic

* Deluxe Balloons is owned by the same people who own Göreme Balloons. I had a nice chat with the General Manager, and he explained that Deluxe tries to live up to its name. Göreme Balloons and Deluxe are like Toyota and Lexus. Flying with Deluxe means spending a little more to enjoy a nicer experience.
* Office in Göreme/Ürgüp
* Contact Information: Email - info@deluxeballoons.com
* Telephone - +90 545 359 4359, +90 384 341 5000

DISCOVERY BALLOONS (www.discoveryballoons.com)

WHEN DID THEY OPEN?	2011
HOW MANY SLOTS?	3/2
WHAT SIZE BASKETS?	10, 28, 32 passengers
HOW MANY PILOTS?	5
PILOT EXPERIENCE?	Minimum 7 years
FLIGHT LENGHTS OFFERED?	60 minutes, 90 minutes
PILOT LANGUAGES?	Turkish, English,
TYPE OF BREAKFAST	Basic
WAITING AREA BEFORE FLIGHT	Tourist Hotel in Göreme
BRANDED GUEST TRANSPORT?	Yes
BALLOON MAKER/MATERIAL	Hyperlast from Lindstrand and Ultra Magic

* Discovery Balloons is owned by the same company that owns Anatolian Balloons.
* Office same as Anatolian Balloons on road between Göreme and Uçhisar
* Contact Information: Email - info@discoveryballoons.com
* Telephone - +90 384 214 2300,+90 541 678 0000

EZ AIR BALLOONS (www.ezairballoons.com)

WHEN DID THEY OPEN?	1987
HOW MANY SLOTS?	2/1
WHAT SIZE BASKETS?	20 passengers
HOW MANY PILOTS?	5
PILOT EXPERIENCE?	3-30 years
FLIGHT LENGHTS OFFERED?	60 minutes
PILOT LANGUAGES?	English, Turkish
TYPE OF BREAKFAST	N/A
WAITING AREA BEFORE FLIGHT	N/A
BRANDED GUEST TRANSPORT?	No
BALLOON MAKER/MATERIAL	Hyperlast by Ultra Magic & Kubicek

* EZ Air, the oldest hot air balloon company in Cappadocia, started in 1987, and Hasan, one of the 5 original Turkish pilots is still flying for them today. They currently are not taking reservations but only serving overflow guests from other companies.
* Office in Çavuşin Village
* Contact Information: None

GÖREME BALLOONS (www.goremeballoons.com)

WHEN DID THEY OPEN?	1997
HOW MANY SLOTS?	6/4
WHAT SIZE BASKETS?	12, 16, 20, 24, 28 passengers
HOW MANY PILOTS?	12
PILOT EXPERIENCE?	Minimum 10 years
FLIGHT LENGHTS OFFERED?	60 minutes, 90 minutes
PILOT LANGUAGES?	English, Turkish, German, & Japanese
TYPE OF BREAKFAST	Basic
WAITING AREA BEFORE FLIGHT	Breakfast hall in Göreme
BRANDED GUEST TRANSPORT?	Yes
BALLOON MAKER/MATERIAL	Hyperlast from Lindstrand, Kubicek, and Cameron

* Göreme Balloons is the only company, as far as I know, that has a basket with handicap access. Around 70% of their customers are from tour groups, about 25% come from hotel recommendations, and just 5% from the internet. They are owned by the same company that owns Deluxe Balloons.
* Office in Ürgüp
* Contact Information: Email- info@goremeballoons.com
* Telephone- +90 530 643 9868, +90 532 416 6461

ISTANBUL BALLOONS (www.istanbulballoons.com)

WHEN DID THEY OPEN?	2011
HOW MANY SLOTS?	3/1
WHAT SIZE BASKETS?	12, 16, 18, 20, 28 passengers
HOW MANY PILOTS?	6
PILOT EXPERIENCE?	From 4-6 years
FLIGHT LENGHTS OFFERED?	60 minutes, 90 minutes
PILOT LANGUAGES?	Turkish, English
TYPE OF BREAKFAST	Open Buffet
WAITING AREA BEFORE FLIGHT	Aydede Restaurant in Göreme
BRANDED GUEST TRANSPORT?	Yes
BALLOON MAKER/MATERIAL	Silver coated Hyperlast from Lindstrand and Ultra Magic

* Istanbul Balloons is owned by the same company that owns Comfort Balloons and Universal Balloons. They get most of their customer reservations from travel agents.
* Office in Göreme
* Contact Information: Email - fly@istanbulballoons.com
* Telephone - +90 384 271 30 62, +90 384 271 30 63, +90 533 025 95 95

KAPADOKYA BALLOONS (www.kapadokyaballoons.com/en/

WHEN DID THEY OPEN?	1991
HOW MANY SLOTS?	10/5
WHAT SIZE BASKETS?	14, 16, 20 passengers
HOW MANY PILOTS?	1
PILOT EXPERIENCE?	4-7 years
FLIGHT LENGHTS OFFERED?	60 minutes, 90 minutes
PILOT LANGUAGES?	Turkish, English,
TYPE OF BREAKFAST	Basic
WAITING AREA BEFORE FLIGHT	Breakfast hall at their offices in Göreme
BRANDED GUEST TRANSPORT?	Yes
BALLOON MAKER/MATERIAL	Hyperlast from Ultra Magic

* Kapadokyaballoons is the second oldest hot air balloon company in Cappadocia and get most of their guests from tour groups. They are owned by Dorak Holding which also owns Atmosfer, Sultan, and Rainbow Balloons.
* Office in Göreme
* Contact Information: Email - fly@kapadokyaballoons.com
* Telephone - +90 384 271 24 42

KAPADOKYA KAYA BALLOONS

(wwww.kapadokyakayaballoons.com)

WHEN DID THEY OPEN?	2005
HOW MANY SLOTS?	7/3
WHAT SIZE BASKETS?	2, 12, 18, 20 passengers
HOW MANY PILOTS?	15
PILOT EXPERIENCE?	From 500-6000 hours
FLIGHT LENGHTS OFFERED?	60 minutes, 90 minutes
PILOT LANGUAGES?	English, Spanish, and Turkish
TYPE OF BREAKFAST	Basic
WAITING AREA BEFORE FLIGHT	In a breakfast hall near Göreme Open Air Museum
BRANDED GUEST TRANSPORT?	Yes
BALLOON MAKER/MATERIAL	Hyperlast from Lindstrand, Cameron, & Ultra Magic

* Kaya Balloons runs the largest pilot training school in Turkey and some of their pilots are trainers in the school. Most of their customers are from tour groups.
* Office in Ürgüp
* Contact Information: info@kapadokyakayaballoons.com
* Telephone- +90 (384) 341 46 48, +90 (533) 498 29 29

RAINBOW BALLOONS (www.rainbowballoons.net/en/)

WHEN DID THEY OPEN?	2012
HOW MANY SLOTS?	6/3
WHAT SIZE BASKETS?	12,16, 20 passengers
HOW MANY PILOTS?	10
PILOT EXPERIENCE?	From 2-15 years
FLIGHT LENGHTS OFFERED?	60 minutes
PILOT LANGUAGES?	English, Turkish,
TYPE OF BREAKFAST	Basic
WAITING AREA BEFORE FLIGHT	Office in Uçhisar
BRANDED GUEST TRANSPORT?	No
BALLOON MAKER/MATERIAL	Hyperlast by Ultra Magic

* Rainbow Balloons' customers are part of group tours or from hotel recommendations. They are owned by Dorak Holding which also owns Atmosfer, Sultan, and Kapadokya Balloons.
* Office in Uçhisar
* Contact Information: Email- fly@rainbowballoons.net
* Telephone- +90 384 219 33 08

ROYAL BALLOONS (www.royalballoon.com)

WHEN DID THEY OPEN?	2010
HOW MANY SLOTS?	5/3
WHAT SIZE BASKETS?	Queen flight max is16, King flight max is 10
HOW MANY PILOTS?	6
PILOT EXPERIENCE?	5-20+ years
FLIGHT LENGHTS OFFERED?	60 minutes (Queen), 90 minutes (King)
PILOT LANGUAGES?	Turkish, English
TYPE OF BREAKFAST	Open Buffet
WAITING AREA BEFORE FLIGHT	Breakfast hall in the main offices in Göreme
BRANDED GUEST TRANSPORT?	Yes
BALLOON MAKER/MATERIAL	Silver Coated Hyperlast by Lindstrand and Cameron

* They get many passengers direct from internet reservations or hotel recommendations. Royal gives a baseball cap or hat as a gift for the Queen Flight and a polo shirt for the King Flight. I have flown with Royal Balloons with my whole family and we had a great experience. I have flown with Royal Balloons multiple times and had great experiences every time.
* Office in Göreme
* Contact Information: Email - royal@royalballoon.com
* Telephone - +90 384 271 33 00, +90 549 271 33 00

SKYWAY BALLOONS (www.skywayballoons.com)

WHEN DID THEY OPEN?	2007
HOW MANY SLOTS?	4/2
WHAT SIZE BASKETS?	12, 16, 20, & 28 passengers
HOW MANY PILOTS?	9
PILOT EXPERIENCE?	From 3-15 years
FLIGHT LENGHTS OFFERED?	60 minutes (standard & comfort), & 90 minutes (deluxe)
PILOT LANGUAGES?	English, Turkish, and Spanish
TYPE OF BREAKFAST	Basic
WAITING AREA BEFORE FLIGHT	Tourist hotel in Göreme
BRANDED GUEST TRANSPORT?	Yes
BALLOON MAKER/MATERIAL	Hyperlast by Cameron, Ultra Magic, & Kubicek

* Skyway Balloons has 1 of the 2 female pilots in Cappadocia. 80% of their customers are from travel agencies or hotel recommendations and the rest are direct through the internet or phone.
* Office in Ürgüp
* Contact Information: Email - info@skywayballoons.com
* Telephone - +90 533 608 0525

SULTAN BALLOONS (www.sultanballoons.com)

WHEN DID THEY OPEN?	2005
HOW MANY SLOTS?	2/1
WHAT SIZE BASKETS?	16 & 20 passengers
HOW MANY PILOTS?	2
PILOT EXPERIENCE?	5-6 years
FLIGHT LENGHTS OFFERED?	60 minutes
PILOT LANGUAGES?	English, Turkish
TYPE OF BREAKFAST	Basic
WAITING AREA BEFORE FLIGHT	Office in Uçhisar
BRANDED GUEST TRANSPORT?	No
BALLOON MAKER/MATERIAL	Hyperlast by Cameron and Ultra Magic

* Sultan's customers come mostly from travel agencies. They are owned by Dorak Holding which also owns Atmosfer, Rainbow, and Kapadokya Balloons.
* Office in Uçhisar
* Contact Information: info@sultanballoons.com
* Telephone- +90 384 353 53 91, +90 533 239 41 72, +90 533 239 37 88

THK BALLOONS (www.thk.org.tr/balon/)

WHEN DID THEY OPEN?	1997
HOW MANY SLOTS?	3/1
WHAT SIZE BASKETS?	2, 12, 15, 20 passengers
HOW MANY PILOTS?	5
PILOT EXPERIENCE?	Minimum 500 hours
FLIGHT LENGHTS OFFERED?	60 minutes
PILOT LANGUAGES?	English, Turkish, Arabic
TYPE OF BREAKFAST	Buffet
WAITING AREA BEFORE FLIGHT	Tourist Hotel in Göreme
BRANDED GUEST TRANSPORT?	Some are and some are not
BALLOON MAKER/MATERIAL	Silver-coated hyperlast from Lindstrand

* They find most of their customers through tour agents and hotels. They began as THK and then became Saray from 2015-2016 before switching back to THK Balloons.
* Office in Ürgüp
* Contact Information: Email- info@thkballoons.com
* Telephone- +90 542 404 72 48

TÜRKIYE BALLOONS (www.turkiyeballoons.com/en/)

WHEN DID THEY OPEN?	2013
HOW MANY SLOTS?	3/2
WHAT SIZE BASKETS?	2, 12,16, 20 passengers
HOW MANY PILOTS?	7
PILOT EXPERIENCE?	1500 hours minimum
FLIGHT LENGHTS OFFERED?	60 minutes, 90 minutes
PILOT LANGUAGES?	English, Turkish, Spanish, French, Italian, & Arabic
TYPE OF BREAKFAST	Open Buffet
WAITING AREA BEFORE FLIGHT	Breakfast hall in the main offices in Göreme
BRANDED GUEST TRANSPORT?	No
BALLOON MAKER/MATERIAL	Hyperlast by Lindstrand and Cameron

* Turkiye Balloons is owned by 3 pilots who came together to start their own company. Their customers come from hotel recommendations and direct through the internet. I have flown with Turkiye Balloons and had a great experience.
* Office in Göreme
* Contact Information: Email - fly@turkiyeballoons.com
* Telephone - +90 533 417 5656, +90 384 271 3222

ÜRGÜP BALLOONS (www.urgupballoons.com)

WHEN DID THEY OPEN?	2008
HOW MANY SLOTS?	4/2
WHAT SIZE BASKETS?	12, 16, 20, and 28 passengers
HOW MANY PILOTS?	7
PILOT EXPERIENCE?	Minimum 5 years
FLIGHT LENGHTS OFFERED?	60 minutes (classic & comfort), & 90 minutes (deluxe)
PILOT LANGUAGES?	English, Turkish
TYPE OF BREAKFAST	Basic
WAITING AREA BEFORE FLIGHT	Breakfast hall in Çavuşin
BRANDED GUEST TRANSPORT?	Yes
BALLOON MAKER/MATERIAL	Hyperlast by Lindstrand and Cameron

* Ürgüp Balloons' guests come from hotel recommendations while 30% are direct from the internet.
* Office in Ürgüp
* Contact Information: Email - info@urgupballoons.com
* Telephone - +90 532 400 07 70, +90 384 341 56 36

UNIVERSAL BALLOONS (www.universalballoon.com)

WHEN DID THEY OPEN?	2013
HOW MANY SLOTS?	3/2
WHAT SIZE BASKETS?	12,16, & 20 passengers
HOW MANY PILOTS?	6
PILOT EXPERIENCE?	Minimum 4 years
FLIGHT LENGHTS OFFERED?	60 minutes
PILOT LANGUAGES?	English, Turkish
TYPE OF BREAKFAST	Open Buffet
WAITING AREA BEFORE FLIGHT	Aydede Restaurant in Göreme
BRANDED GUEST TRANSPORT?	Yes
BALLOON MAKER/MATERIAL	Hyperlast by Cameron, Ultra Magic, and Lindstrand

* Universal is owned by the same company that owns Comfort and Istanbul. Their customers come from hotel recommendations and the internet.
* Office in Göreme
* Contact Information: fly@universalballoon.com
* Telephone- +90(531) 386 50 50, +90(384) 271 27 54

VOYAGER BALLOONS (www.voyagerballoons.com)

WHEN DID THEY OPEN?	2008
HOW MANY SLOTS?	6/3
WHAT SIZE BASKETS?	4, 10, 12, 16, 20, & 28 passengers
HOW MANY PILOTS?	10
PILOT EXPERIENCE?	Minimum 1000 hours
FLIGHT LENGHTS OFFERED?	60 minutes
PILOT LANGUAGES?	English, Portuguese, Japanese, & Turkish
TYPE OF BREAKFAST	Open Buffet
WAITING AREA BEFORE FLIGHT	At their breakfast hall in Avanos
BRANDED GUEST TRANSPORT?	Yes
BALLOON MAKER/MATERIAL	Ultralast by Ultra Magic

* Voyager also owns Atlas Balloons. Voyager Balloons gets most of their guests from hotel recommendations and travel agencies. Voyager has a sitting basket (passengers sit down during the flight) that holds up to 4 people. This flight includes champagne and breakfast and costs 550 Euro per person.
* Office in Göreme
* Contact Information: Email- fly@voyagerballoons.com
* Telephone- +90 532 347 1514, +90 532 717 5050, +90 384 271 3030

CHAPTER 11

RECOMMENDED TRAVEL/TOUR AGENCIES

A quick search reveals hundreds, even thousands of travel/tour agencies that are happy to serve you in Cappadocia and throughout Turkey. I'm sure many of them are excellent, but I am not capable of vetting all of them. Thus, I have listed below a few quality companies that I know will provide excellent value.

All of these companies can help with day tours as well as your whole Turkey trip. They will arrange as little or as much as you like.

As with everything in this book, I receive no material profit for making these recommendations, but you get a discount if you mention that you heard about them through the book.

If you book a trip with any of these companies and have a problem that they don't fix, please let me know. Up to this point I have only received positive feedback from the people who have used the services offered by the companies below. Enjoy.

CAPPADOCIA TRAVEL AGENCY - GÖREME

* (Talk to my friend Efe- pronounced Eh-fay)
* Website: www.cappadociatravelagency.com/
* Email: info@cappadociatravelagency.com
* Phone Number: +90 535 648 5167

Personal anecdote: *I have sent many of my friends and acquaintances to Efe and all have been pleased.*

HERITAGE TRAVEL - GÖREME

* Website: www.Göreme.com/turkish-heritage-travel.php
* Email: info@Göreme.com
* Phone Number: +90 384 271 2687

Personal anecdote: *This is a top-quality service. They charge a bit more but deliver.*

SOJOURN TURKEY CUSTOM TRAVEL – ANTALYA

* Website: www.sojournturkeytours.com
* Email: info@sojournturkey.com
* Phone Number: Turkey: +90 242 311 5961 US: +1 770 783 0167

Personal anecdote: *Run by foreigners, Sojourn understands the foreign mindset and provides great service to all their customers.*

ARGEUS TOURISM & TRAVEL - ÜRGÜP

* Website: www.argeus.com.tr/
* Email: info@argeus.com.tr
* Phone Number: + 90 384 341 4688

Personal anecdote: *We use them for a host of services including airport shuttles and tours, and they have never let us down.*

PETER SOMMER TRAVELS

* Based out of England their expert guides lead tours throughout Cappadocia and all of Turkey.
* Website: www.petersommer.com
* Email: info@petersommer.com
* Phone Number: UK: 01600 888 220 US/Canada: 855 443 3027 (toll free) Australia: 00 11 44 1600 888 220

Personal anecdote: *I met Peter online and am impressed with what they offer, but I have not actually used his services personally.*

CHAPTER 12

WHAT TO DO AND SEE

As has been mentioned, Cappadocia is an expansive region with numerous attractions and activities to fill days and even weeks. Most of these are outdoors which means that weather is important.

Today as I am writing this the weather is not cooperating. It is mid-March and snow is falling, low clouds are obscuring any view, and the ground is wet. This means that the many visitors will be making the best of whatever plans they had and dealing with cancellations (balloons and tours). This happens and at this time of year weather conditions are unpredictable.

Last week was sunny and 70 degrees fahrenheit with balloons flying every morning. So, if you are a crazy adventurer, then today is a great day; but for most of us, today is a day to snuggle up in a cozy cave room and enjoy good movies.

Fortunately, today is not the norm. The balloons fly around 250 days per year and Cappadocia is known as a dry, sunny region. This means that most of the year you will be out and about taking advantage of all that Cappadocia has to offer. And what is that?

I have divided this into 2 parts:

1. Attractions (what to see)
2. Activities (what to do)

A good combination of these will make your time in Cappadocia full and memorable…

WHAT TO SEE

Since everyone has different tastes I have avoided claiming some definitive order, but instead have listed what I consider to be the best sights in the region. If I listed every sight, the book would be over 1000 pages. Most people stay for 1-3 days which makes even seeing all of these very difficult.

You may put the valleys first? Or perhaps you love the towns? Or is it the beautiful cave churches that capture your fancy?

Read the list and put them in the order you want.

NOTE: For the sights that are included in tours, I have added those listings in parenthesis either next to the title or at the end of the description if it required explanation. Hopefully this helps in your planning as well.

NOTE: See the Maps in Appendix 7 to locate these sites in the region.

GÖREME OPEN-AIR MUSEUM (RED TOUR)

In a relatively small area you will see a lifetime's quota of cave churches whose walls are covered with beautiful frescoes. This is one of those places you must see once, but like a suspense movie it loses its allure once you know the ending.

An audio tour is available but since they have detailed signs in multiple languages the need is questionable. Only you know if you prefer to read or to listen. There is one church within the park, the Dark Church, that you pay extra to visit. I recommend paying it. Most people agree that it is worth it.

UNDERGROUND CITIES: DERINKUYU, KAYMAKLI (GREEN TOUR)

There are many underground cities in the region, but these are the two most famous, most visited. Derinkuyu is the deepest (around 8 stories- 100 meters) and Kaymaklı is the broadest (more like a honeycomb).

There is no signage in either so hiring a guide is recommended. If you go on your own, you will find a guide waiting near the entrance. You can negotiate a price. These underground cities will blow your mind and should be considered as "Don't leave Cappadocia without seeing this" attractions. You only need to see one of these.

TOWNS

The towns of Cappadocia each have their own unique flavor. They are worth visiting for the shopping if you are looking for gifts or something to remember your time. A bonus is that this helps the local economy since most of the shops and restaurants are locally owned and operated.

GÖREME

Fairy Chimneys, hotels, restaurants, carpet and antique shops and those who work in them is what you will find in the quaint town of Göreme, barely bigger than a village. The people are friendly and this is a good place to buy a carpet if you are looking for one. If you are in Göreme around sunset you must climb the hill to Sunset Point and capture the scene on film or just sit with someone special and take in the overwhelming beauty. (Green Tour stops for a photo at a spot above the town.)

AVANOS

This riverside town is the Mecca for pottery with master potters setting up shop on every corner. You should definitely visit one of the shops but be careful not to get ripped off. If you go to a big shop, only buy a piece made by the master as it will be the only unique item in the shop. Also, feel free to take advantage of the opportunity to get a free lesson and try to throw your own pot.

If you have some spare time, taking a stroll along the river and having tea at one of the cafes while the river flows by, the ducks and geese honk, and the town goes about its business is a memory worth making. With all the chaos in the world, this kind of peaceful setting is worth experiencing when possible. And for those desperate for America fast food, Avanos has the only McDonald's in the area.

ÜRGÜP

The biggest of the three towns, Ürgüp is full of shops, cafes and hotels like Göreme, only five times bigger. The main shopping area of the town is hurting as fewer and fewer tourists walk the streets.

Tour groups generally do not just walk to random shops as they have tight schedules and set stores. This means that Ürgüp's shop owners are feeling a bit desperate. If you are a good bargainer, you should be able to get some deals.

This is one of the few places in which you will find unique antiques and other trinkets among the quotidian items located on every stand. Another great view is from Temenni Hill which overlooks the town and the valley; have a glass of tea at the cafe while taking it all in.

MUSTAFAPAŞA (BLUE/UNDISCOVERED CAPPADOCIA TOUR)

This old Greek town is a fascinating anachronism. The Greeks left in 1923-4 and were replaced by Turks. Many of the Greek houses remain at different levels of dilapidation as well as at least one church (not a cave). It is better to see it with a guide but works on your own as well. It is about 10 minutes outside of Ürgüp but buses go regularly.

GULŞEHIR

About 15 minutes down river from Avanos sits this sleepy town with some cool sights. Just outside of town is the Mushroom Rock (Mantar Kaya). This is a fairy

Chimney shaped like a huge mushroom. Within the town you will find friendly people, some good food (if you're adventurous), and a large Greek Orthodox church (not refurbished, get the key from the office across the street), and St. Jean's Cave church which dates to the 13th century and is beautifully restored. Buses go to Gulsehir regularly from the mall in Nevşehir.

HACIBEKTAŞ

This town requires more effort but many would say it is worth the effort. The man, Haci Bektas, lived around 700 years ago and is buried here. Visiting the museum is a spiritual and cultural experience giving interesting insights into the Alevis, a minority Muslim sect. If you have an extra day, it is something to consider.

VALLEYS: LOVE, ROSE/RED, IMAGINATION, PIGEON, ZEMI, & SWORDS

These seven stunning valleys are centrally located between Uçhisar and Çavuşin. If you have a couple of hours, pick one and hike it. Be sure to bring your camera and a bottle of water.

Our family loves hiking all of these wonders. You will need good footwear and to be in decent shape since each valley includes some hills and rough terrain. If it has been raining within a day of your visit, expect to find some muddy places.

I have included a Hiking Guide with Google Map coordinates at the end of this book. Check it out and ask your hotel for help if you are interested in hiking. Transportation will need to be worked out since most of the valleys are not loops.

ÇAVUŞIN CHURCHES

Living in this village means we have spent many hours hiking around these churches. The upper church, St. John's, reportedly dates back to the 4th century. It has not been renovated and is free to the public although not so easy to navigate. You can barely make out old frescoes that used to cover the walls.

Put away your fear and hike around the Swiss cheese rock. You will find the views and the hidden rooms quite worth the risk. Going to the top of the cliffs/hill allows for a great view of the valley from Göreme to Avanos.

The lower church, Nicephorus Phocas, dates from the 10th century and is beautifully renovated. If you have seen the Open Air Museum, you will not see anything new here. I only recommend this church if you are way into cave frescoes and need to see as many as possible; perhaps you are getting a PhD. Otherwise, save your money.

HISARS: ORTAHISAR AND UÇHISAR

Two more towns in the center of the region (near Ürgüp and Göreme respectively) are worth visiting for their climbable rock towers. Be sure to go on clear days as the view is breathtaking. (The Red Tour stops for picture taking of Uçhisar but does not enter it.)

IHLARA VALLEY (GREEN TOUR)

This is a bit harder to get to but is well worth it. Start in Ihlara and descend into the valley. From the bottom you follow the river through lush vegetation with steep cave-filled cliffs rising up to the sky on both sides. About halfway you will find a cafe. From there you can keep walking and hope to catch a ride back or turn around.

The Green Tour takes care of transportation so if you go on your own you have to figure out transportation beforehand. Ihlara is relatively in the middle of nowhere so hitchhiking is a risky venture. You may not see a car for long stretches of time. This is one of the more peaceful places on earth.

PAŞABAG & ZELVE OPEN-AIR MUSEUM

Most people would put these higher up the list. In Paşabag you will find maybe the best collection of Fairy Chimneys. A bonus is no entry fee. I love Paşabağ and could spend a couple of hours there every time I go. There is much more to see than what first meets the eye. Zelve is like the unwanted step-sister to Göreme's museum. It is a nice place to hike around and explore but does not have the frescoes so is generally not included in most tourists' itineraries. (The Red Tour goes to Paşabağ and gives people 30 minutes to walk around and take pictures. No tour includes Zelve.)

RHYTHMS OF LIFE BY ANDREW ROGERS

On the hills near the university off the Nevşehir - Avanos road, you will see some strange, humongous man-made rock-walled figures. They came from the mind of Andrew Rogers and were formed by hundreds of locals working together.

You are welcome to go up to them and walk around and enjoy the view of the area from the hill as well as try to figure out what each one is. The best way is probably to rent a scooter and go see them.

SOBESOS, KEŞLIK MONASTERY, & SOĞANLI VALLEY (BLUE/ UNDISCOVERED CAPPADOCIA TOUR)

These three options included in the Blue Tour or Undiscovered Cappadocia Tour are rarely visited but well worth the time. I describe each in detail in the tour section so will not repeat it here.

WHAT TO DO

You will notice from this list that almost everything is outdoors and very little water is included (no beaches). You could stay active in Cappadocia for weeks, but since most of you are taking 1-3 days this list should serve you well.

As with the "Attractions" section, I have listed these activities in no particular order. After reading this you will have a better idea of what is available in Cappadocia. The next step is to play matchmaker for yourself and prioritize.

For most of these items your hotel should be able to help you get set up, but be sure to check on the internet (or face to face if you can) to confirm that you are getting the best deal (I am assuming that most people are looking for a good deal, but I understand that for some people the best deal is not having to waste time confirming everything).

And with that let's get to it...

HOT-AIR BALLOON RIDE

This is by far the most popular thing to do in Cappadocia and for good reason. Apparently more balloon trips are made here than anywhere else in the world. The landscape is crazy and the view from above is a great way to see it.

There are 25 hot air balloon companies and as of this writing that number has been capped. They are not allowing any more companies. By reputation, Royal Balloons, Türkiye Balloons, and Butterfly Balloons are the best **(Royal, Butterfly, Türkiye, Saray, and Voyager give a discount if you tell them you bought this book- that pays for more than the price of the book!)**. I wrote about all of this in great detail in the Hot-Air Ballooning section of the book so go to that section before making a reservation.

HORSEBACK

For those who like to ride horses, Cappadocia is a great place. Having hills and valleys with few trees, the landscape is perfect for riding. Make sure you get a good horse and know what you are doing. This is not for beginners.

You are free to trot or gallop as you wish. The guide shows the way but every rider is on his or her own leading his or her horse. They have a few different options from which to choose. The Price List section of the book has more information as well.

4-WHEELER (ATV)/MOTORCYCLE

Just as the landscape is good for horses, the motorcycle & ATV enthusiast will enjoy the dirt trails between Göreme and Çavuşin. For ATVs, guided tours are generally the only option as the authorities fear people will drive onto private property and suffer the wrath of local land owners and most visitors do not know the best places to go.

However, the problem with guided tours is that the leader (the guide) is the only person who does not get dust in his face the whole time. Regardless, everyone seems to enjoy the time. My brother did this with his wife and daughter with a guide and had a great time.

Cappadocia is a perfect place for ATV riding with a good balance of hills and flats, great scenery, and dirt roads stretching for miles in every direction. I have not seen rental places outside of Göreme and Çavuşin so expect to start from there. The Price List section of the book has more information as well.

Motorcycles are also available and do not require a guide.

> **NOTE**: Businesses in Göreme rent ATVs, motorcycles, scooters, and bicycles. They are one-stop shops in a manner of speaking. You can also find ATVs in Çavuşin but not the other options. There are at least 14 different places in Göreme that will rent these to you so feel free to talk to each of them to get the best deal. Silk Road Rentals and Öz Cappadocia (both are near the bus station) will give you a discount if you have bought this book.
>
> * www.silkroadrentacar.com/index.html
>
> * www.ozcappadocia.com/en/index.html

SCOOTER

If you are not with a tour and want to get around in good weather, a scooter may be the way to go. The price is reasonable if you plan on covering the area. Two people can ride one if money is tight. The Price List section of the book has more information. **Silk Road Rentals will give a discount if you bought this book.**

BICYCLING

I met a guy who visited, rented a bike, hit the trails and hills and canyons, found a cave and slept in it for the night. How does that sound to you? If you are this kind of person, Cappadocia is the place to be. If you do not bring your own bike, you can rent one from the places mentioned above. The Price List section of the book has more information.

HIKING

For those who love simple nature and/or on a small budget, Cappadocia offers endless trails for the hiker. Pick a valley, pack a lunch and some water, and go for the day. You will find endless caves and rock climbing opportunities. The main valleys between Uçhisar and Göreme are Pigeon, Love, Zemi, Red, Rose, and Swords. Monks Valley is near Zelve Open Air Museum.

More distant options are Ihlara and Monastery Valleys. One great thing about every valley except Ihlara is that they have no entrance fees, and you can spend a whole day exploring or zip through them in 2 3 hours. If this interests you, check out the Hiking Guide at the end of the book.

GREEN/RED/BLUE TOUR & SIGHT-SEEING

Of course, most people come to Cappadocia for the sights, and you could spend days seeing them. The local tour companies divide the region into different sections and offer day tours. If you do not like the tour option, there is plenty to see in the Göreme – Avanos – Ürgüp triangle that is easily accessible by public transportation.

Go to the Tour Section of the book to learn more. The Price List section of the book has more information as well.

SHAVE

This is my first choice for activities in Cappadocia but since it only applies to half the population, I did not feel I could put it at the top of the list. The barber (berber or küaför) shops are segregated so make sure you go into an Erkek (male) Küaför and ask for a shave ("sakal traj").They will sit you down in the comfy chair, lather your face with a horsehair brush, and shave you clean with a straight razor two times. Then they will massage your face and shoulders as you turn into putty. So relaxing!

I take all my guests, and everyone so far has loved it. I recommend Küaför Şehit in the town center of Ortahisar. He gives the best, most luxurious treatment. A shave and massage is only 10TL and is quite addictive.

NOTE: Be sure to set the price beforehand as I have heard stories of barbers ripping off tourists.

TEA DRINKING

Turks drink a lot of tea and usually they sit and talk while drinking it. Another wonderful way to spend your time is to grab an hour-glass shaped glass of steaming black tea, pull up a chair, and connect with a local English speaker. Chances are your hotel manager, restaurant waiter, or shop owner speaks some English and is eager to practice with you. Take the time; you will not regret it.

In fact, it is my contention that the relationships you make with Cappadocians will be the most memorable part of your trip.

OPEN AIR MARKET (PAZAR)

Depending on where you are from this should be a real treat- Farmers' Market Gone Wild! You can find them only once per week in each of the main towns. Göreme - Wednesday; Avanos - Friday; and Ürgüp - Saturday. The Göreme market is quite small, but the Avanos and Ürgüp options are large and wonderful. These are not touristy in any sense of the world.

The majority of what's available are fruits and vegetables (most grown locally or at least in Turkey), but you can also find plastic goods, farming equipment, coal stoves (in the winter), shoes, cow bells, chain saws, and lingerie.

It is a cultural experience worth enjoying. As you walk through the stall one thing to be aware of is that if someone is standing at a table (usually male), they are most likely a seller, not a farmer. If they are sitting on the ground (usually a woman with a headscarf), they are most likely from nearby villages selling items from their gardens.

VOLCANO - HIKING, SKIING, AND SLEDDING

As you probably know Cappadocia's unique landscape is the result of volcanic eruptions and the erosion that followed. In the summer, tours are offered to climb one of the two volcanoes (Hasan Dağ near Aksaray and Erciyes near Kayseri).

Join a group for an overnight climb to the top. None of the volcanoes in the area are currently active so you do not need to fear an eruption. I have only heard of this but have not done it and do not know which tour agents offer it.

Here is a link I found with some information:

* www.summitpost.org/erciyes/150247

Another option in the winter is skiing and sledding. Work out transportation to the slopes on Erciyes and spend the day shredding. They have all the equipment you will need on the mountain for rent so dress warmly and have fun. You can also opt to sled or just play around and have a snowball fight. Taking the gondola to the top of the mountain is a great way to see for miles. There are hotels near the slopes as well.

And lastly on this topic, while you are there you can stop in Kayseri and experience civilization again. Kayseri is the only place around that has Starbucks and movie theaters with movies in English.

GO SWIMMING AT A POOL WITH WATER SLIDES.

For a couple of months in the summer the weather gets hot enough to make us wish we had a pool. If you are here during this time and just want to relax by a pool instead of seeing the sights, then you have many options. If your hotel does not have a pool, then I recommend Ada Aquapark (in Avanos on the road to the Double Tree Hotel), Göreme Camping (not far from the Goreme Open Air Museum) or Kuş Adası (outside of Avanos off the road to Gulşehir near the river).

Many of the hotels and campgrounds charge a daily fee for non-guests. I like the three options mentioned because they have water slides. The Price List section of the book has more information.

JET BOAT & GONDOLA

If you are interested in having fun on the river, this is the activity for you. Go down to the river in Avanos and sign up or have your hotel or travel agent make a reservation for you. Or you can make a reservation at kapadokyajet.com.

The jet boats hold up to 22 people. We loved this crazy ride all the way up the river and back (took over an hour) at top speeds with 360 degree spins and water spraying everywhere.

Note: Both of these only function in certain seasons (mainly summer but the gondolas are open more in the fall and spring).

The Price List section of the book has more information.

TURKISH NIGHT

All you can eat and drink while watching an array of Turkic/Ottoman folk dances. This usually goes from around 8-11pm. This will be one of the more memorable experiences of your trip.

And then other places only do Whirling Dervishes but no other dances (see below). See the link or turn to the section for more information on venues. Your hotel will be happy to make a reservation for you.

> **NOTE**: Be aware that the Turkish Night shows do not include the Whirling Dervish dancers.

The Price List section of the book has more information.

WHIRLING DERVISH

These shows last about an hour and do not include food. Also taking photos is not allowed. This is a religious service as well as a religious experience. After the performance concludes, the guests are allowed to meet the dancers while enjoying tea and a sweet treat. See the more detailed Whirling Dervish section of the book for reservation and price information.

The Price List section of the book has more information.

WINE TASTING

For those who like to partake of the "fruit of the vine", Cappadocia has some good options for you. Although you can find options in Göreme and Avanos, Ürgüp is the best place with Uçhisar following. In Ürgüp you will find the Turasan winery on the Nevşehir road just barely out of town. You are welcome to taste their many varieties.

Kocabağ is based in Uçhisar, but you can find a shop in the center of Ürgüp that will allow you to taste all their options. Another option is the Mahzen Şarap Evi (Wine House) located behind the hamam (Turkish bath) near the center of town. Mahzen is like a micro-winery run by the Sarkaya family who make their wines locally.

I am not a wine connoisseur so don't listen to me for wine advice, but I really enjoy the Sarkaya fruit wines- mulberry wine, cherry, blackberry, green apple, raspberry, pomegranate, and so on. They also make red and white wines. Besides these three options there are a number of other tasting rooms scattered about Ürgüp and in Avanos on the road up to the Duru Hotel above the town.

"THROW" A POT

In Avanos and Çavuşin you will find countless pottery shops making and selling their wares. Stop in and they will give a demonstration as well as allow you to try your hand at "throwing" a pot on the wheel. It is free with no obligation to buy any of the products. The specialty is the Hittite wine jug which is very difficult to make and comes in a variety of sizes and colors.

> **NOTE**: When shopping for pottery recognize that the shops normally are selling to tour groups and their prices reflect this. Tour agents take a large commission for bringing their groups to the shops.

If you are not with a group, then they do not have to cover any commissions so you should pay anywhere from 1/3 to 1/2 the advertised price.

As an example, when I went to a number of shops to test this idea, I asked about the same piece (size, finish, and color) in each shop. The listed price was 600TL, and they were willing to sell it to me for anywhere from 200 to 350TL.

HAMAM (TURKISH BATH)

For those times when you have taken a good hike or finished a long tour, few things are more relaxing than a hamam. Ürgüp, Göreme, Avanos, and Nevşehir each have working hamams. They generally include a sauna and hamam (the room with the heated platform in the middle and sinks on the surrounding walls), and some have a steam room and/or pool. You pay a few lira to enter and use the different rooms and for a bit more you can get a scrub down and massage.

Most of the hamams have either different rooms for men and women or different times, except for Avanos which is co-ed. Expect to spend at least a couple of hours and bring a bathing suit although you may not use it. Some hamams expect you to use towels they provide and others assume you will wear your own bathing suit.

JEEP SAFARI

A quick look online shows that the so-called "Jeep Safari" has not been commodified just yet. These tours cover many of the valleys in the area as well as Çavuşin, Ürgüp, Ibrahimpaşa, Mustafapaşa, and even Hamsa Dam and the lake it created.

Each company seems to take a different route and includes different attractions. You will be sitting in an SUV with 2-3 other people (the price is much higher if you want to do it alone) as you gaze at the unique rock formations and beautiful landscapes (don't let the "safari" title fool you; there are no animals to see).

Some tours include lunch and some do not. They go at different times of day and are different lengths. These tours vary widely depending on which company you choose. See the link or turn to the Jeep Safari section of the book for more details on each company. The Price List section of the book has more information.

BONUS

One thing that is desperately needed here is a rock climbing / rappelling tour. Much of the rock is difficult because of the flaky sandstone but for people who know what they are doing, this is a great place to test your skills.

As I read over this list I get excited myself. Most of the activities on this list are fun regardless, but when done in this unique moonscape they are awesome! Let me know which ones you enjoyed.

THINGS TO DO WITH KIDS

Cappadocia is a paradise for children because most everything to see is outside and exploring is encouraged.

In the following list I tried to think of activities specifically appealing to kids. I am not listing the normal touristy activities like the Open-Air Museum, hot-air balloon ride, or the underground cities. I am assuming you will see those if you visit. Here I have tried to highlight the activities that are not so obvious.

Parents will not have to worry about prying their kids away from the ipad here. This place is like living in a video game.

HIKING

Go for a hike off the beaten path in one of the many valleys or, even better, up one of the many mesas in the area, especially those around Çavuşin. I cannot stress this opportunity enough. Cappadocia has no fences or walls. You can go almost anywhere. Don't be conventional; go off the path. This is your chance.

The flat top behind Çavuşin? Go for it.

The hill with the weird rock sculptures near Nevşehir University? Go for it.

There are caves everywhere. Just stop on the side of the road in a place that looks interesting and see what you discover. Take a picnic and spend the day exploring. This is a great feature of Cappadocia for kids. My kids and I have been out exploring countless times and still have plenty to see.

TRY YOUR HAND AT POTTERY

Find any potter in Avanos and have your kids "throw a pot" for free. The master potter will give a short demonstration, and then your children (and you) will be allowed to sit at the wheel and see what they can do with a lump of clay. The potter will sit with them and make sure they form something presentable. There is no obligation to buy anything, but you should look around the shop to be courteous.

Living in Çavuşin, I recommend Çavuşin Seramik. Ask for Hakan and tell him you know Duke from Captivating Cappadocia, and he'll take good care of you. I do not get any commission if you do end up buying anything, so don't pay more than half the listed price. (I know this is listed in main Activities section, but it is something children enjoy more than adults.)

BICYCLE RENTAL

Bring or rent a bicycle and go riding on the hundreds of trails in the area. Finding trails that do not include steep hills is not so difficult. I recommend the road/trail that goes through Çavusin and out past the cemetery or the dirt road between Çavuşin and Göreme.

Love Valley may be too steep but parts of it are very doable. For kids 16 and older, renting an ATV (4-wheeler) is also an option. I recommend Silk Road Rentals in Göreme.

See the Price List at the end of the book for prices on ATVs and mountain bikes. They will give you a discount if you bought this book.

ICE CREAM

Go to Mado on the river in Avanos and order one of the amazing desserts. They have wonderful ice cream, chocolate soufflé, creme brûlée, or hot salep, and on and on. If you are in Ürgüp, go to the Merkez Pastanaleri right across from the bus station and enjoy one of their many homemade ice cream flavors.

FEED THE DUCKS/GEESE IN AVANOS

Since you are in Avanos eating ice cream, enjoy another great activity that my younger kids love. Buy a loaf of bread and feed the hundreds of ducks and geese that live on the island in the middle of the river.

RIDE A CAMEL

Historically camels played an important role in the Ottoman Empire and even in the early days of the Turkish Republic. At one point there were more than 50,000 camels in the country. However, that number has dwindled to just a few today and most of them are used for either wrestling (do a Google search) or tourists.

In Cappadocia you will find camels at the Göreme Open Air Museum, on the road below Uçhisar, and at Paşabağ (not far from Çavusin). See the Price List at the end of the book for prices. Looking at them and taking pictures is generally free.

HORSES

Go to the horse corrals near the Göreme Open Air Museum and let the kids sit on the horses. You can walk them around within the spacious pen for a minimal fee, maybe even for free if you sweet talk the owner. Besides horses you will see pigeons, a peacock, dogs, cats, and chickens.

IHLARA VALLEY SWIMMING

For those of you who are especially adventurous and have kids who can hold their own in water, go to the **Ihlara Valley** in July/August and take your swimsuit. Park in the village center and enter the park.

Not far after you descend the stone steps into the valley you come to a small waterfall where the pool is a bit deeper. Take off your shirt and shoes and jump in. This may have been our funnest experience in Cappadocia so far. Google coordinates for the waterfall/pool: 38.247752, 34.312372

CAVE CAMPING

For the truly adventurous parents out there, take your tent and sleeping bags, choose one of the many caves, and spend the night. If this were my family and we wanted to do this, I would take the kids while my wife stayed in the hotel room. Regardless, keep your hotel room so you can return in the morning and shower and have some breakfast! This will be a memory your kids will never forget.

BAYRAMHACI HOT SPRINGS - WINTER ACTIVITY

A few clicks outside of Avanos you will find a hot springs facility that is heavenly if you can get past the 1-star facilities. Honestly, they don't get many foreigners because it is off the beaten path and is lacking in terms of comfortable changing rooms and bathrooms.

However, if you go in expecting this, you should be pleasantly surprised. They have an outdoor pool and an indoor pool. One of our most enjoyable experiences is sitting in the steaming outdoor pool with snow all around us.

You will have to work out transportation and be sure to have your hotel call and check to make sure the pool is full. Every 3rd or 4th day they empty and refill the pool with fresh hot water.

FILM A CAPPADOCIA MOVIE

Video them doing all of these things and then let them help you edit the final product. You can write out a mystery or plan a music video or even a documentary and then film it with the kids as the main characters. My kids love doing this, and it shows off some cool Cappadocian scenery.

GONDOLA BOATS AND/OR JET BOATS

Go to Avanos and take a ride in a gondola boat. The boats hold up to six people. This is a very calm ride on the river. It is not Venice, for sure, but will be a fun memory for your kids. The same company that does gondola rides also offers Jet Boat rides in warm weather, which your kids will love. The boat speeds up and down the river doing 360 degree spins and spraying water everywhere. The ride lasts about an hour and includes a stop to climb around in some ruins on the riverbank.

Signing up for these is doable online (kapadokyajet.com) and they don't run in the winter. But the best way is to ask your hotel or travel agent or to go down to the docks on the river and book it in person. See the Price List at the end of the book for prices

SHOPPING MALL

Nevşehir's Forum Shopping Mall provides a good diversion, especially in bad weather. The mall has many stores for shopping as well as a food court and "game" room that includes bowling and billiards/pool. Right outside the mall you will find a Go-Kart track. Nevşehir's second mall, Nissara, is in the center of the city and offers similar fare to the Forum.

If you want more, then head down to Kayseri where you will find a couple of large malls. These malls (Forum Kayseri and Kayseri Park) have Starbucks and Caribou Coffee, game rooms, theaters with movies in English (animated movies are only in Turkish), large food courts with a mix of western and Turkish food, as well as all the stores that malls generally have selling overpriced clothes, electronics, and toiletries.

I only mention these for those desperate parents who are looking for something to do on a rainy day. At the same time perhaps you are curious to see what a Turkish mall is like. Public transportation goes directly to the Nevşehir Forum mall, but for Kayseri you will need to work out transportation. The cheapest way is probably to take the intercity bus to Kayseri (20TL per ticket as of January 2018) and then take a taxi from the Kayseri bus station to the mall. Be sure to get round trip bus tickets.

ERCIYES SKIING AND SLEDDING

Erciyes is the volcano in Kayseri that is quite visible from central Cappadocia. It is one of the volcanos responsible for Cappadocia looking like it does. In the winter it provides a great opportunity to do some skiing or sledding. They rent all the equipment you need so just show up and enjoy the day. You can also take the gondola to the top of the mountain which provides an amazing view on clear days.

Even in warmer weather you may want to head to Erciyes and hike around on the mountain. With so much to do in Cappadocia, I would not put this high on the list but if you are here for a few days and are not interested in another cave, how many people can say they climbed around on a volcano? Of course, this volcano is dead, but you don't have to tell anyone that!

There you have it. After reading this you will most likely need to add a couple of days to your trip. My one warning is that many of these activities will not work in the winter, of course. November to March is cold in Cappadocia and being outside is not so fun. There is still plenty to do, but you will have the most fun when the weather is warm.

As a contingency in bad weather be sure to have a plan for the kids whether it be iPads, Kindles, movies on the computer (all the hotels have free wifi as do many of the coffee shops), board games, or whatever your family enjoys. Since Cappadocia is mostly outdoors, bad weather means braving the elements or staying in your hotel room a lot, except for the few indoor activities listed above.

SECTION II:

ON THE GROUND IN CAPPADOCIA

CHAPTER 13

ON THE GROUND IN CAPPADOCIA INTRODUCTION

Up to this point in the book, the assumption has been that you have been planning your trip. I tried to think about it progressively and give you what you needed to know before arriving.

Now you should have a good idea of where you are going to stay and what you are going to do and see. If you used the companies that give discounts to readers, then this book has paid for itself a few times over.

With all of that taken care of, it is time to be in Cappadocia. Section II of the book gives you the key information you need once you are here.

SECTION II COVERS:

* **Public Transportation:** What you need to know to use the public bus system
* **Food:** A wide range of restaurants as well as an introduction to Turkish food
* **Shopping:** Descriptions of many of the items you can purchase here either as keepsakes or gifts
* **Emergencies:** What to do in case of emergency

CHAPTER 14

CAPPADOCIA PUBLIC TRANSPORTATION GUIDE

Cappadocia public transportation is relatively comfortable, cheap, slow, and generally dependable. Most but not all of the main attractions can be reached using the public system, although for some of the options you will need to transfer to a second bus in Nevşehşir. The bus drivers are usually helpful, but they do not speak English. Fortunately, the transfer points are close to each other.

Here's an outline (not exhaustive) of the public bus system in the area. As with many things in Turkey this is subject to unannounced changes. All times are estimates. Please ask the driver to confirm your destination when you board.

AVANOS – NEVŞEHIR BUS

Large city buses leave **Avanos** on the hour every hour from 8:00-19:00 (times vary seasonally). You can catch them in front of the PTT building off the center of town.

These pass through **Çavuşin** (15 after the hour), **Göreme** (20 after the hour) and **Uçhısar** (25 after the hour) and end in **Nevşehir** with various stops in each place. They often have signs in the front window listing their stops. They leave every hour from **Nevşehir** as well and follow the opposite route.

There is a large city bus leaving **Avanos** and **Nevşehir** on the half hour starting at 8:30 and ending at 18:30. This generally has the sign ***"Kısa yol"*** (short route) in the front window and takes a different road which goes straight to **Nevşehir** or **Avanos**. It passes by the main street corner in **Nevşehir** from which many other public buses leave and goes by the university.

GÖREME - NEVŞEHIR

Across the parking lot from the **Göreme** bus station sit a few midsize buses heading for **Nevşehir**. They leave around every half hour and make stops in **Uçhisar**.

AVANOS – ÜRGÜP

There are mini-buses that connect **Avanos** with **Ürgüp** leaving every hour as well. These pass through **Zelve**(10 past), **Çavusin**(15 past), **Göreme**(20 past), and **Ortahısar**(25 past) and then make various stops in **Ürgüp** ending in the center of town at the bus terminal. The **Ürgüp** – **Avanos** route passes through the villages in reverse order.

AVANOS – ÖZKONAK

From Avanos there is a big city bus going to **Özkonak** (the site of an underground city) on the half hour from 9:30 to 16:30. The last return bus back to **Avanos** is 16:30.

NEVŞEHIR – DERINKUYU & Kaymaklı

From **Nevşehir** to **Derinkuyu**, buses start at 7:30 and run every half hour. The last return bus is 19:00 from **Derinkuyu** to **Nevşehir**. This bus is about 40 minutes. On Sunday it only runs on the hour. (**Kaymaklı** is on the way to **Derinkuyu**.)

In **Nevşehir** the bus stop where you can pick up **Kaymaklı** and **Derinkuyu** buses (as well as other village buses and return buses for **Ürgüp** and **Avanos**) is a block uphill from the Otel Altınöz, around the corner from Dominos and on the street parallel to the main street running through **Nevşehir**.

NEVŞEHIR – HACIBEKTAŞ

From **Nevşehir** to **Hacıbektaş**, buses start at 9:00 and run every hour. The last return bus is 17:00. This bus is about 40 minutes long and can only hold 14 people so be in line early in the busy season.

Not many tourists use the public transportation, but it is a good option if you have time and want to save money. Please write me if you use it and let me know about your experience so I can better serve other travelers.

Prices are listed in the Price List at the end of the book.

CHAPTER 15

FEED ME!

Since beautiful views and magical landscapes do nothing for the stomach, and hiking the valleys generates a good appetite, we have dedicated a section to culinary satisfaction. Fortunately, Cappadocian cuisine will not disappoint. Your stomach will be as happy as your eyes.

But with the hundreds of restaurants in Cappadocia how do you choose?

That is another reason you bought this book. Below you will find restaurants that satisfy every taste and budget. The question remains as to what to order? I'm not leaving you hanging there either. See how many foods you can try from our list.

As the Turks say, "Afiyet olsun!" (Bon appetit).

[And you should reply, "Elinize sağlık" (Bless your hands) if you are speaking to the cook.]

RESTAURANTS

Over 2.5 million visitors is a lot of mouths to feed!

No worries. Cappadocia's restaurants are up to the challenge.

However, not all of the restaurants are satisfying. With hundreds to choose from I have listed my favorites. Many of the owners are my friends. If you have a problem at any of these places, let me know, and I will do my best to make it right. As is the case with everything listed in this book, I receive nothing for recommending them. My only incentive is earning your trust. If you prefer a restaurant not on this list, tell me about it and maybe we will add it to future editions.

Many of the restaurants on this list will give you a DISCOUNT if you show them that you bought this book (Logo Page).

INSTRUCTIONS

I've gone back and forth about how to do this section. In the end I have decided on giving you a quick easy list of the 7 restaurants in Cappadocia that serve the best food at the best value followed by a longer list of my favorite eateries.

This way if you are here for 2-3 days, pick from the first list and enjoy. If you are here for longer and/or want to include lunches or maybe are on a tight budget, then the longer list will provide all you need.

I guarantee satisfaction at the places I list. There are many wonderful restaurants in Cappadocia not listed here as well as many places you'll be sorry you chose.

One thing to be aware of if you go to a place not on either list is that the places that are most easily accessed are usually not that great. There are some exceptions but if they get lots of traffic, then they do not have to work hard for customers. Being a touristy area they are not counting on repeat business. For this reason finding places a bit off the beaten path is a wise way to go.

TOP 7 RESTAURANTS

1. Seten Restaurant Anatolian Cuisine

LOCATION: GÖREME

Serving gourmet Turkish dishes, this is perhaps the nicest restaurant in Göreme . The elegant dining area has an antique, classy feel. I have ordered a variety of dishes at Seten and always been impressed. They also have a wide selection of wines from Turkey and internationally.

I recommend calling ahead for a reservation, but it is not necessary usually. The restaurant sits next to Sultan Cave Suites.

www.setenrestaurant.com/
Telephone: +90 384 271 3025
Google map coordinates: 38.641284, 34.826018

2. Ziggy Cafe & Restaurant

LOCATION: ÜRGÜP

Ziggy's is a unique gourmet restaurant in Ürgüp. The owners are lovely people who fell in love with Cappadocia many years ago, moved here, and eventually opened this restaurant. In 2018 the wife died but the husband continues to run it well. The dining room is small (so make a reservation) and the atmosphere is cozy. The food is excellent. I love the Beef Tortellini and the Ember-Grilled Aubergines (eggplant), but everything is good.

www.ziggycafe.com/
Telephone: +90 384-341-7107
Google map coordinates: 38.633009, 34.907094

3. Topdeck Cave Restaurant

LOCATION: GÖREME

This is a strangely named restaurant given that it sits in an underground cave. The name refers to the food rather than the setting. And the food is excellent-homemade, traditional Turkish dishes cooked to perfection. Their menu varies from night to night so it is hard to list what they serve.

The best thing I can say is that you have to make a reservation or you will not get a seat. I asked the owner about interviewing him so I could write about him, and he said he did not want the extra press since they already have more customers than they can seat each night. They are consistently #1 on TripAdvisor.

> www.facebook.com/TopdeckCave
>
> Telephone: +90 382-271-2474 (whoever answers the phone should speak English).
>
> Google map coordinates: 38.641804, 34.827488

4. Pumpkin Göreme Restaurant and Art Gallery

LOCATION: GÖREME

This restaurant is aptly named with decorative lighted pumpkins and gourds lining the walls and windows. The food is excellent as well and the owner is eager to serve. They serve a set menu that changes regularly, but is always exquisite. The place is small with only 6-8 tables so I recommend making a reservation. (**Show the LOGO and they will give you a discount.)**

> Telephone: +90 542 808 5050
>
> Google map coordinates: 38.640673, 34.828856

5. Caverna Restaurant

LOCATION: ÜRGÜP

Set on the hill above Ürgüp, Caverna is part of Yunak Cave Hotel. The food is delicious, the decor is elegant, and the setting is beautiful with a gorgeous view of the valley looking towards Ürgüp. This is a favorite date night spot for many of my friends.

> Telephone: +90 384 341 69 20
>
> Google map coordinates: 38.633220, 34.907796

6. Dibek Traditional Home Cook

LOCATION: GÖREME

The name says it all. You get to sit on cushions by a low table enjoying delicious homemade Turkish cuisine. The decor is somehow both elegant and rustic. I recommend making a reservation. Dibek is easy to find right near the center of town.

www.dibektraditionalcook.com/tr/index.html
Telephone (land): +90 384 271 2209
Telephone (cell): +90 535 424 4570
Email: info@dibektraditionalcook.com
Google map coordinates: 38.642636, 34.829232

7. Old Greek House

LOCATION: MUSTAFAPAŞA

Another aptly named restaurant sitting in an old Greek house in the old Greek village of Sinasos which was renamed Mustafapaşa after the Greeks left in 1923-24. The layout of the dining area of the house gives the feel that you are eating in private rooms with just 2-4 tables in each.

They offer a set menu each night with a few options from which to choose. The traditional dishes are delicious and eating here is a memorable experience. You will need to arrange transportation, and I recommend calling to make sure they are open and have available seating.

www.oldgreekhouse.com/en/index.html
Telephone: +90 384 353 5306
Google map coordinates: 38.581448, 34.899793

AND FOR THE REST...

If I were to visit Cappadocia for just a few days, I would go to the previous restaurants. But there are other options and for those of you looking for more, these are the next tier eateries I recommend.

The restaurants below are broken down by town and each includes contact information. Only a few restaurants in Cappadocia require a reservation, and we have noted that on their descriptions.

The prices in Cappadocia are reasonable even at the nicer restaurants- an "expensive" entrée is $15-$20 and most are closer to $10. For this reason I have only mentioned price when it is unique. The letters on the maps below correspond to the letters for each restaurant in the list.

GÖREME RESTAURANTS

A. Fat Boys Restaurant

Owned and operated by Yilmaz Şişman (Shishman means fat) and his Australian wife, Angela, Fat Boys serves a mix of Turkish and foreign cuisine. All the basic Turkish restaurant options - chicken shish, guveç, grilled meatballs, and so forth - are available as well as nachos (made with Doritos), sausage rolls, and even Vegemite.

They also sell alcohol (which is not the case at many restaurants in Cappadocia). My wife and I often go here for date nights and are never disappointed. Prices are reasonable, the atmosphere is comfortable, the food is tasty, and outdoor seating is available. No reservation is necessary. It is located just around the corner from the bus station in the center of town.

(Show the LOGO and Yilmaz will give you a discount.)

www.facebook.com/pages/Fat-Boys-Bar-Cafe/384940121529206
Google map coordinates: 38.642990, 34.829317

B. Viewpoint Cafe

Viewpoint delivers with one of the best views in Göreme. The food is tasty but not gourmet. Expect to find Turkish dishes with some interesting twists that are not available everywhere. Only go here in warm weather.

Be sure to call for a reservation and ask for a table on the edge of the terrace so as to maximize the view. If you are standing near the center of town and look up the hill to the right facing the bus station you can't miss the Manzara sign.

* Telephone: +90 384-271-2712.
* Google map coordinates: 38.642227, 34.827584

C. Mozaik Restaurant

Mozaik was opened in 2018 by friends who tried to do something a bit different. I cannot say they fully succeeded, but I like the food and atmosphere. Their menu is not the normal Turkish fare and it is a bit limited, but what they serve is tasty. I recommend the cheese plate and stuffed pumpkin flowers. (**Show the LOGO and they will give you a discount.)**

Telephone: +90 384 271 21 19
Google map coordinates: 38.643425, 34.829259

D. Göreme Kale Terrace Restaurant

The Kale Terrace has a wide variety of tasty Turkish dishes including chicken shish, güveç, saç tava, köfte, and many more. The prices are reasonable, the service is good, and the food tastes good. This is not the kind of place you go to celebrate your wedding anniversary, but if you are looking for a satisfying meal while on vacation, this is a good option.

It is located near the center of Göreme where the road forks to go behind the bus station.

www.kaleterrasserestaurant.com/
Google map coordinates: 38.642613, 34.829590

And for a coffee or tea break...

E. Nazar Börek Cafe

Be prepared for the unusual at Nazar Börek. The food is unique including dishes like apple börek. At any minute, Refik, the owner, may break out in song playing his saz and entertaining his guests.

This is a great place to go for lunch or tea and dessert. Sit, eat, and enjoy being in Turkey with friends, and/or be entertained by the owner. They serve Turkish food but you will not find these particular dishes at many places.

Google map coordinates: 38.643392, 34.831371

F. Cafe Şafak

Right next door to Nazar Börek, this family run cafe is another great place to go for lunch or just to have a cup of tea and pass the time. Especially in warm weather it is nice to sit outside and watch the hustle and bustle of Göreme.

This is another family business serving homemade delicious Turkish food. It is located to the east side of the bus station across the canal not far from Voyager Balloons.

www.cafesafak.weebly.com/
Google map coordinates: 38.643392, 34.831371

G. Mydonose

If you are in Göreme looking for a cup of coffee, the best place is the quirky Mydonose. Go behind the bus station and across the street then upstairs and you will find a unique cafe serving a wide variety of hot drinks (teas, hot chocolate, specialty coffees, and more) in an offbeat atmosphere.

If I want to get some work done or meet a friend or just hang out and relax, this is high on my list of options.

Google map coordinates: 38.643044, 34.830234

AVANOS RESTAURANTS

A. Bizim Ev

Bizim Ev (Translation: Our House) is one of the more memorable restaurants in Cappadocia. Tucked away in a back alley directly after crossing the river, the entrance is a museum of sorts that mazes around until finally leading you upstairs to the comfortable dining room which has coves that give it the feel of eating in private rooms without doors. You will find excellent Turkish food on the menu.

I recommend the eggplant (aubergine) salad as an appetizer; but if eggplant is not your thing, no worries, I have not had anything here I did not like.

www.bizim-ev.com/tr/
Google map coordinates: 38.717807, 34.843680

B. Dayının Yeri

Sitting right off the river welcoming everyone to Avanos, Dayının Yeri offers a Turkish menu specializing in grilled dishes. The grilled onions and garlic in pomegranate sauce are blow-your-head-off good. This was the first restaurant we visited when we moved to Cappadocia, and it was a nice welcome.

www.dayininyeri.com.tr/AnaSayfa-EN.aspx
Google map coordinates: 38.716907, 34.843353

C. Sofra Restaurant

Located right in the center of town, the Sofra is a mainstay in Avanos. I eat breakfast here once a week with friends and know the owners and staff well.

They have a basic Turkish menu and specialize in the famous Testi Kebap - http://www.captivatingcappadocia.com/cappadocia-testi-kebap/.

zelvehotel-restaurant.com/en/restaurant.shtml
Google map coordinates: 38.719008, 34.847784

D. Köşem Döner

Okay, you may be wondering why this place is on here. I understand. There are 1000 döner places, and one is pretty much indistinguishable from the others. I chose this one because Galip is a good friend and a great guy and will treat you right if you go to his place.

The food (döner, soup, french fries) is fast, cheap, and tastes good. If you are on the go in Avanos, stop at the corner (Köşem means corner) across from the big mosque in Avanos and grab a sandwich or wrap.

www.youtube.com/watch?v=5cjmP-3hoP4
Google map coordinates: 38.718586, 34.847670

E. Konak Çorba & Kebap

This konak (2-3 story square Ottoman house) is a historic landmark in the center of Avanos. Everything on the menu is tasty and the service is good. They change the menu daily, making a variety of soups and traditional dishes. I love the kuru fasulye (Turkish baked beans).

I saw this place every time I went to Avanos but did not eat here until my 4th year in Cappadocia when a friend took me. I felt I had missed out. I listed it here so you would not make the same mistake.

https://www.facebook.com/Konak-kebap-ve-çorba-salonu-686385934812018/
Google map coordinates: 38.719616, 34.847498

F. Mado

This is my favorite restaurant in Cappadocia. It is not the best, but it is my favorite. You'll have to visit it to see what I mean.

Mado is a national chain, and I find that people coming from Istanbul are not as high on it because they feel it is not as "special". This is one of those places you find in mall food courts in Turkey. However, without a Starbucks in Cappadocia, this is a great place to sit by the river with good friends and/or family, enjoy ice cream or chocolate soufflé (wow!), and relax.

Their menu includes some dishes you won't find elsewhere in Cappadocia like calzones and fruit/chocolate fondue. Their desserts are great, and we enjoy their "normal" food as well. The tomato soup with a salad is delicious and their Köy Kahvaltisi (village breakfast) is amazing. They have wifi, and I enjoy going there some days just to get some work done while watching the ducks and drinking tea.

en.mado.com.tr/mado-cafe/mado-cafe-about.aspx
Google map coordinates: 38.717264, 34.849116

IBRAHIMPAŞA RESTAURANTS

A. Babayan Village House

Ibrahimpaşa is off the beaten path a bit, but this makes it the best chance to see an authentic village in Cappadocia. To say it has not been touched by foreign influence would be a lie, but you have to look hard to find it. Within this little hamlet lies a special experience at the Babayan Village House.

Babayan was the former name of the village as I understand it. They changed the name to honor the Ottoman Grand Vizier who hailed from Nevşehir and apparently brought running water to the village. (I can't verify this is true, but it is what I was told by more than one of the villagers.)

And the Babayan Village House could not be more appropriately named as it is one of the village houses turned into a restaurant. They serve traditional homemade Turkish dishes, of which most of the ingredients are grown/raised locally. The food is delicious and the experience is unique. Be sure to call before going, and if you don't have a car/ride, you will need to take a taxi.

Telephone: 0384-362-6001
Google map coordinates: 38.599278, 34.842341

UÇHISAR RESTAURANTS

> **NOTE**: These are both low-budget places that will satisfy your taste buds and your wallet.

A. House of Memories

Another memorable experience in Cappadocia awaits you at the House of Memories in Uçhisar which has a panoramic view of the beautiful Pigeon Valley and Erciyes Mountain in the distance.

Bayram Abi, the owner and chef, will serenade you throughout your meal with a smile and beautiful baritone voice. The food is normal Turkish restaurant food (kebabs, köfte, soups,...), but the atmosphere is anything but normal.

Google map coordinates: 38.629294, 34.805748

B. Centre Cafe

A surprising find right in the heart of Uçhisar is the aptly named Centre Cafe. A Turkish friend from Istanbul took me here the first time, and I was in for a surprise. I had the best salad I have had in Turkey, and I have had some good salads since we arrived in 2007.

I've been back a few times since and been impressed every time. Each dish has been deliciously satisfying. This is not gourmet, but it is cooked to perfection. In the past they have closed in the winter so double check if you want to go between December and March.

Google map coordinates: 38.627963, 34.804138

CHAPTER 16

TURKISH FOOD & DRINKS

To say that Turkish food is delicious would be trite; better words are delectable, scrumptious, delightful, yummy. The breads, the kebabs, the salads, the pides, the sarmas, the dolmas, the sweets, the tea and coffee...

When you visit feel free to use this list of 68 Turkish foods and drinks as a guide. Make sure you order something different every meal. If you gain a few kilos, think of it as taking a bit of Turkey home with you.

The list consists of 68 different Turkish foods and drinks divided into the following 11 categories:

BREAKFAST
BREADS/PIZZAS (GÖZLEME)
APPETIZER (MEZE)
SOUPS (ÇORBA)
SALADS
MEAT DISHES
SIDE DISHES
DRIED FRUITS/NUTS/SEEDS (KURUYEMIŞ)
DESSERTS/SWEETS
SPECIAL TREATS
DRINKS

BREAKFAST

Turkish breakfast is a real treat, one of the legacies of the Ottomans. It includes eggs, breads, tomatoes, cucumbers, olives, cheeses, jams, honey, thick cream, sausage, cold cuts, cereals, juices, tea and/or coffee, and more.

Most hotels that serve buffet breakfast will have all of these items and may allow special order omelets and other egg dishes. I have highlighted a few items below that may not be so familiar to the foreign visitor.

1. Menemen – My favorite! Chop tomatoes, onions, & peppers, and cook them with some oil in a frying pan (sausage too if you desire). Add salt and pepper and scramble some eggs. Enjoy!

It appears under-cooked, but it is not. This is a common dish among locals and in restaurants but is not as often found at hotels. If you can get it, try it. Try requesting it if you don't see it being served already.

2. Pekmez - This grape molasses is sweet and delicious. The locals make it in the fall after the grape harvest. They spend a day stomping on grapes (while wearing special boots) to get the juice, then mixing the juice with dirt, and eventually straining out the juice (removes bitterness).

Once the juice is collected they start boiling it in huge pots over open fires. Hours later the thick, tasty pekmez is all that remains in the pot. We use it as a sweetener on granola and other cereals as well as in some recipes. For a real treat take a banana and cover it with a mix of peanut butter and pekmez. Delicious!

3. Börek/Su Böreği – Take yufka (like a huge tortilla but paper thin) and put white cheese (think feta) in between the layers with some spices and butter and bake it until golden brown. It is optional to include ground beef- I recommend it. Another option is what they call sigara böreği which is a cigar-shaped pastry stuffed with white cheese.

BREADS/PIZZAS (GÖZLEME)

Turks have not eaten a meal if bread is not included. If you require a gluten-free diet, it is possible but not easy in Turkey. They have many different kinds of breads, and the best recommendation I can give is to try them all. Below I have highlighted the main items you will find as you travel.

4. Pide (flat bread) – The basic pide (pronounced "pee-day") bread is a flat bread with no toppings. We get it warm at the Çavuşin bakery. It does not last long! This is different than the pizza-like pides listed below.

Pide at restaurants is a Turkish version of pizza without tomato sauce. They are usually long, oval shaped like a flat American football or even a broad sword, but by the time you receive them they are cut into rectangular shaped pieces. I have listed the 6 most common varieties below.

* **Kaşarlı Pide** – The basic version contains kaşarlı cheese (no tomato sauce) and an egg. You end up with something resembling a meatless Egg McMuffin – crust, cheese, and egg – but delicious. The egg is optional on all pides.
* **Karasık Pide** – A mix of vegetables and ground beef.
* **Mantarlı Pide** – Mushroom and cheese – Wow!! So delicious.
* **Sucuk Pide** – Turkish Pepperoni.
* **Kuşbaşı Pide** – Chunks of beef with cheese.
* **Kiymalı Pide** – Ground beef mixed with a bit of chopped tomato, onion, and green pepper.

5. Lahmacun – An Anatolian specialty. This inexpensive pide consists of crust and a mixture of vegetables (no cheese). Honestly, I am not sure what is in the mixture but it tastes good and often has a bit of a spicy kick. They serve this with parsley, fresh spinach leaves, sliced tomatoes, and lemon. I recommend putting a little of each on top, rolling up the crust and enjoying.

6. Simit – This sort of resembles a sesame seed bagel except it is thinner and the hole is bigger. Like bagels these are heavenly with cream cheese. They are sold by street vendors as well as in bakeries and grocery stores. They are either browned and harder or golden colored and soft to the bite. I could eat these all day, every day.

We made a video showing how these are made: www.youtube.com/watch?v=LHYEFEpm-JA

7. Pogaça – A delicious light roll made plain or stuffed with olives, cheese, or potatoes. They melt in your mouth- a real treat.

8. Yufka – A very thin bakery dough (similar to a crepe but about 4 times bigger) used for making pastries (my wife uses it for lasagna) like baklava and börek. Find a Yufkacı and watch them make the thin sheets from scratch- fascinating.

9. Trabzon Ekmeği – This is a special bread, one of many specialty Turkish breads, that is famous around the country. You will see Trabzon Ekmeği stores devoted to these round, country-style loaves.

10. Gözleme – Take the yufka, fill it with one of a number of items- cook it on a hot flat surface (frying pan with no oil) until the yufka has hardened a bit and the filling is hot/melted. Filling options: potatoes, spinach, kasarlı cheese, white cheese, or a mixture.

The closest comparison is a quesadilla but the flavor does not remind you of Mexico in any way.

11. Tost – This is basically a grilled-cheese sandwich, sometimes including Turkish pepperoni. They take two huge pieces of bread, stick some cheese in the middle and place it in a sandwich press/maker. They press down as hard as they are able to flatten and melt it and the resulting creation is delicious.

> **NOTE**: When an American hears toast he thinks of bread cooked in a toaster. That is not what a Turkish person thinks when he hears the word tost. I mention this so you don't order it thinking the grilled cheese sandwich variety is a special kind of tost.

APPETIZERS (MEZES)

In most restaurants a variety of small mezes or appetizers are served with bread while you wait for your food. I have listed many of these below. But the most popular way to enjoy the mezes among the non-religious crowd is to go to a Meyhane and enjoy them with Raki and friends.

12. Hummus – This mashed chickpea spread is usually served along with other appetizers and is wonderful with flat bread.

13. Ezme (Salsa) – This mix of tomatoes, peppers, spices, and sprinkled pomegranate sauce (Nar Eksisi) will run the gamut on the "spicy" index depending on the restaurant. We have tasted it everywhere from so hot we went without taste buds for the rest of the meal to so mild they must have used bell peppers.

14. Grilled Baby Onions & Garlic – They sprinkle these with the viscous, sweet pomegranate sauce (Nar Eksisi) as well. Grilled to a golden brown, they melt in your mouth and are usually served as a free appetizer (although some restaurants charge so it is best to check).

15. Yoğurt – Turks eat a lot of plain yogurt, and this is an area in which we have acclimated well. For us it has taken the place of sour cream, but we eat it with granola as well. I know yogurt seems like a plain item, but I mention it because most people don't know that it originally comes from Turkey and that it is thick and delicious. This is one of the food items our college-aged daughter misses most.

16. Homemade Pickled Vegetables - Sometimes this is just pickled cucumbers but in some locations it includes various vegetables. My favorite is cabbage. Turkish pickles have a different flavor from their American cousins; stronger may be the best way to describe it. We love them.

17. Mercemek Köfte – These are vegetarian meatballs made out of red lentils (instead of meat) mixed with bulgur wheat, dried onion flakes, red pepper paste (think tomato paste except with red peppers), tomato sauce, cumin, parsley, green onion, lemon, olive oil, salt & pepper.

Of course, different locals will have their own varieties and every recipe may not match this one exactly. They are usually served cold as appetizers wrapped in crunchy lettuce. I love them, but not everyone in my family agrees.

ÇORBA/SOUPS

Turks love their soup and even eat it for breakfast sometimes. You can find restaurants that serve nothing but soup, and I think literally every restaurant and cafe in Turkey serves lentil soup. I have enjoyed most every soup I have tried with one exception listed below. If you are looking to have a light meal, soup and salad is the way to go.

18. Mercemek (Lentil) – This is my favorite soup and a Turkish staple. Each restaurant has their own special ingredients, but the red lentils are the distinguishing factor. Commonly, people add some lemon juice and either red pepper or mint and sometimes when we make it at home we add yogurt.

A version of this soup is called Ezo Gelin, which is mercemek with bulgur and tomatoes added. I expect that different people have their own varieties.

19. Işkembe (Tripe) – I assume some people like this or else it would not be offered. Personally, I am not a big fan of the lining of a cow's stomach. Once we were at a local restaurant and were finishing our meal as closing time approached. The owner brought out a bowl of tripe soup and with a big smile said it was on the house. We looked at each other wondering what to do (yes, we did think of spilling it so it would literally be on the house!).

We would never have ordered it, but here we were stuck with it. It would have been very rude not to eat it. I ended up eating the broth and leaving the tripe. The broth was good.

20. Tarhana – Tarhana is made from a mix of yogurt, vegetables, and flour which is fermented and then dried. Mix it with rice and broth and make it into a delicious soup. Every summer our landlords dry this mixture on our porches in order to have a good supply to take with them to Germany.

SALADS

Turks know how to make salad, and we love eating them. The vegetables and fruits are so full of flavor and when you order a salad in Cappadocia you can expect that most everything in it was grown locally.

21. Çoban Salatasi – This "Shepherd's salad" is a mix of greens and shredded carrots and tomatoes and cucumbers and oil and vinegar dressing. It is a bit more than a basic green salad. Tastes like health in a bowl.

22. Kısır Salatasi (Taboulli) – You have probably had taboulli before, and the Turkish version is not that different from common recipes we used in America. You will find it at some restaurants as an appetizer, but I like it best when our neighbors share it. It is often an orange-ish color in Turkey.

23. Patlican Salatasi – Eggplant (aubergine) salad is made with grilled eggplant, garlic cloves, yogurt, olive oil, and lemon juice. The eggplant interior is used and the skin is discarded. Mix it all together and out comes something unique and delicious.

MEAT DISHES

When ordered at restaurants these dishes are usually served with rice (or bulgur) and a salad along with a grilled tomato, a grilled hot pepper and plenty of bread.

24. Testi Kebab – This is the quintessential touristy food in Cappadocia. Cooked in a ceramic pot, broken open at the table, and served with rice, this stew is delicious. However, it is a restaurant/tourist dish, and you will rarely find it served at anyone's home these days. It includes beef, peppers, tomatoes, onions, garlic and various spices. Honestly, the experience is greater than the food, but the food is good.

How often do you get to watch someone break a sealed pot and pour what was inside on your plate? Traditionally, this dish dates back for as long as potters have been using the clay along the river in Avanos (over 1000 years, for sure). We made a video at a local restaurant to show how this is prepared: https://www.youtube.com/watch?v=mWAuxL-ue0U

25. Adana Kebab & Urfa Kebab – Take ground beef and shape it like a flat footlong hot dog, put it on a skewer and grill it, add some hot spice and you have this delicious dish. (Urfa Kebab is the same without the hot spice.)

26. Erciyes Kepab – Shoestring potatoes, with a creamy garlic yogurt, flank steak and demi-glaze sauce shaped on the plate like Erciyes Mountain covered with snow. You will only find this at a few restaurants.

27. İzgara Köfte – These grilled Turkish meatballs are on my list of personal favorites. Turkish köfte varies from place to place, but you can usually expect to taste some combination of lamb or beef, onion, garlic, salt & pepper, parsley, paprika, as well as oregano, mint, and ground sumac.

28. Saç Tava – This is Turkish stir fry. Take meat strips, peppers, tomatoes, onions, and garlic, stir fry them (no soy sauce or peanut oil) in vegetable oil, and sprinkle in salt and pepper.

29. Tavuk Şiş – These seasoned grilled chicken pieces are probably our kids' favorite meal when we eat out.

30. Iskender – Many Turkish restaurants serve this dish which consists of bread covered with döner meat and smothered in a special Iskender sauce. Add some tomato slices, a dollop of yogurt, and a chile pepper to complete the dish.

31. Tavuk/Et Durum – Take chicken or beef döner, put it in a tortilla like flat bread (some places serve thicker bread than others), add some lettuce, onions, and tomatoes, wrap it up and you have a delicious, economical lunch.

32. Tavuk/Et Döner Sandwich (Turkish: Ekmek Arası) – This is the same as the durum (above) except the ingredients are put in Turkish Ata Ekmek (similar to French bread); thus, it becomes a sandwich.

33. Beef Güveç – A stew-like dish with garlic, onions, eggplant and mushrooms, baked in a clay dish. This is similar to Testi Kebap but no clay pot.

34. Balık (Fish) – We prefer the grilled salmon (somon) but the sea bass (levrek) and trout (alabalık) are also readily available as well as anchovies (hamsi). The fresh fish markets are scattered throughout the area with every town having at least one.

35. Ciğer (liver) – I am not a fan myself but liver is very popular among Turks. In some shopping mall food courts in Turkey, you can find restaurants that only serve an astounding array of liver dishes. If you enjoy it, be sure to take advantage of the Turkish varieties.

36. Kiremet Chicken or Beef – Take an oval ceramic dish about 3 centimeters deep, fill it with meat, peppers, onions, tomatoes, garlic, and spices, and broil/bake it. The result is heavenly. In English, Turks often translate this casserole, but that does not give a good equivalent of this dish.

37. Sarma Beyti – Ground beef (Urfa Kebap) wrapped in a tortilla (Turkish: Lavaş) covered with an oily tomato sauce and served sliced with yogurt. This is a family favorite.

38. Mantı – This dish was made famous in Kayseri. Turkish mantı is stuffed with meat and there is a cheese version that looks similar to ravioli. The normal meat mantı is made by taking a small square of rolled-out dough, putting a bit of meat in the middle and then closing it similar to a Hershey's kiss except a bit smaller (if you have been to Russia, think pilmeni).

They cook them and serve them in the broth and with yogurt. Many people like to sprinkle red pepper and/or mint on top.

39. Ali Nazik – According to Wikipedia this is a specialty of Antep province in southeastern Turkey. Fortunately, you do not have to travel there as it is readily available in Cappadocia. The staples of this dish are eggplant puree, lamb or beef, and garlic. You will usually also find it with tomatoes and onions.

40. Hünkar Beğendi – (Sultan's Delight or Sultan Loved) This is patlican puree with tomatoes, peppers, and garlic, topped with kuşbasi (cubed lamb). Hünkar is another word for Sultan so the literal translation is "Sultan loved". There are different legends surrounding this dish, but everyone agrees the Sultan liked it.

41. Imam Bayıldı – (Imam Fainted) Eggplant (aubergine) stuffed with sautéed tomatoes, peppers, onions, and garlic, but NO meat of any kind. The legends on this one say that either the imam liked it so much he fainted, or he fainted when he realized he was out of the ingredients and could not make it, or he fainted when he saw the price of the ingredients. I have no idea which is true, but I know that I enjoy it.

42. Karnı Yarık – Stuffed eggplant with ground beef, tomatoes, peppers, onions, and garlic; the main difference between this and Imam Bayıldı is the inclusion of beef in this dish. This may be my favorite Turkish dish.

43. Kokoreç – Grilled lamb intestines. I have eaten some crazy stuff in my life... balut in the Philippines, lamb ear, eye, brain, cheek, and tongue in Kazakhstan...

But I have not found the courage to try this delicacy. From what I hear it tastes much better than the above mentioned items, but I just cannot bring myself to do it. You will be hard-pressed to find it in a restaurant. Mostly it is sold by street vendors.

Good luck!

44. Biftek – This is like a flank steak; the thinly cut beef can be served as an entree or cut into strips and served on salad or cut into strips and served as fajitas.

SIDE DISHES

In most Turkish restaurants you will not have a choice of side dishes as the entree comes with rice and maybe some garnish. Often these will be listed as appetizers or included in a Set Menu. The items listed below are delicious. I recommend ordering them if you have the chance.

45. Grape Leaf Sarma – Two keywords to learn regarding Turkish food are *sarma* which means wrapped and *dolma* which translates stuffed. Take a rice based mix with herbs and spices that vary from recipe to recipe, family to family, wrap it in a grape leaf and steam it. The result is a wonderful finger food that quickly disappears.

46. Kabak Çiçeği Dolma (Stuffed Pumpkin Flower) – Every late spring as the pumpkin flowers blossom you will find local ladies in their fields harvesting. They take the flowers, clean them, and stuff them with the same mixture described above, steam them, and just as quickly they disappear.

Both this dish and the grape leaf sarma are seasonal so you have to be here at just the right time to enjoy them.

47. Mushrooms Baked with Cheese – They fill a ceramic plate with mushrooms and cheese and bake it until the shrooms are soft and the cheese has melted into a nice blanket. If you are too eager, expect to burn your mouth, but sometimes it is hard to wait. They are so yummy!

48. Sigara Böreği – This is another favorite among our kids and was mentioned in the breakfast foods. Take a pastry fill it with white cheese (think feta) and some spices, roll it up like a cigarette, and fry it in oil.

DRIED FRUITS/NUTS/SEEDS (KURUYEMIŞ)

The Kuruyemiş stores around Cappadocia are wonderful places to visit, especially in Ürgüp's main square. My kids call them candy stores. We love to go in and sample everything. I can never leave them without buying something. They have unique items that are difficult to describe without seeing them so I recommend you go. I list a few of my favorite items (very basic examples) below:

49. Dried Apricots – Malatya is best known for their apricots but Cappadocia has no shortage and if you are here in August you will be able to pick them ripe off of the trees as you walk through the valleys. Most people grow too many to consume so they dry them. The open air markets have them in abundance. They make a wonderfully healthy snack food.

50. Walnuts – We have at least 5 of these trees in our yard and enjoy them each October when they are ripe. They are plentiful in the open air markets (pazars) and are delicious if you like to work for your food!

51. Leblebi – We love this snack food, although I think we are in the minority. This is the stuff they put in the dried food mixes to add weight without value. They are roasted chickpeas, and I like them most when they have the hard, white coating which adds a little flavor and makes them crunchier. I find them addictive which is why I have to measure out a certain amount. Otherwise, I will eat a whole kilo before I realize it!

52. Pumpkin Seeds – These may be my favorite snack. The yellow oblong pumpkins are harvested in September for the seeds. Everyone has their own special recipe and the results are addictive. I always look forward to sitting with my neighbors in the fall and eating homemade spicy pumpkin seeds. They are sold at the open air markets in each town.

DESSERTS/SWEETS

I love savory Turkish food, but their desserts are lacking, especially for Americans. They do have some good sweets, and their chocolate competes with the best in the world, but their post-meal desserts need some work. With that said, except for the künefe, I greatly enjoy the items listed below.

53. Künefe – This is a very popular, very Turkish dessert. It originally comes from Antakya. We tried it there when we visited. Take shredded wheat, stuff it with melted cheese, and cover it with syrup. If that sounds good, go for it. You may be surprised. Most people enjoy it, especially with a scoop of vanilla ice cream.

54. Maraş Ice Cream – Look for the guy in the fez at most tourist stops, and you will find this unique ice cream. It has a chewy texture caused by the addition of salep (flour made from purple orchid roots) and mastic (a resin).

The sellers are usually from Maraş and spread out around the country selling the gooey frozen treat. The show they put on for their customers is as good as the ice cream.

55. Baklava – This very, very sweet treat is best enjoyed with a cup of tea or some non-sweet liquid to wash it down. I guarantee you will be thirsty after partaking. Take thin pastry and stuff it with nuts and cover it with syrup. The result is a sweet sensation.

The Turks and Greeks fight over who originally made this. Since I live in Turkey, I'm happy to say it originated here; but, honestly, I have no idea.

56. Lokum (Turkish Delight) – This sweet treat was made famous in the Chronicles of Narnia. The closest taste and texture is that of a marshmallow mixed with a gumdrop. Lokum has many varieties/flavors in which they add nuts or other dried food to the sweet treat.

57. Helva – Tahin and sesame seed paste mixed with whatever you want- pekmez, chocolate, almonds, etc. This sort of reminds me of Bit-o-honey. I like it.

SPECIAL TREATS

You will not find these 2 items in restaurants and Aşüre is only made a few days each year to mark a certain holiday (see below). They do not really fit in any other category but are worth mentioning so I made a special category for them.

58. Aşüre (Pronounced Ah-shure-ay) – Legend has it that when Noah and family and animals exited the ark in eastern Turkey they took all the remaining food, mixed it together, and the result was aşüre.

Thus, today we have a strange mix of foods including saffron, rosewater, chickpeas, white beans, hulled wheat, rice, raisins, figs, apricots, sugar, walnuts, almonds, peanuts, and water.

Given this list the Noah story sounds as reasonable as anything else. What you get is a delicious soupy dish that is sweet, chewy, crunchy, and wet.

If you have read the *The Flea Palace* by Elif Şafak, you will recognize the foreign wife who spent her days trying to make the perfect dish of aşüre and never succeeded.

59. Ceviz Sucuk – This is a freaky thing you get in stores which consists of a gelatinous substance similar to tree sap with walnuts mixed throughout. It is long and cylindrical, thus the name walnut sausage. Some people love it. I cannot say I crave it. If you have a chance, you should taste it, but be careful not to eat the string that runs through the middle!

DRINKS

With the food list ended we have come to the last section of our list. This is not an exhaustive list of drinks but does cover the main concoctions found in Cappadocia. I have not listed sodas (Coke, Sprite, Fanta, ...) even though they are sold in abundance here.

60. Ayran – This salty yogurt drink could be considered the national non-alcoholic drink of Turkey. I love it and highly recommend it (most of my kids hate it). Apparently, it is a similar taste to buttermilk in America.

61. Turkish Coffee – This is the ultimate energy drink. Usually it is served in a miniature coffee cup about the size of a shot glass which is appropriate given the shot of caffeine contained within. Think espresso on steroids.

62. Turkish Tea – Black tea (add your own sugar) served in an petite tulip shaped glass has been the catalyst for more deep conversations than can be counted. Turks drink tea like lungs inhale air making it impossible to visit Turkey without staining your teeth at least a little bit.

63. Apple Tea – This is strictly a tourist drink. I have never seen a local Turk drink it. Usually it is not tea but just a sugary, apple-flavored powder served in hot water. The taste is similar to a weak cider. Nonetheless, most visitors enjoy it.

64. Efes Beer – I am not a beer drinker, but I am told that Efes is a good brew. Of course, this beer is not Cappadocian, but it is Turkish. You will find it in any restaurant that serves alcohol.

65. Şarap (Wine) - Cappadocia wines are growing in quality and fame and if you enjoy the fruit of the vine, then Ürgüp is the place to go (although you can buy wine in all the towns). Turasan and Kocabağ are the two best known Cappadocia wineries but you can get free tastings at any number of places in and around Ürgüp. We like the unique flavors of the "micro-winery" whose wines are sold at the Mahzen Şarap Evi in Ürgüp behind the hamam.

66. Raki – Atatürk's bane or "Lion's Milk" as it is better known is popular all over Turkey and is best enjoyed with a table full of Turkish mezes (appetizers) as described by Stephen Kinzer in his book, *Crescent and Star*. It is usually mixed with water to give it a cloudy appearance and it tastes like black licorice.

67. Salep – This is similar to egg nog for those who have had it. We buy it at the store in a box and heat it on the stove adding some cinnamon. You can also find it in restaurants. It is made from orchid root.

68. Şalgam – Fermented carrot or beet juice. I prefer the beet.

This list was not difficult to make but was wonderful to discover. Now it is your turn. Try as many as you can and let me know your favorites.

CHAPTER 17

SHOPPING

Most visitors to Cappadocia want to take something home to remember their experience. Perhaps you want to take gifts as well. There are no shortage of items from which you can choose. In this section of the book I want to give you an idea of what you will find and hopefully save you from being ripped off.

Every popular attraction will be littered with souvenir stands/shops and then each town will have more with Göreme and Ürgüp leading the way in this category. Most of the standard shops will have the same items with one out of every 10 having something unique.

As you can imagine if someone gets a unique item that sells well, then everyone else will supply it as soon as possible. This means you do not have to work too hard to find items. You will see the same things countless times during your stay. For certain items- carpets, pottery, wine - you will be better served going to a store specializing in those items.

I have divided this section into the following categories:

*** Carpets**
*** Wine**
*** Pottery**
*** Unique Items**
*** Cheap Gifts**

It is impossible to list everything sold at the stalls in Cappadocia, but with the products I mention you can devise a good strategy for taking care of your shopping needs while here.

THINK ABOUT THIS BEFORE BUYING A TURKISH CARPET

If you are reading this section, you must be interested in buying a Turkish or Persian carpet or rug. Well done. These works of art are available in abundance in Turkey and there are many reputable dealers in Cappadocia. However, there are just as many dealers trying to take advantage of tourists which makes for a potentially frustrating experience.

The information gap between buyer and seller is as wide as the Grand Canyon. My aim is to narrow that expanse to a manageable width. I spent time with a local seller learning how to recognize the differences that set nicer carpets apart.

Below I point out 10 characteristics to be aware of when shopping. I recommend that you visit a few shops, plan on spending at least an hour in each, and once you buy something, don't keep looking unless you want to be remorseful. Also, expect to spend at least $1000 and up to many thousands for a nice rug (perhaps a small quality prayer rug can be found for cheaper). Low quality pieces are available for a few hundred dollars.

You will see below the different factors that affect price. In the end, if you like it and are happy with the price, then it was a good deal. But I must warn you that if you show your purchase to locals and tell them what you paid, they will tell you that you paid too much even if you got it for free!

So, don't listen to them. Personally, I cannot think of a better way to cement your time in Cappadocia in your long-term family history than with one of these pieces of art displayed in your home or office. Your grandkids will still be using it when they are your age, and it will be as beautiful as it was when you bought it!

DON'T GET RIPPED OFF!

Now, let's get to the heart of the matter. There is a problem. A large percentage of carpet-buying tourists are at the mercy of the salesman who wants to get as much money as possible out of them. The tourists spend much more than they need to, especially if they buy in Istanbul. You will get a much better value in Cappadocia if you know what you are doing.

I have heard of people who paid $10,000 for a carpet in Istanbul only to find out they could have purchased its equal for $3,000 in Cappadocia. Let that sink in.

Now, if you know what you are doing, buyer's remorse will not be a worry. Let me explain the system you are entering, a system of commissions. You probably think that the price reflects the carpet plus the expenses of the shop. Usually that only tells a small portion of the story.

UNDERSTANDING THE SYSTEM

I am probably going to get in trouble for telling you this, and if you are with a tour group, then you are stuck in the system. But if you are shopping apart from a group, then you need to understand this.

The prices you see in many of the shops reflect the commissions that have to be paid to the tour agency, the tour guide, the hotel that recommended that shop, and maybe more people. On top of that the expectation of negotiating increases the price. All of this is to say that you should immediately take off 30% from the quoted price and then go down from there. If you are in Istanbul make that 50%.

How can you do that and not get laughed out of the shop? The rest of this section will explain what you need to know to get the perfect carpet for your tastes and preferences at a fair price.

But keep 2 things in mind: these are each unique works of art (the handmade pieces) and setting prices for art is tricky. Whatever someone will pay is what it is worth. And the salesmen are professional negotiators who are experts at reading people and knowing how thick their wallets are.

10 CARPET CHARACTERISTICS YOU NEED TO UNDERSTAND

Before going to the carpet shops you need to think through what you want and what you want to spend. I have made a video to show these ideas visually. If you are interested in watching it (30 minutes), here is the link: Turkish Carpet Buying Guide (www.youtube.com/watch?v=F7TFWcaxEPs)

1. Price	**6. Style/Motif**
2. Size	**7. Age**
3. Material	**8. Handmade?**
4. Type	**9. Region**
5. Color	**10. Product**

1. Price - The first rule is to never tell the seller what your budget is or, if you do, give a lower number than the actual minimum you are willing to spend (they assume you are doing that). Telling them will guarantee that you end up with a carpet for a little more than that price whether the carpet is worth that much or not.

Also, recognize that the seller expects you to negotiate and the initial price takes this into account. Also, if you are serious about buying a carpet remember that relationship is important. Do not walk in and ask for a price. Instead, talk to the salesman, get his story, ask about the shop and its history and the carpets, drink a cup of tea. Then you can ask about price.

2. Size - What size carpet do you want? The better you know the size, the better service you will get because the seller knows that you are serious. Ideally, you can measure the space before you leave your house. Remember that they use the metric system here so measure in meters. (Note: 1 inch = 2.55 centimeters)

3. Material - Turkish carpets are made of wool, cotton, silk, or a combination. Silk is the most expensive with the wool-cotton combination generally being the least expensive. Another price delineator regarding the material is the quality of the materials used. Hand spun wool and silk are much more valuable than machine spun fibers. You can feel the difference. The price difference can be 2-4 times more for the better material (all other things being equal).

4. Type - There are basically four types of Turkish and Persian rugs or carpets. The Turkish words are Halı (rug with pile), Kilim, Cicim (pronounced jee-jeem), and Sumak. The halı is probably what you are thinking of when you read Turkish rug/carpet. This fits everything from petite prayer rugs to large living room rugs with intricate motifs. They are thicker (pile) due to the double knot method of production.

The kilim (basic flat weave), cicim (flat weave plus extra wrapping), and sumak (flat weave, extra wrapping, and embroidery) are all made without knots so that they are thinner and lighter. These are used as wall hangings as well as throw rugs and come in many sizes, colors, and motifs.

5. Color - As with size, knowing the colors you want in your carpet will help your seller to better serve you. But when it comes to price, beauty, and duration the type of dye used is important. Natural dyes are more valuable and hold the color better than chemical dyes. Also, if you spend enough time looking, you will realize that different regions tend to use different colors.

Thank you to Ikman Galeri in Göreme for this chart.

6. Style/Motif - What do you see when you look at a Turkish carpet? The obvious answer is colors and shapes. Every shape and color has a meaning, a purpose, tells a story. Experts can glance at a carpet and immediately know its region of origin and the story its creator wanted to tell. Perhaps the young woman wanted a blessing of fertility or protection over her house. Or maybe she was hoping for peace and love in her coming marriage. Or more likely she wanted a bit of everything and mixed it all in the design of the carpet.

Be sure to take the time to discover the story told in the hieroglyphs of your chosen masterpiece. However, this is only true for older carpets made by women who planned to use them in their homes. The patterns on newer carpets handmade by women working in "factories" for big carpet shops do not have the same significance.

7. Age - Another important characteristic is age. Of course, the older the carpet, the more valuable it is as the note above about "factories" makes clear. The older carpets made in the villages are antique works of art, and their price reflects this.

However, the newer carpets can still be high quality, but you must realize the differences in the two products. One was made for a home with much care and purpose while the other was made (with much skill) to be sold to a foreign tourist. In the end you will buy what you like, but for some people the backstory affects the enjoyment.

8. Handmade? - This is probably the biggest price differentiator but there is a caveat you should be aware of. Most people ask if the carpet is handmade not understanding that there are two kinds of handmade rugs. The most expensive carpets are made by young women in the mountain villages of Anatolia (Turkish), Iran (Persian), and Central Asia.

They use natural dyes and hand-spun wool or silk. However, today very few carpets are still made this way. More common now are small workshops that employ women to make carpets. The difference is difficult to see for the novice; but for those who know, it is clear. This is one of the key ways that tourists are taken advantage of.

I expect your salesman will tell the truth if you ask a direct question. If this is important to you, ask whether it was made in a workshop or village home. It will give you some negotiating power. Also, an easy way to tell if it is really handmade is to look for defects. Check the corners and other details. If it is handmade it will not be perfect. Only machines can make it perfect.

9. Region - One of the ironies of Turkish carpets is that many of them do not come from Turkey. The average Turkish carpet seller will have rugs from Anatolia, Iran (Persia), Afghanistan, Armenia/Caucasus, Uzbekistan, and Turkmenistan. They each have a distinctive style and feel and within a few minutes you can expect to recognize the differences.

One NOTE here: Some sellers are importing "Turkish" carpets from China and pretending they are made here. I heard one town in China was renamed a

Turkish name so they could write on the carpet that it was made in that town and people would think it came from Turkey (search it on Google). For this reason I would stay away from the big tourists sellers.

Most of the places in Göreme are safe as far as I know. I feel confident with Ikman Galeri as well as with my friend Faruk who has carpets at his Kismet Cave Hotel.

10. Product - Lastly, the most important aspect of buying a Turkish or Persian carpet is to recognize that you are not buying a carpet only. You are buying history, culture, art, and a story (when you buy an old carpet – made before 1970). The good salesmen know the people who made their carpets. They can tell you about their lives, and the region in which they live.

If the age is clear, then you can easily learn about what was going on during that time. In the end you have a piece of art to display in your home or office, a conversation starter that will bring hours of enjoyment for years to come. And when all is said and done, if you are happy with your purchase, than you did not get ripped off.

Lastly, in terms of picking your shops, as I said above, I would discourage you from going to the shops that cater to large groups/tours. It is a different experience in the smaller outlets: more personal.

I know this section sounds a little negative. I hate writing it in this tone, but don't kill the messenger. I pray you are able to enjoy the process and find the perfect piece for you. If you like beauty, you will definitely enjoy all that you see in the shops.

WINE

Cappadocia boasts at least five local wineries, each with their own style and variety. The big two are Turasan, based in Ürgüp, and Kocabağ, in Uçhisar. You will see these bottles all over the region in shops and restaurants.

Kapadokya and Şenol Wineries are smaller and produce their product in Mustafapaşa. You can stop by for a taste and can find their wines in Mustafapaşa, but they mostly sell to restaurants and hotels throughout Turkey and not in retail outlets. Lastly, the Sarıkaya family produces their own brand in Mustafapaşa and sells it at the Mahzen Şarap Evi in Ürgüp behind the hamam. We love their "fruit" wines.

Turkey's wines are still lacking in reputation but are growing from what I've been told. I am not a connoisseur so my opinions can't be trusted, but I do enjoy the local wines and have heard that they are improving each year. There is definitely no shortage of grapes in Turkey.

The dry red wines are usually made from two different grapes, Öküzgözü and Boğazkere, which come from the region around Elaziğ and Diyarbakır in southeast Turkey. Most wineries make varieties using only one of these as well as a mix. I prefer the mix. I recommend you taste them all to form your own opinion. Another variety of red grape, Kalecik Karası, is used as well but not as much in Cappadocia wines.

I am not a fan of white wine so can't speak to it as much. The grapes are grown in Cappadocia, and I think some come from western Turkey around Izmir.

Now, I must confess here that I am not a big drinker. I don't drink beer and may have only 2-3 glasses of wine in a month. I am not the one to give expert opinions. However, I have tried everything I mention below and am happy to give my thoughts on them.

Cappadocia's wines are worth trying. I think you will be pleasantly surprised if you partake. You can find most of them in their own branded stores in different towns as well as in wine tasting shops that feature many different wines. Below you will find a short description of these five producers...

TURASAN

The first and largest winery in Cappadocia produces over 25 wine varieties. They make their wines in Ürgüp, and for a small fee you can take a tour of the winery which includes an opportunity to taste the different types. They began crushing and fermenting grapes in 1943, and today their products are ubiquitous in Cappadocia and throughout Turkey.

Their winery and tasting room is above Ürgüp on the road that leaves the main square heading towards Nevşehir, but they have sales points throughout the area that will allow you to sample their wares.

KOCABAĞ

Opened in 1972 and still going strong, Kocabağ has special tasting rooms in Ürgüp and Uçhisar. They make about 17 different wines. If the bottle has the Kocabağ brand name it means the grapes were grown in Kocabağ's vineyards which are located in different regions of Turkey.

They also make wines using lower grade grapes from local growers.These bottles will be branded with another name and have the Kocabağ name in a tiny font somewhere on the bottle.

Their shop in Uçhisar is near the Pigeon Valley overlook. The Ürgüp sales point is right off the main square in the center of town.

KAPADOKYA

Opened in 1956 this family-run winery out of Mustafapaşa makes four wines including three dry red wines and Emir, a white wine made from locally grown grapes. They produce their wine using a unique process in which they wait to separate the juice from the pulp until after the fermenting process. This gives their wines a strong bouquet, reminiscent of grape juice.

The flavor is distinct and my guess is that connoisseurs will not find it as appealing. However, it is worth trying if you can find it. I have only seen it in Mustafapaşa.

ŞENOL

Opening their doors just three years later in 1959 in Mustafapaşa and operated by the same family since that time, Şenol is a small winery producing only four wines and a total of 300,000 liters annually, a relatively small amount. Again, you will probably have to go to Mustafapaşa to sample their products since they sell most of their wines to hotels and restaurants outside of Cappadocia.

SARIKAYA

Last but not least is our favorite of the group. The Sarıkaya family sells wine mainly at the Mahzen Şarap Evi in Ürgüp behind the hamam. They are more like a micro-winery producing their own unique blends as well as the normal red and white varieties.

I mentioned above that we love their fruit flavored wines. They make pomegranate wine and green apple wine, as well as mulberry, blackberry, raspberry, and cherry varieties. They add the different fruits in with the grapes during the fermenting process and the result is wonderful. Think alcoholic fruit juice. I recommend you stop by Mahzen and sample their unique offerings.

With these five wineries Cappadocia offers a variety of wines for your palate. Try them and let me know what you think.

POTTERY/CERAMIC SHOPPING

Local Cappadocians have been using the perfect red clay of the Red River (Kızılırmak) to make pottery for millennia. The skill of local masters is world class which is a boon to visitors who can buy replicas of Hittite objects found by archaeologists as well as more common items ranging from beautifully painted plates to bowls, cups/mugs, miniatures, pitchers, vases, and many unique items.

Items can be purchased at tourist stalls throughout the region but the centers for production are the town of Avanos and Çavuşin village with more shops than can be counted.

The normal routine when you visit a shop will be to watch a little demonstration in which the master potter "throws" a pot from a lump of clay. He will then offer you the chance to try your hand at sitting at the wheel and making something. Once you have washed your hands you will be free to look around the shop.

There is no obligation to buy anything, but most people find something that will look good in their home and remind them of their visit to Cappadocia.

BEWARE

If you plan on shopping for pottery when you visit Cappadocia, I can give you a few cautions:

1. Tour Price Hike: If you are part of a tour during which you visit a shop, know that prices will be higher due to commissions that have to be paid to the different agents. The tour does not randomly pick a shop but has signed an agreement.

2. Handmade By Master? Not every item you see is handmade and not every item in a shop was made by the master potter. Around Avanos are a number of "factories" in which potters are employed to churn out items all day. These potters are very talented but are not "masters".

Also, for some items like the Hittite wine jug which are quite difficult to make, some potters have developed molds into which they pour the clay. The way to tell is to look at the base. If it is open (underneath), the piece was handmade. If it is closed, the piece was made from a mold. I think the handmade are a much better option (outward appearance is identical) but you should be able to get a molded piece for cheaper. This is a way that sellers will take advantage of tourists' ignorance and overcharge them for pieces that are not handmade.

Also, the white clay pieces come from other parts of Turkey like Kutahya so verify the origin of the piece you want if it matters to you.

3. Price: If price matters to you, shop around. Prices vary significantly from shop to shop and never settle for the listed price. The given price is for tour groups so you should try to negotiate down to at least half price. I went to four shops next to each other and asked about a similar piece in each shop and the quoted prices varied by 150TL!

4. Relationship: Be relational. Generally tourism is deadly to the soul. Locals see visitors as walking wallets and visitors are wary of being ripped off. The best way to fight this is to take your time, have a conversation with the potter, hear his story, have a cup of tea.

If the potter does not seem interested in connecting, then find one who does. It will be good for your soul and will give you a better story to tell when you are showing off the piece to your friends back home.

5. Region: As mentioned above some of the items will come from other parts of Turkey, namely Kutahya. Cappadocia is known for its red clay which means that most of the red clay items are locally made. The white clay comes from other areas. Generally, the Turquoise items come from other parts of Turkey. Of course, some of the potters procure white clay and make their own items. Ask the potter where the items were made if it is unclear.

Keeping these notes in mind will help you choose the perfect piece for you. I pray you enjoy the experience as well as whatever you pick to decorate your home.

INEXPENSIVE GIFTS & KEEPSAKES

In Cappadocia you will find hundreds of shops with all kinds of interesting items at varying price points. But often travelers are looking for inexpensive items to serve as memory-markers or to give as gifts.

Maybe you need to get something for a knickknack shelf, or for each of your workmates, or for your nieces and nephews or your neighbors or (fill-in-the-blank).

You do not want to blow your budget, but you would like something they will appreciate. I am sure this list contains something to fit the bill at a price you will appreciate.

1. Pottery - You can find a host of handmade ceramic items from small bowls to mugs to statuettes, trivets, and magnets for around $5 to $10.

2. Cappadocia Sculpture - This is the white elephant gift you have been searching for all your life. The problem is fitting it in your bag. I find that our kids love these, but, in my opinion, these rule the world of tacky. They do come in all sizes but be aware that they chip very easily.

3. Whirling Dervish - These provide minutes of fun. If you attended a Dervish night while in Turkey, one of these is worth purchasing as a memento. Put it on the coffee table in your living room, and you will be able to talk about Turkey with everyone who visits you and asks about it.

4. Hanging Decorative Ceramic Balls - I have no idea what these are for besides decoration or why they were first made, but they must be popular as they are sold everywhere. This is the gift for the person who has everything, I guess.

5. Bejeweled Dagger - These are cool and make great gifts for teenage boys. Make sure NOT to pack it in your carry-on bags!

6. Onyx - The onyx stones come in all shapes, colors, sizes, and prices. How about a pair of onyx dice instead of the fuzzy kind?

7. Magnet - Every shape and theme imaginable. If you took a hot-air balloon ride, this may be a good trinket to bring home.

8. Money Purse - These make wonderful gifts and are easy to pack. I use them for business cards and coins. My kids use them to store their little treasures. They are less than $1 each.

9. Turkish Carpet Bookmark - Another perfect gift for the traveler with no luggage room. The Turkish designs are unmistakable. You can also find these as mouse pads which also work well as dollhouse rugs.

10. Pepper Grinder - These distinctly Ottoman looking items are fun to use and make classy gifts. Whose table would not be improved with a nice pepper grinder?

11. Fairy Doll - After visiting Fairy Chimneys you will have a story to tell your niece when you give her one of these dolls. They are made more for display than as a toy, but most little girls will enjoy them.

12. Picture - This is sort of cheating, but since everyone comes to Cappadocia with digital cameras these days, you should be able to take at least one nice picture of your time. Print it, get a frame at Target, and give it to a loved one.

13. Coasters - A nice addition to your living room may be a set of coasters with a colorful hot air balloon drawing or Turkish carpet design.

14. Cappadocia Playing Cards - For just a couple of dollars you can get playing cards with pictures of Cappadocia. We took these home as gifts, and they were well received.

15. Cappadocia T-Shirt - Many shops carry a variety of Cappadocia t-shirts for under $10.

16. Turkish Carpet Covered Journal - These come lined and un-lined and serve a double purpose of recording your thoughts while reminding you of your time here.

17. Tea Glasses or Turkish Coffee Set - Leaving Turkey without drinking a glass of tea in the tulip-shaped glasses or sipping a cup of Turkish coffee is a real challenge. Why not take a set home to enjoy?

18. Scarves - Many tourist shops will carry a variety of beautiful scarves. They are good prices and can be used for casual or formal occasions.

19. Purses/backpacks - Girls of all ages will proudly sport the colorful pursed and bags found at many gift shops.

20. Local clothing - Village ladies wear a special type of pant called shalvar. The pants are very roomy and look much like a skirt. Local tourist shops carry these traditional pants as well as a variety of more modern and fashionable ones for the tourist. Our daughter wears them at her college dorm and has received a lot of requests for her to bring some back from Turkey.

21. Keychains - Lastly, if you have waited until the last minute, you should have no trouble finding a keychain with a Cappadocia theme.

There you have it, something for everyone. Now, for those of you looking for nicer items, the next section is for you.

UNIQUE GIFTS & SOUVENIRS

In earlier sections I explained how to buy carpets, wine, pottery, and reasonable gifts, but many visitors are looking for other unique items that will go just perfectly in their office or on their living room mantle or coffee table (next to this book, of course!). I hope one of the items listed below fulfills that desire. I have been to almost every shop and tourist stand in Cappadocia, and have listed a few options here.

You will find literally hundreds of items in this region. What you find at the ubiquitous stands will be pretty similar throughout. If you do not find what you're looking for there, then I recommend going to the antique shops you will find near the town square in Ürgüp. Göreme has a few as well but you have to search to find them.

Regardless, here are a few items worth mentioning:

1. Mosaic Glass Hanging Lamps - These beautiful pieces can be creatively displayed in myriad ways in your home. Every color imaginable can be found and the sizes vary as well. These are a favorite gift of my wife.

2. Ottoman keys, jewelry, and other antiques - Many stands and shops will have unique Ottoman antiques including large keys, jewelry, and other ancient knick-knacks.

3. Kurdish wall hangings and Susannehs - These come from the southeast, from both Kurds and Uzbeks. They are unique and make a beautiful addition to any room. My daughter has one of these hanging in her dorm room and we have several in our own home.

4. Turkish Coffee or Tea Set - These sets will be great reminders of your time in Turkey. Be sure to buy the coffee or tea as well so you can make it when you get home. You may want to get a Turkish tea pot and/or a cezve (special Turkish coffee pot).

5. Chess Set - These come in many shapes and sizes but the variety in Cappadocia is lacking. If you

CHAPTER 18

IN CASE OF EMERGENCY

What happens when you get to Cappadocia for your dream vacation and get sick? Perhaps you forgot to pack medicine... or you ran out. What will you do?

Or maybe you have heard that medicine is cheap in Turkey so you want to pick some up before you return home. Do not tell anyone, but we think this is a good idea. I am not saying we have done it, I am just not saying.

PHARMACY = ECZANE (Pronounced Edge-zahn-ay)

The first step is to find the pharmacy. If you are looking for Rite-Aid or Sav-on, an all-in-one drugstore, you will join Odysseus on his 10 year journey as they do not have such stores here. Instead look for the glowing "E" which stands for Eczane. These are generally small (about the size of a barber shop) and have shelves brimming with drugs with names you probably will not recognize.

Some brand names are available like Advil but not all. Instead look for the active ingredient name. Paracetamol is Tylenol and Ibuprofen is Advil, for instance.

The store will have some beauty supplies and baby products like pacifiers and bottles. But I am guessing that most tourists will not be interested in these. These are generally over-priced and can easily be found in other stores. They will also have condoms (also found in grocery stores) and saline solution for contacts but expect to pay close to $10 per bottle!

Also, you need to know that they are open during normal business hours from Monday through Friday. If you need something in the middle of the night or on weekends, you will need to do a little work as only one eczane will be open in your town. You can find which one by going to any of them. If it is not open, it will have a sign in the front window listing which one is open. However, this will still be difficult since you won't know the addresses. The best bet is to ask someone at your hotel for help.

MEDICINES

I went by one of the pharmacies we use in Avanos to get some prices for a few basic items (prices may vary but this gives a general range):

* Opti-Free contact lens saline solution - 355ml - 30TL (This is expensive because very few Turks use contact lenses.)
* Paracetamol (Tylenol) - 20 500mg tablets - 2.50TL

* Children's Paracetamol Syrup - 150ml - 5TL
* Thera-Flu - 20 tablets - 5TL
* Amoxicillin - 16 1000mg tablets - 10TL
* Ben-Gay - 50g - 5TL

> **NOTE**: The eczanes have hundreds of medicines for every sort of malady. I just listed a small sample to give an idea.

As you can see the prices are not so bad, especially for the children's meds. The pharmacist will most likely speak very little English so you will need to know what you are looking for when you arrive. By pointing to the area of your body that is sick, you should be able to make them understand your need.

And you do not have to see a doctor first. If you want an antibiotic, just buy it, no prescription necessary. If you are not comfortable self-diagnosing, then you will be able to find a doctor during the day. Just ask your hotel for help.

If you are more on the adventurous side, trust the pharmacist to pick the right medicine for you or get the name beforehand from a Turkish friend (hotel managers should be able to help).

My hope is that you do not get sick while here, but if you do, you do not need to despair. Help is right around the corner at your neighborhood Eczane.

NEED A DOCTOR?

If you think you need a doctor, the best advice is to ask your hotel for help. Generally in Cappadocia doctors work at hospitals, not in their own offices. Thus, you can either catch a taxi to one of the hospitals in Nevsehir or ask your hotel to arrange it. There are two private hospitals, Versa and Kapadokya, and one public hospital. The private hospitals provide better care, but charge a lot more for it. You will be expected to pay the amount and then get reimbursed by your insurance company when you return to your home country.

> **NOTE**: The eczanes have hundreds of medicines for every sort of malady. I just listed a small sample to give an idea.Note: The eczanes have hundreds of medicines for every sort of malady. I just listed a small sample to give an idea.Note: This is true for America. I am not sure how it works with European and Asian countries. Our family has had several experiences at both private hospitals and we have been really pleased.

SECTION III:

1, 2, & 3 DAY ITINERARIES

CHAPTER 19

1, 2, & 3 DAY ITINERARIES INTRODUCTION

The vast majority of visitors to Cappadocia stay 1-3 days. I have listed all the things to do in previous sections of this book, but to better serve you I want to give basic outlines for these stays.

I break each of them down into 2 alternatives:

1. "Others Serve You" - This includes the package tours and guides and such.
2. "Do It Yourself" - This is for those who prefer to "wing it", like adventure, and/or have a low budget.

Whichever you prefer, this section should help you arrange your days so as to maximize your time in this amazing region.

CHAPTER 20

24 HOUR PLAN

I pity you if this fits you, but I understand that you want to see Cappadocia and can only spare one day so let's make the best of it.

You are probably arriving late at night or early in the morning and have a full day before departing again. I assume you are here for at least one morning which is why I include the balloon flight.

Let us start in the morning. With one day you will not have time to dilly-dally so every moment will be full. You can sleep after you leave. I strongly encourage staying in Göreme to keep transportation times to a minimum.

I have not included descriptions for the activities since they are written in other sections. Either click the links or check at the listed page number if you need more details.

Jump to the end of this section for my ideal day in Cappadocia.

OPTION 1

THEME: LET OTHERS SERVE YOU

5am – 9:00am – Hot Air Balloon Flight & Breakfast

> You will be up around 5am and heading to the hot-air balloon launch. Once you have received your certificate and returned to your hotel, you can down a quick breakfast and proceed to…

Guided Tour

9am – 5:30pm – Green or Red or Blue Tour

> The transport will pick you up at your hotel and traverse the region with a guide.

5:30pm – 7:30pm – Göreme Open Air Museum

> This is here in case your tour did not include this museum and it is summer with long days, otherwise this is your chance to do some strolling and window shopping in whichever town you are staying. When someone offers tea, accept the invitation.

[Note: Depending on the time of year and the weather, this could be the time to head up to the cliffs overlooking Göreme to get your sunset photos.]

7:30pm – 10:30pm – Turkish Night or Whirling Dervish- Dinner and a Show

Some Turkish Night shows include the Whirling Dervishes along with belly dancers and folk dances from many different regions of Turkey while others include everything but no dervishes. The Whirling Dervish show only includes the dervish dances.

THE END: Head to the bus station or airport

I like this schedule but not everyone is into the guided tour thing. I cannot take everyone into account and so much is available here. Below I give a DIY alternative to the above plan.

OPTION 2

THEME: CONTROL YOUR DESTINY

5am – 9:00am – Hot Air Balloon Flight & Breakfast

Same as above.

9am – 11am – Göreme Open Air Museum

This allows you to fill your lifetime quota of cave churches and paintings.

11am – 1pm – Hiking

Love, Pigeon, Devrent (camel rock), or Red Valleys are truly captivating. Pick one and enjoy yourself. For some of you, renting a mountain bike and taking in your chosen valley while catching serious air will be the way to go. For others an ATV will do the trick.

1pm – 2pm – Lunch

2pm – 5pm Visit Underground City, either Derinkuyu or Kaymaklı

These are at least a 30 minute drive from Göreme, 60 to 90 minutes if you take the bus. Therefore, I recommend either renting a car or a driver or hiring a taxi (or scooters if you are adventurous and the weather is nice-in this case rent them right after you finish the ballooning so you can use them all day).

Derinkuyu is deeper and Kaymaklı is wider, otherwise they are similar. This is one place I recommend hiring a guide as there are no signs explaining anything except which direction to walk (guides are usually waiting at the entrance to the underground city and will negotiate a price).

5pm – 7:30pm – You Choose

Upon returning from the underground city, you have a number of options depending on your tastes/preferences and the season/weather.

I would recommend one of the following:

* Wine tasting and shopping in Ürgüp – you can find good gifts in the shops in the center of town and enjoy some locally made wines.

* Pottery in Avanos or Çavuşin – Go see a pottery demonstration, try your hand at it, and pick out some nice Hittite ceramic wine bottles for your living room. Recognize that the selection will be better at one of the big places but you will get a much better deal and maybe even make a friend at one of the smaller shops.

* Shopping for Carpets in any of the Towns – Most every town has carpet stores. However, you do not want to be rushed in this purchase, and with only one day in Cappadocia, you will feel rushed. But if you do buy one here, remember this advice: If you are happy, then you got a good deal.

* More Hiking - If you did not get enough in the morning, you can try to satiate that urge now. Pick one of the other valleys, put on your hiking shoes, grab your camera, and head for the rocks. (Red/Rose, Love, Pigeon, and Zemi Valleys)

* Pick a site - Within a few kilometers of Göreme the following towns/ sights are available to you: Çavuşin with its swiss-cheese rock churches; Ortahisar and Uçhisar with their towering rock castles (amazing views); Paşabağ with its perfect fairy chimneys bunched in one small area; and Zelve Open Air Museum, which is probably a bit repetitive if you went to the Göreme Open Air Museum.

* Drink some Tea – Probably the most memorable thing you could do is meet a local who speaks your language and drink some tea with him or her.

SUNSET VIEW

Sunset Point - If the weather is clear, and the season is right, go up to sunset point above Göreme and enjoy a breathtaking scene as the sun descends over the hill and the lights slowly come on in the town below. Or rent an ATV and go up to one of the high points for a beautiful sunset scene and then a return ride in the dark.

7:30pm – 10:30pm – Turkish Culture Night

Either the Whirling Dervishes or the Turkish Night (belly dancing,...) as explained above.

THE END: Head to the bus station or airport

One last note: I did not mention the Ihlara valley even though I think it is at the top of my list in Cappadocia. The reason is that it will take the whole day and does not capture the essence of the region, in my opinion.

If you stay longer, I put it in the must category. I wanted to mention this as most people will have heard of Ihlara, but may not understand the distances and times involved. (It is included in the Green Tour mentioned above. On that tour you at least get to see it and hike a bit).

WHAT IF I ONLY HAVE 12 HOURS?

After I wrote the above someone emailed me saying they only had 12 hours in Cappadocia and asked for an itinerary. This means no hot air balloon because they are arriving in the morning and leaving in the evening. Here is what I wrote them:

"Here is my ideal day in Cappadocia for you but it may be too expensive. Have the tour company pick you up at the airport and go to Derinkuyu underground city. Then head to Ihlara for the valley hike that ends with lunch. From lunch go to Selime monastery (these 3 are all part of the Green Tour). From there head back to the Göreme Open Air Museum and then to Pasabag (these 2 are from the Red Tour)). If you have any time left you can do the following: Uçhisar kale or go to see a pottery demonstration.

I would then go to Göreme for dinner and be sure to head up to sunset point. End with strolling through Göreme before heading back to the airport. That allows you to make the most of your 12 hours seeing all the best/key sites."

> **NOTE**: This day will be significantly more expensive than the Green Tour and choosing from some items as listed above. The problem with the Green Tour is that you miss the Open Air Museum and by the time the tour ends, the museum will be closed. But with only 12 hours, you have to make these hard choices. You are not paying for a hotel room in Cappadocia so maybe that makes it possible to justify spending more?

CHAPTER 21

TWO DAY PLAN

You have 2 days in Cappadocia, how are you going to spend them? Let's walk through a schedule that will maximize the time. I'm counting this as 2 full days so adjust according to what you actually have.

OPTION 1

Theme: Relax and let others take care of you – Guided Cappadocia Tours

DAY 1

5:30 – 9:00am Cappadocia Hot-Air Balloon & Breakfast

More balloon rides occur in Cappadocia than anywhere else in the world. Balloon flights are cancelled a few days per month due to windy conditions. For this reason I recommend booking your trip on day one. This way if the weather is bad, you will still have a chance the next day.

9:30am – 5:30pm – Red, Green, or Blue Tours

The van will pick you up at your hotel and return you to the same spot. The tour usually includes transportation, a guide, and lunch. This is probably the best way to see as much as possible in a short time.

5:30pm – 7:00pm – Sunset/Hike/Shop/Tea/Rest

Depending on the season and the weather you will have some time between the tour and dinner that can be spent outside. Only you know what you can handle at this point.

Here are some good options:

* Pick one of the valleys (Red, Pigeon, Love, and Devrent) and go for a hike. Make sure to check which valleys are included in your tours so you pick one you will not see on day 2. Where you are staying will play a role in this as well since transportation can be a problem. If you are in Göreme or Çavuşin, this should not be a problem.

* This is a good time to do some shopping around your hotel if you were not able to shop enough on your tour.

* After a long day of touring you may want to rest before the big night. In this case you can either sit in your hotel lobby/courtyard and have some tea or take a nap.

SUNSET VIEW

Go take pictures of the sunset from the cliffs overlooking Göreme. This will depend on the season and weather, but is worth doing if conditions are right.

7:30pm – 10:30pm – Turkish Night or Whirling Dervish- Dinner and a Show

Some Turkish Night shows include the Whirling Dervishes along with belly dancers and folk dances from many different regions of Turkey while others include everything but no dervishes. The Whirling Dervish show only includes the dervish dances.

DAY 2

Sunrise – 9am – Morning hike & Breakfast

Since you are not ballooning you can sleep in or you can take advantage of the beautiful, quiet mornings and go for a walk/hike. I can speak from firsthand experience about this. Besides the balloonists, only the dogs are up early in Cappadocia.

The scenery is truly captivating as the first rays of sunlight hit the rock formations and the serenity is life-giving. This is a wonderful opportunity to prepare your soul for the day ahead. Of course, if everyone does this, than it will not be so peaceful and serene! But I do not think we need to worry about that.

9:30am – 5:30pm – Tour

Same as above, just a different tour.

5:30pm – 7:00pm – Sunset/Hike/Shop/Tea/Rest

Same as above; you decide what is best for you.

7:00pm – Bedtime – Dinner and Debrief

If you truly love watching Whirling Dervishes and did not get enough at the Turkish Night, then you can go see more. However, since most of you will not fall into this category, I would recommend that you pick a nice Cappadocian restaurant close to your hotel and debrief your trip.

Talk about your highs and lows, what you would do differently, how glad you are that you read this book and list the five people to whom you want to give it, what you would recommend to someone else, and what five things you want to remember. This will provide some closure before you head off to your next adventure and cement the best memories in your mind.

OPTION 2

Theme: You are the ruler of your destiny!

If you are not one to take a guided tour, you would prefer to explore and do your own thing on your own schedule, then let me give you some pointers/ guides to help you at least know the key sights, activities, and towns.

DAY 1

Hot-Air Balloon

DURATION: Flight is 60-90 minutes. Add at least another hour for transportation and waiting.

If you have the money this is a must.

Göreme Open Air Museum

DURATION: Give yourself 2 hours with transport.

This fascinating area gives you the opportunity to see beautiful centuries-old religious cave paintings in what was once a thriving community. The Open Air Museum will most likely satisfy your need to see caves and wall paintings.

Hiking – Red/Rose, Love, Pigeon, Swords, and Zemi Valleys

DURATION: You could spend all day but at least 2-3 hours.

Hit as many valleys as you can or take your time meandering through one. Be sure to bring a camera, some water, and good hiking boots or sturdy shoes. This is not mountain climbing but the ground can be a bit slippery from the sandy stone ground, and you can expect to find muddy spots especially October through late April.

Another option is to do this with either a mountain bike, an ATV/Quad or on horseback.

Underground City

DURATION: Exploring the rooms and tunnels takes around 45 minutes. Transportation from Göreme is 45-90 minutes.

After lunch head to either Kaymaklı (wider) or Derinkuyu (deeper). If going by public transport, catch the bus to Nevşehir and then transfer to the Derinkuyu bus. If you are not sure what to do, ask your bus driver- just say the name of your chosen destination with a questioning look, and he (or someone on the bus) will direct you. Or get detailed instructions from your hotel.

Sunset/Shop/Tea

DURATION: As much time as you want to/can spend.

Same as above (Option 1, Day 1)

7:00pm – 11:00pm Turkish Night or Whirling Dervish- Dinner and a Show

Some Turkish Night shows include the Whirling Dervishes along with belly dancers and folk dances from many different regions of Turkey while others include everything but no dervishes. The Whirling Dervish show only includes the dervish dances.

DAY 2

1/2 Day – All Day – Ihlara Valley

Ihlara is my favorite place in Cappadocia. The trail goes 12 kilometers in total, and you can go as much or as little of it as you wish. A gentle stream flows through the length of the valley and with the lush greenery, high cliffs, and dearth of visitors and civilization, this is one of the most peaceful "tourist" attractions you will visit anywhere on earth.

There are cafes along the trail so bring some money, but I would still plan on bringing water and even a picnic if you like. If the weather is hot, you may want go for a swim in the stream (it is actually somewhere inbetween a stream and a river in terms of size). Take your bathing suit if you think you may be tempted.

Working out the transportation logistics for Ihlara is not easy but worth the effort. One option is to hire a driver and have them drop you off at one end, then meet you at the other end. You are then free to hike through the valley at your leisure.

If you do not have a driver or two cars, then you will need to either hike part of the way and return or do what we did which was to hike halfway, climb out of the valley, and hitchhike back to your car. Don't expect to find public transportation from Göreme.

Sunset/Shop/Tea/Rest or see more Attractions

At this point you can choose to do any of the options as were listed above, or, if you have time, you may want to see some more sights. Go to the "Attractions" and/or "Activities" sections to get more ideas.

Dinner and Debrief

Same as above

And with that 48 hours have flown by and you are trying to catch up on sleep and focus on whatever is next.

CHAPTER 22

THREE DAY PLAN

3 days in Cappadocia…ahhh…sit back and relax…it's like a lifetime… Or Not!

I have to admit that with three days you can at least do a bit of justice to this place, but the time will be full so it is best to have a good plan.

I am going to change the format a bit for this length as the daily schedule will be a bit tedious. I am still going to give the options but will not be so detailed in the timing. If you are unclear as to how long activities last, please look back at the 2-Day Plan.

OPTION 1

Theme: Guided Tours – Breadth instead of Depth

GREEN - RED - BLUE/UNDISCOVERED CAPPADOCIA

If you are the kind of person who wants to see the most things in the most efficient way and likes structure, then this is the option for you. Taking a different tour each day will allow you to canvas the region and at least get a taste of most of what is available.

The tours last from around 9am to 5:30pm The cost is 100TL-120TL (except for Undiscovered Cappadocia) depending on the tour. This gives you some time in the morning and evening to fill in the missing pieces.

HOT-AIR BALLOONING

On one of the days you will want to do the hot-air balloon ride. Cappadocia is perhaps the best place in the world for this with its unique landscape, dry climate, and relatively calm early mornings. The rides start at sunrise and last 60-90 minutes. This means you will need to be up early in order to get to the launch site (they will pick you up at your hotel).

You should be back to your hotel in plenty of time to catch breakfast and be ready for the tour bus pickup. The cost for a one hour flight is around 150 euros depending on the company. You can book directly online or through your hotel or tour agency.

Check the hot air balloon section of this book to learn more and to see which companies offer discounts to you for purchasing this book.

Important note on balloons: I would recommend booking the flight for the first morning you are here so that you will have opportunities in the following days if the weather is bad.

MORNING WALKS

If you are a morning person, I recommend getting up early on at least one of the non-ballooning mornings to enjoy the view from the ground before the world wakes up. Except for the ballooners Cappadocia is quiet in the early morning, making for a glorious time of enjoying nature. Being the only people walking around such a beautiful place with the birds singing and the balloons floating will be a sweet memory for your mental scrapbook. Personally, morning walks have provided many of the highlights of my time living in Cappadocia.

TURKISH NIGHT or WHIRLING DERVISH SHOW

You have two choices here. One option is to go to the Whirling Dervish show- a spiritual and cultural experience. These shows usually do not start until after 8pm and last for 45-60 minutes.

The alternative is a mixed cultural show which includes dinner and lasts close to three hours. Every 15-20 minutes a different Turkish cultural group (actually same dancers in new costumes doing different dances) enters the room to entertain you. Whirling Dervishes, belly dancers, folk dancers, and on and on. These shows go from 7:30pm – 10:30pm.

SUNSET PHOTOS, DINNER & DEBRIEF

On the other nights you are free to do some shopping and strolling about. There is really no night life to speak of in Cappadocia. If the weather is nice, be sure to head up to the point overlooking Göreme and take in the sunset.

I strongly encourage you to take some time on your last evening to debrief your trip. If you are alone, schedule in time to journal/blog. If you are with family or friends, spend dinner discussing your time in Cappadocia. Here are some questions to get the conversation going:

* What was the best experience of our time here in Cappadocia?
* What was the worst experience?
* What will we remember 5 years from now?
* What can we recommend to other visitors?
* What do we wish someone had told us before coming?
* What do we wish we had done that we did not get to do this time?
* What's the most interesting historical fact we learned?

* Which sight/activity was our favorite?
* Who should we buy this book for?

OPTION 2

Theme: Frank Sinatra – I did it my way!

If you are not the guided tour type (or at least not the three tour type), then you have plenty of options. If you are fully open to whatever and do not like to be pigeon-holed, then you can set your own schedule and make it happen. Three days gives you enough time to hit the key attractions and pick some of your unique preferences without feeling rushed.

The morning and evening will be the same as above (hot-air balloon, serene morning hikes, Turkish cultural night, sunset photos, dinner and debrief). The difference is how you spend the time that would have been a tour. By not choosing the tour you are saying that you want to choose a few things and focus on them, go deeper, really explore and enjoy them.

TWO MUST-SEES

Everyone who comes should see the GÖREME OPEN AIR MUSEUM and an UNDERGROUND CITY (Derinkuyu or Kaymaklı are the most popular).

ONE MUST-DO

Cappadocia's fairy chimneys make it one of the more unique destinations in the world. Many of the chimneys as well as networks of caves are located in the many beautiful valleys in the area. This means hiking should be part of your plan. This is generally not strenuous as long as you go the downhill direction.

Since you have 3 days, I recommend the IHLARA VALLEY (see the section for details) but because transportation is a bit of a hassle, you may consider doing the GREEN TOUR as your one tour during your visit. Otherwise, the many valleys between Uçhisar and Zelve could take your whole trip, but I think one or two will do the trick.

If you are looking for more "off the beaten path" valleys, there are a few between Ürgüp and Mustafapaşa that very few people visit.

SUMMARY SO FAR

With these three activities/attractions you have spent a day and a half to two days. It is possible to do the museum and underground city in a half day if you hustle and then Ihlara in 2/3 of a day the next day.

I would not recommend doing all three in the same day as you will feel quite rushed, but you could fit in one of the valleys surrounding Göreme in the same day as the museum and underground city if you are really energetic. This means you have 1.5 to 2 days remaining. Here is where your individuality blossoms...

Choose from the following (Read details in the What to Do & See Section):

* DRINK TEA with a local- this will be one of your most memorable times and will help to forge a friendship that could last for years. You may want to do this more than once.

* HIKE another valley

* ATV/QUAD, BICYCLE, HORSEBACK RIDING

* SHOPPING - Check out the shopping section for gift ideas and quality souvenirs as well as information on carpets, pottery, and wine.

TOWNS & SIGHTS

Perhaps you have chosen from the above list and still have some time. If so, here are a few more choices, some of which are not on the normal itineraries.

UÇHISAR & ORTAHISAR – These two towns are named for their landmark rock towers that jut into the sky and offer a wonderful view of the surrounding valleys. As in all of the towns, they have plenty of shops and restaurants as well.

ÇAVUŞİN, PAŞABAĞ & ZELVE OPEN AIR MUSEUM – Church in a "swiss-cheese" cliff, perfect fairy chimneys and more cave churches for those who have not fulfilled their quota.

HACI BEKTAŞ – Named after the Alevi saint and spiritual leader, this town is about a 45 minute drive from central Cappadocia. The museum and culture center give an excellent picture of 13th century life as well as an understanding of the teachings of Bektaş. Every mid-August is their big three day festival when visitors from around the world descend on the town for singing, dancing, political speeches, and a generally festive atmosphere.

MUSTAFAPAŞA & GULŞEHİR - These two towns are located in opposite directions a few kilometers from the central area. Mustafapaşa or Sinasos, as it was called by its former Greek inhabitants, still has some Greek buildings and churches. Gulşehir as well has a large Greek church, the beautifully frescoed St. Jean Cave Church, housed in a fairy chimney, and Mushroom Rock that is worth seeing, if you have the time.

FINAL THOUGHTS – MY PERSONAL PLAN

I did not intend to list everything like this, but I realize that everyone is different with different tastes. There is something in here for everyone. Unfortunately, you will have to choose as you cannot do it all in three days.

Personally I would recommend doing the museum, the underground city and drink some tea/do some window shopping on day one along with the hot-air balloon ride in the morning. On day two I would go to Ihlara and do the Turkish Night. On day three I would hit one or two of the valleys and then do some shopping for whichever item I most fancied. That includes a little bit of everything, and I would leave fulfilled but not exhausted.

SECTION IV:
CAPPADOCIA DETAILS

CHAPTER 23

CAPPADOCIA DETAILS INTRODUCTION

For many readers the book is done. I have covered most everything you will do and see in Cappadocia, helped you with hotels and restaurants, given you shopping tips, and even given some 1, 2, and 3 day templates to help you plan your time.

This section is a free bonus for those looking to go deeper. If you are the curious type, hungry for learning, then this chapter is designed to feed your appetite.

Many authors put these kinds of sections at the beginning of their travel books, but my priority has been to help you plan your trip to Cappadocia, and thus, I have waited to put this information until the end.

This section includes:

*** Cappadocia History**

*** Geography/Geology**

*** Towns**

*** Books About Turkey**

*** Photos**

*** Hiking Cappadocia's Valleys**

*** Off the Beaten Path**

*** Göreme Open Air Museum**

*** Brief History of Hot Air Ballooning**

*** Underground Cities**

*** Horseback Riding**

*** Jeep Safari Tours**

*** Turkish Night Cultural Show**

*** Whirling Dervish Show**

CHAPTER 24

BRIEF HISTORY OF CAPPADOCIA

People have inhabited Cappadocia for thousands of years and many kingdoms and empires have claimed this region.

As you walk through the valleys and visit the towns, imagine yourself back in time living under the Hittites, Eastern Mushki, Persians, Macedonians, Romans/Byzantines, Seljuks, Karamanids, Ottomans, and finally the Republic of Turkey. Wow!

But today's Cappadocia boundaries have not always defined the area. At one point Cappadocia extended north all the way to the Black Sea and south to the Taurus Mountains, but currently its name is not even an official region in Turkey.

The historical name of the area has been kept for tourist reasons and what people visit today is only only 150 miles by 250 miles touching five Turkish provinces (Kayseri, Nevşehir, Kirsehir, Aksaray, and Nigde).

HITTITE BEGINNINGS

According to most sources the current name comes from an adapted form of Katpatuka which it was called by the Persians. With the fall of the Hittites around the 12th century B.C., the Eastern Mushki ruled the area. The next we hear is of King Croesus, he of fabulous wealth and ill-fated oracles, who takes the area but is quickly defeated by the Persians in the 6th century B.C.

EMPIRE - KINGDOM - EMPIRE - REPUBLIC

The Persians ruled the area using locals as their representatives until Alexander the Great defeated them. Then in the chaos of Alexander's death, Cappadocia became an independent kingdom. Ariarathes I was king from 331-320 B.C. His sons followed him, and Cappadocia was ruled as a kingdom until 17 A.D.

At that point the Romans were in control and the emperor decided to change it to a province. The Romans had allowed the Cappadocians to rule themselves since 188 B.C., but that changed when the Emperor Tiberius flipped their status in a fit of anger at the Cappadocian king.

The Romans, who became the Byzantines, controlled the area until the Seljuks moved into the area after the battle of Manzikert in 1071.

The Seljuks of Rum ruled for a time until they were defeated by the Mongols and the Karamanids (from Karaman southeast of Cappadocia) took over in their rivalry with the growing Ottoman dynasty. (During your time in Cappadocia, you may visit a caravanserai as they are popular on many of the tours. You have the Seljuks to thank for this. Be sure to note the unique architecture they introduced to this land.)

With the fall of the Ottoman Empire after WWI, the Republic of Turkey was formed and Cappadocia has become a tourist destination.

CHRISTIANITY

But in all of this changing of empires, you may have noticed that I did not mention Cappadocia's renowned cave communities. The first Christians arrived in Cappadocia shortly after the resurrection of Jesus and the birth of the Christian religion. They are mentioned in the Bible in Acts at Pentecost and when the apostle Peter writes them in his first epistle.

The Cappadocian Fathers, Basil the Great, Gregory of Nazianzus, and Gregory of Nyssa, played a significant role in the development of Christian theology in the 4th century. They also established monastic communities that would survive for hundreds of years (you'll see some of their work at the Göreme Open Air Museum).

The majority of the cave churches you visit here date to the 9th-11th centuries. At this time Byzantine rule was weak and Arab raiders were often terrorizing the Cappadocia region. This is when the underground cities were greatly expanded. Apparently, they had begun with the Hittites, but the Christians were the first to use them for more than animals and storage.

Once Ottoman rule became strong and peace reigned in the area, the need for the underground areas diminished and by modern times they had been forgotten until accidentally discovered and turned into tourist attractions.

ISLAM

Islam arrived with the Seljuks (Turks) and was continued with the Ottomans (also Turks). Both ruling groups built mosques and madrasas, some of which you can still see today.

During Ottoman times there was a mix of religions living together under Islamic rule, but that ended with the forced people swap between Turkey and Greece in 1923-24. You may visit Mustafapaşa while you are in Cappadocia and see the remnants of the Greeks who inhabited the area.

NEW CITY

One other note worth pointing out was the creation of Nevşehir, the provincial capital. This town was first famous as Nyssa, the home of Gregory mentioned above. Then it fell off the map and was just a small village until Damat Ibrahim Pasha became Grand Vizier to the sultan in 1718.

He poured money into the region transforming his small village into a "new city", thus the name Nevşehir which translates new city. The mosque and hamam complex he built are still in use today.

And so you have 3000 years of human history in a few paragraphs. Much is left out, of course, but this should give you a good structure within which you can view the fascinating sights of the region.

** Most of this information came from Wikipedia.*

Cappadocian Fathers Introduction

> **NOTE**: These sections on the Cappadocian Fathers were written by my friend, Aaron Moss.

To understand the Cappadocian Fathers it is necessary to know the context and times in which they lived. Let us take a look at the cultural milieu in which the Cappadocian Fathers entered the scene.

Socrates of Constantinople (not to be confused with the great Classical Greek Athenian philosopher) records in his early Church History an encounter of 80 Christian clergy with the Roman Emperor Valens (364-378 AD) over a theological dispute. Valens was apparently so angered by these 80 men's complaints of ill-treatment, because they did not hold the same theological view as Valens, that he ordered them to board a ship immediately.

Assuming that they were being led away to join their other like-minded friends who had been systematically exiled under the rule of Valens, they must have been more than surprised when the crew carried out their secret orders to set the vessel afire and then jump ship to secure their own safety, while effectively killing all 80 clergy! (Ecclesiastical History 4.16)

When we read of such ludicrous and inhumane acts perpetrated by insecure and downright evil rulers it may cast a doubt in the reader's mind as to the importance of the subject of debate. The way these "grown, mature men" handled these issues makes me think of my 3 year old son and 2 year old daughter as they struggle for possession of a stuffed animal, which neither of them wanted until they saw the other one reach for it.

But, you are coming to Cappadocia (or, at least interested in it) and in your initial research you find out that there are three important early Christian church leaders, all venerated by both Eastern and Western Christianity, who hailed from this area: St. Basil of Caesarea (Kayseri), St. Gregory of Nazianzus and St. Gregory of Nyssa – the Cappadocian Fathers.

You do a little research on the internet to figure out what these guys did to make them so important in church history, and you feel like the article writers are speaking a different language (that's because they are – it's called Koine or patristic Greek!). You might have seen words like homoousian, homoian, homoiousian, Arian, Nicene, hypostatis, ousia, and to top it all off, one of my personal favorite words, Sabellianism.

How do we make sense of the day when leaders of a religion who purportedly follow the teachings of Jesus of Nazareth, who commanded his followers to love their enemies, instead kill those who believe something different from them?

I want to quickly present three things that we need to keep in mind as we seek to understand the importance of each of the Cappadocian Fathers.

4TH CENTURY CAPPADOCIAN CULTURE

By the time the Cappadocian Fathers come on to the scene Christianity had been legalized for almost 20 years (Edict of Milan, 313 AD). Up until this time Christians had been experiencing sporadic and localized persecutions for the past two and a half centuries at the hands of the state. Basil and his brother Gregory of Nyssa grew up knowing the cost of following Jesus as they were told stories of their own grandfather and his martyrdom.

Because of the state's increasingly favorable position toward this "cult", culminating in it becoming the official state religion of the Roman Empire by 380 AD, every theological debate became a concern of the state as the emperor's role was to bring "divine favor" and protection to the empire and her citizens.

So, when we read of emperors exiling (and in some cases murdering) bishops, and empire-wide church councils [e.g. Nicea (325 AD), Constantinople (381 AD)] being called to discuss heretical ideas, we must understand that politics and spirituality were interwoven, leading to a mixed bag of conclusions.

This mingling of "religion and state" does not negate the rightness of what they were trying to do, which was to preserve and better understand the Gospel, the central message of the Old and New Testaments. "Who is Jesus?" was the question on the lips of his initial 12 disciples as they witnessed him calming the wind and seas with a single command (Mark 4:35-41); it was the question the early church wrestled with; and it comes to us today in the 21st century. Their inability (not that we would do much better) to navigate these turbulent waters in a way that reflects the spirit of Jesus actually proves the truth of His words.

He said, "I am the vine; you are the branches. If you remain in me and I in you, you will bear much fruit; apart from me you can do nothing." (John 15:5) The politicians of the day offered their own versions of what would bring life and hope (still true today). When the religious leaders were torn between following Jesus and the emperor, life became ugly for many.

FORMATION OF INSTITUTIONALIZED RELIGION

Not only were these church leaders trying to come to agreement on what the Bible revealed, but they were also trying to create a standard language for Christians that could withstand the vast distances within the Roman empire.

They could now legally assemble in public places; they were no longer on the run from state authorities. They had the luxury of becoming the "majority" in their communities, and they could now communicate with Christians from different regions of the empire.

The church was not "centralized" yet and as time went on, there were more and more heretical threats to the understanding of the Gospel, which was passed down from the apostles and their disciples. Thus, letters and treatises were being written to not only clarify their understanding of the Biblical text, but also to solidify alliances between church leaders. No one wanted to be "hung out to dry" in that day and age when emperors were very eager to "protect" the empire's citizens from false teaching.

PROGRESS

In the West, our present-day education system is based on innovation. Originality and creativity are the two foundations upon which we are to construct a better, more enlightened culture. In the 4th century, however, cultural progress was founded upon the truths and interpretations discovered in the classic books and texts. Thus, exploring, clarifying, studying and interpreting the texts of the canonized Christian scriptures were the "Christian" counterpart to the Roman empire's attempt at cultural development.

CONCLUSION

These three cultural realities, which were the air the Cappadocian Fathers breathed, hopefully bring a bit of "color" to the "black & white" world of the 4th century as we attempt to not only understand "what" they did, but "why" they did it. These are the sociological factors that contributed to the actions of the players during this time. But I believe life consists of more than sociological factors and St. Basil agrees. He would have put more stock in the idea that what was propelling the establishment of orthodox belief, of which he was just a small part, was the Holy Spirit.

He wrote that the Holy Spirit brings illumination to souls from which then comes "foreknowledge of the future, understanding of mysteries, apprehension of what is hidden, distribution of good gifts, the heavenly citizenship, a place in the chorus of angels, joy without end, abiding in God, the being made like to God, and highest of all, the being made God." (On the Holy Spirit 9.23)

> *Disclaimer: I do not pretend to be an expert in church history, as I am but one who is on a journey to better understand the religious history of this great area. Many of my thoughts have been influenced by two introductory works that I would highly recommend if you want to learn more about the people and events of the 4th century in Cappadocia.*
>
> *Thank you, Aaron Moss*
>
> * The Cappadocians (Outstanding Christian Thinkers) by Anthony Meredith
>
> * Basil of Caesarea: A Guide to His Life and Doctrine (Cascade Companions) by Andrew Radde-Gallwitz

ST. BASIL OF CAESAREA: THE GREAT

The Emperor Valens caused quite a commotion when he visited Caesarea (present day Kayseri) for a Christian festival one winter.

Up until this time Valens had been exiling and deposing Nicene-supporting bishops *(see footnote at bottom regarding their position on the deity of Jesus) all over the empire. He had been successful even in removing the leading proponent of Nicene theology, Athanasius the Great.

One of the few still standing was Basil of Caesarea, a stalwart and vocal defender of Nicene theology, and it just so happened that he was to be leading the liturgical service on the particular Sunday that the emperor came a-calling.

The stage was set for a showdown: the people's favorite, dissonant, rebel bishop against the cruel, unbending sovereign. What would happen when the proverbial unstoppable force met the immovable object?

Basil's friend, Gregory of Nazianzus, in his eulogy for the Caesarean's funeral, records that as Valens entered the sanctuary with his entourage:

> *"he was struck by the thundering roll of the Psalms, by the sea of heads of the congregation, and by the angelic rather than human order which pervaded the sanctuary and its precincts: while Basil presided over his people, standing erect, as the Scripture says of Samuel (1 Samuel 19:20) with body and eyes and mind undisturbed, as if nothing new had happened, but fixed upon God and the sanctuary, as if, so to say, he had been a statue, while his ministers stood around him in fear and reverence. At this sight, and it was indeed a sight unparalleled, overcome by human weakness, [Valens'] eyes were affected with dimness and giddiness, his mind with dread...he was staggering, and had not someone in the sanctuary reached out a hand to steady his tottering steps, he would have sunk to the ground in a lamentable fall."* (Oration 43.52)

It seems as though the immovable object won this time.

EARLY YEARS

One might think from his upbringing that the great saint from modern-day Kayseri was groomed for such a power struggle. Born into a Christian family (329/330 AD) with a rhetoric teaching father, Basil was preparing for a life of learning in Constantinople and Athens (where he met his friend Gregory of Nazianzus).

He was brother to 9 siblings, 4 of which have been canonized in the Church, including his elder sister, Macrina. He eventually left his studies in search of a happiness which he found to be "empty" in Athens. (Oration 43.18)

Thus, he began a year-and-a-half tour in the eastern Mediterranean, following the highly self-disciplined religious devotees, or ascetics, of the area. In the end he returned to his family retreat home on the Iris River (in present-day Sivas). Far from wanting to engage in ecclesiastical affairs, his search was more private.

"CONVERSION"

It was at this time spent with his sister at her make-shift monastery that his life decidedly changed, according to his brother, Gregory of Nyssa. Basil saw his coming to faith as an awakening.

> *"Much time had I spent in vanity, and had wasted nearly all my youth in the vain labour which I underwent in acquiring the wisdom made foolish by God. Then once upon a time, like a man roused from deep sleep, I turned my eyes to the marvelous light of the truth of the Gospel, and I perceived the uselessness of the wisdom of the princes of this world, that came to naught. (1 Corinthians 2:6) I wept many tears over my miserable life and I*

prayed that guidance might be vouchsafed me to admit me to the doctrines of true religion." (Letter 223.2)

BIRTH OF CAPPADOCIAN 4TH CENTURY MONASTICISM

During this retreat time what he was pursuing was not to be found in a life of being physically cut off from the world, which is what he saw in the ascetics in Egypt. Instead, he diagnosed himself in this way: "I carry my own troubles with me, and so everywhere I am in the midst of similar discomforts." (Letter 2.1) He couldn't escape himself, so there was no considerable benefit from sequestering himself from society.

Out of this was born Basil's vision for a community of believers who sought after a "quiet mind" in the midst of a community of like-minded persons. This was his great contribution to the development of the monastic movement: communal living, on which he wrote extensively, later becoming known as Basil's Longer Rules.

This was his call to the ascetics who had been wandering the Cappadocia valleys, such as those you might hear about during your trip to Cappadocia, who sat atop fairy chimneys (monks similar to st. Simon of Paşa Bağı of the 5th century) in order to commune with God.

This was Basil's "conversion": from the pursuit of worldly wisdom, personified by the academy in Athens, to the life of a "quiet mind", where one can put himself in an atmosphere where he can see the "light of the Gospel" and thus be transformed by the Holy Spirit.

Question: So, did Basil found the monastery at the Open Air Museum in Göreme?

As Basil later became Bishop of Caesarea, his teachings and influence began to spread; thus, his call for communal living in all probability influenced people who were already living in the valley. So, in an indirect way he did "found" it, but I personally doubt that he came out to Göreme in order to physically set up the monastery. His teachings however, without a doubt, governed the communal setting.

SOCIAL JUSTICE

Around 367/368 AD a severe famine broke out in the Cappadocia region. Basil summed up the dire situation very succinctly: "The hungry are dying." (Homily 6.6) How did he respond?

Basil addressed the rich to open their stores of food (quite possibly referring to the naturally refrigerated caves near Ortahisar and other villages) to the poor by delivering a series of sermons and writings on the subject, as well as personally becoming involved. Below is Gregory of Nazianzus' account of Basil's actions:

> *"For by his word and advice he opened the stores of those who possessed them, and so, according to the Scripture dealt food to the hungry, and satisfied the poor with bread, and fed them in the time of dearth, and filled the hungry souls with good things. And in what way? for this is no slight addition to his praise. He gathered together the victims of the famine with some who were but slightly recovering from it, men and women, infants, old men, every age which was in distress, and obtaining contributions of all sorts of food which can relieve famine, set before them basins of soup and such meat as was found preserved among us, on which the poor live. Then, imitating the ministry of Christ, Who, girded with a towel, did not disdain to wash the disciples' feet, using for this purpose the aid of his own servants, and also of his fellow servants, he attended to the bodies and souls of those who needed it, combining personal respect with the supply of their necessity, and so giving them a double relief."* (Oration 43.35)

A few years later (372 AD) Basil opened a hospice for those still recovering from the famine a little ways outside of Caesarea, known as the Basileias, where they cared for the leper and the poor. They also supplied those who were able with employment and training in various trades.

Basil called it a ptochotropheion, "a place to feed, nurture and patronize the destitute poor". The complex included apartments for the bishop, his guests, needy travelers and of course, the poor. (Letter 94)

THEOLOGICAL CONTRIBUTION

The Cappadocian Fathers filled a unique place in the history of the church. Those who were before them hammered out the orthodox Nicene Creed, which in its original form, and/or slightly amended form, is accepted by all three major expressions of the Christian faith: Orthodox, Catholic and Protestant.

How the divine and human natures of Jesus of Nazareth co-existed and what their relationship was to God the Father was of primary focus at the Council of Nicea (325 AD),which was instigated by the heretical teachings of Arius, a presbyter at Alexandria.

The fact that this man was exonerated 10 years later is proof that the debate was still far from over. Not only was Basil continuing to defend and uphold the "of one essence" Nicene teaching, but a new front was forming: the Holy Spirit. What was it? How did he/it relate to God the Father, and God the Son?

In my reading of church history no other time was more pivotal in the orthodox recognition and explanation of the Triune nature of God as revealed in the Old and New Testaments than during the years of St. Basil.

So, what did Basil have to say about the Holy Spirit? He began this debate in response to Eunomius (born in the small village of Dacora, near Mt. Argeus (Erciyes) in Cappadocia), bishop of Cyzicus, culminating in his opus, *On The Holy Spirit*, a few years later. Essentially, Basil says that because the Spirit is so closely tied with the Father and the Son in worship, liturgy and hymns, the Spirit too must share in a common nature with the others. The text he loved to quote to uphold this belief was Matthew 28:19:

> *"Therefore, go and make disciples of all nations, baptizing them in the name of the Father and of the Son and of the Holy Spirit."*

It was in one name that believers were to be baptized, not three different names.

Interestingly, even though Basil goes to great lengths to point out that the Holy Spirit is equal in rank and deserving of the same glory as the Father and the Son, he never fully comes out and declares that the Holy Spirit shares in the same "essence/consubstantiation" with God in any of his writings. Because of this he was criticized by others in his day, as they must have interpreted this omission as being an indicator that he didn't believe in the deity of the Spirit.

Even Gregory of Nazianzus called him out to be clear about this, to which Basil replied, "but now I am sick of the subject, and will say no more about it." (Letter 71) There is debate among some church historians as to why this reticence, but most suppose that Basil was leery of introducing yet another controversy to the greater church. Let the divinity of the Son, as espoused in the Creed of Nicea, become firmly established in the realm before tackling another huge doctrine.

Outside of St. Augustine, there is no one in early church history that we know more about than Basil of Caesarea. This brief biography only scratches the surface in conveying all that we know of this man through the historical record.

Basil's fingerprints on Cappadocia are indelible, even in the present time when there are few active Christian communities in the region. His influence can be seen in the frescoes that grace the walls of ancient caves, preserving the story of when the Triune God visited humanity through His Son, and presently testifies through the work of the Holy Spirit as he illuminates our minds to the Scriptures.

* *[Nicene Creed and the bishops that supported it held to what is the orthodox position of the Christian church that Jesus the Son was "of one essence", or "of one substance"[homoousios] with God the Father , as opposed to him being "unlike the Father": a separate, subordinate, created being.]*Basil's fingerprints

on Cappadocia are indelible, even in the present time when there are few active Note: These sections on the Cappadocian Fathers were written by my friend, Aaron Moss.

GREGORY OF NAZIANZUS

What would cause a mob of people to storm into an esteemed clergy's quarters, and deposit a pale, bedraggled youth before him?

What would behoove this long-haired young man to cling to the feet of the (almost) bishop of Constantinople?

When asked, "Who are you and where are you from? What do you want?" the boy only tightened his grip, wailing and sobbing inconsolably.

Not being able to get a word out of the youth, Gregory of Nazianzus looked to one of the juvenile-chasing townsmen who declared: "This man is your assassin."

EARLY LIFE

Gregory (c.326-389/390) was born in present-day Güzelyurt (Arianzus) in the Aksaray province, near the Ihlara Valley. His parents were from wealthy families, and his father was the bishop of a nearby city known as Nazianzus. He was one of three children; he had an older sister and a younger brother. They grew up exploring their large estate, known as Karabala (the namesake of the monastery-turned-hotel in today's Güzelyurt). Throughout Gregory of Nazianzus' life, Karabala remained a fixture of refuge and solace to which he frequented often.

Near the center of Güzelyurt today you can find a beautiful early church that was converted into a mosque (Cami Kilise) in 1924, known as st. Gregorius Church. The belief is that Gregory had this built for the people of Arianzus and its date of construction is thought to be 385 (restored in 1835).

Also, located on the road between Çiftlik and Niğde, in the village of Sivrihisar, the ruins of another church (Kızıl Kilise, or Red Church) stand, dating back to the 6th century, which is also dedicated to St. Gregory. The location of the church is said to be very close to the family estate, Karabala.

At a young age he was sent with his brother to be educated in Iconium (Konya), Caesarea (Kayseri), and then to the other Caesarea in Palestine. Their educational pursuits led them to Alexandria where Gregory left his younger brother, focusing on medicine, for the Hellenistic rhetoric halls of Athens. It was here where his life-long bond with St. Basil the Great burgeoned.

When Gregory of Nazianzus left Athens he was a changed man. He recounts a tale of being out at sea when his ship was overcome by a tremendous storm. It was so bad that he desperately feared for his life, and in those intense moments he cried out to God:

> *"I am yours now, too, as before. Accept me a second time [his mother wanted a boy and when Gregory was born he was dedicated to serve God similar to Samuel of the Old Testament], the possession of those dear to you, a gift from both land and sea, consecrated by my mother's prayer and by overpowering fear. For your will I live if I escape the double danger, but if you abandon me you will lose a servant. Now again one of your disciples is in a storm: for my sake shake off your sleep and walk; let fear be stilled."* (On His Own Life)

From then on Gregory's educational trajectory was altered, and along with Basil they pledged themselves to a life that centered on "God and a desire for higher things". (On His Own Life) Gregory eventually returned to Cappadocia desperately seeking the quiet life, including celibacy, a simple lifestyle and a focused resolve on study and prayer.

FOLLOWING DAD?

When Gregory returned from Athens his father would have been in his mid-eighties and in much need of help to serve the believers of Nazianzus. Gregory recognized the pressure his father was putting upon him to be engaged in public ministry, and responded in a pattern of behavior that followed him throughout his life: flight.

> *"I made for Pontus, seeking a remedy for my pain from that holy friend of mine. For he was there practicing communion with God, concealed in a cloud like one of the wise men of old. Basil it was, he who is among the angels now through him I hoped to soothe the agony in my soul."* (On His Own Life)

STRONG IN WEAKNESS

In my study of the Cappadocian Fathers, Gregory of Nazianzus has become my champion. I do not warm up to the commanding presence of Basil, who seemed to exude confidence and an unwavering assurance. Also, I tend not to gravitate toward Gregory of Nyssa, as his intellect and ability to express complex theological and philosophical constructs make me feel like a stupid ox.

But, in Gregory of Nazianzus, I find a man who is acutely aware of his frailties and weaknesses, with whom I can relate. It was this trait that spurred on these temporary flights from responsibility as he was overcome with his inadequacies.

He did not allow his fear to paralyze him though. After a few weeks he returned from Pontus and plunged himself into the harmful occupation of ministry, aiding his ailing father in the duties of bishop. This was not his first choice as his heart yearned for a life of "retirement" where he could solely focus on study and prayer, but he was faithful to honor his father.

Early in 372 A.D., when Emperor Valens restructured the borders of Cappadocia in order to lessen Basil's influence as bishop over the province, Gregory was hurled into a very unwelcome position. In order to counteract Valens' "attack", the ecclesio-political Basil pressured his brother Gregory and Gregory of Nazianzus to be ordained bishops for two newly created sees within the Cappadocia region.

Through the urging of his father, Gregory accepted the appointment but not with joy as he saw through Basil's plan – he was merely a pawn in his political game.

> *"There is a staging-post halfway along the highway through Cappadocia, where the road divides into three, a place without water, without vegetation, completely uncivilised, an utterly dreadful and cramped little settlement. It is all dust and noise and chariots, cries and groans, officials, instruments of torture and shackles, a population consisting only of visitors and vagrants. This was Sasima, my congregation! This was what he [Basil] appointed me to, he who was surrounded by fifty suffragan bishops – what magnanimity on his part! He did this so that by creating a new see he would get the upper hand over another man [Valens] who was trying to seize it by force."* (On His Own Life)

But Gregory was not a pushover. He passively rebelled against his best friend and apparently never set foot in the village of Sasima, but remained alongside his father in Nazianzus, who died shortly thereafter.

Gregory became de facto bishop even though he was never canonically installed in his father's place. He was chastised by Basil for this, being accused of laziness and inactivity, but he refused to be used by his best friend for his own "private ambitions". (On His Own Life)

After another "flight" to the region south of Cappadocia, known as Seleucia, where he took refuge in a women's monastic community, he became more and more involved in the post-Nicene battles over the identity of Jesus the Son and the Holy Spirit through his writings.

During this time he emerged as the leading voice in articulating the classical doctrine of God for orthodox Christianity: an irreducible Trinity of consubstantial Son who was begotten of the Father, and a consubstantial Holy Spirit, who proceeded from the Father and was sent by the Son.

CONSTANTINOPLE

He was pressured once again to engage in public church administration, and in of all places the request was coming from the imperial capital, Constantinople! Thus, he proceeded to present-day Istanbul, and he was there in time to be invited to participate in the coronation of the new emperor, Theodosius, a subscriber to the Nicene creed.

He was placed immediately behind him in the procession, the place reserved for the high bishop, even though he had yet to be canonized as bishop of Constantinople, and he describes his deplorable states as such:

> *"The moment had arrived. The church was in the hands of armed soldiers who had secretly taken up positions there. A seething mob of townspeople confronted them, like the sand of the seas or a snowstorm or the waves' ebb and flow, torn between anger and entreaties, anger directed at me, entreaties to those in power. The market places were full, the colonnades, streets, every place, two and three storey houses were full of people leaning out, men, women, children, the very aged. There were scuffles, sobbing, tears and cries, all giving the impression of a town taken by force. I, the hero and the commander, with this sick and broken body of mine which could hardly breathe any more, caught between the general [Theodosius] and the army, my gaze directed upwards, moved on, supported by hope, until I entered the church, I don't know how."* (On His Own Life)

The great city of Constantinople had been under the rule of Valens for the past 14 years and had become a bastion of anti-Nicene sentiment. Now, Gregory was stepping once again into harm's way by essentially filling the role of bishop in a hostile environment until a new one could be installed by Theodosius.

It was during this time that our opening assassination caveat took place. The assassin stood before Gregory of Nazianzus, repenting that he had been charged with the duty of his assassination, but was overcome with a guilty conscience and could not carry out the deed. With the power to snuff this young man's life out Gregory instead chose forgiveness. *"May God save you. That I, who have been saved, should appear kind to my assassin, is nothing special. Your recklessness has made you mine. Consider how you might become a credit to me and to God."*(On His Own Life)

According to Gregory his reaction to his would-be murderer spread throughout the metropolis and he began to have his way with the believers. This was the way of Gregory of Nazianzus: a tender theologian who saw himself as a reconciler of disparaging parties, unlike others who seemed only bent on promoting their own viewpoints. *"I could act like a chorus leader between two choruses...I could blend them with myself and thus weld into a unity what had been so badly divided."*(On His Own Life)

COUNCIL OF CONSTANTINOPLE

In 381, a council of 150 bishops was called by the new emperor Theodosius in order to help establish doctrinal unity throughout the eastern empire. Whereas at Nicea, some 66 years earlier, the discussion centered upon the status and activity of the Son, this council's main concern was upon the Holy Spirit. At the end of the main theological discussions the subject turned to the election of a new bishop.

Even though he was breaking a prohibition established at Nicea in 325 A.D. that forbade the transfer of bishops from one see to another by being the bishop of Sasima (as well as being de facto bishop of Nazianzus since his father's death), he consented to the appointment. But after discovering that *"some bishops from Egypt objected to the election, he withdrew his consent. He surrendered his appointment to the bishops when it was required of him, and never complained of his many labors, or of the danders he had incurred in the suppression of heresies."* (Sozomen, Church History 7.7)

Thus, again Gregory turned to "flight" and went back to his family home at Karabala in Cappadocia, where he remained until his death in 390.

CONTRIBUTIONS

There is so much to Gregory of Nazianzus' life that has been omitted from this summary. For the sake of brevity I am embarrassed at what has been withheld: his desire to create a recognizably Hellenic body of literature for young believers, his writings on the difficulties of ministry, the scores of poems that have been studied throughout history because of the exquisite Greek forms he employed, or his five Theological Orations which have been considered as *"the clearest, most economical, and perhaps the most paradoxical parameters for articulating [the mystery of the Trinity] and [which] most insistently emphasized the centrality of this Trinitarian confession for the whole of Christian life."* (Daley, 41.)

Gregory's contributions extend well beyond the lines of poetry and theological prose he wrote during his stay on this earth. Personally, I believe his greatest contribution is his recognition and insightful portrayal of his plight on this orb, which helps bridge the gap of 1600 years that divide us from him.

It is his humble heart that captures those who have divested energy and time to consume his writings, in which we relish the discovery that he was so quick to admit his own inadequacies for the roles and positions in which he was being placed.

> *"I am myself preoccupied with these considerations [his inadequacies] night and day...They depress my soul and contract my thoughts and put a leash on my tongue; they do not lead me to considerations of leadership, or of reproving and directing others – but rather to thinking how I myself might 'flee the wrath to come', and in some small way scrape from myself the rust of wickedness. One must first be purified, and then purify others; first be made wise, and so make others wise; first become light, and then enlighten; first draw near to God and then lead others forward; first be made holy and then sanctify others, lead them by the hand, offer them understanding counsel..."* (Oration 2.71-72)

Oh how I, as a follower of this same Jesus of Nazareth, need to hear this call to humility in light of such prolific religious hypocrisy around the world! It reminds me of something Jesus once said:

> *"Why do you look at the speck of sawdust in someone else's eye and pay no attention to the plank in your own eye? How can you say, 'Let me take the speck out of your eye,' when all the time there is a plank in your own eye? You hypocrite, first take the plank out of your own eye, and then you will see clearly to remove the speck from the other person's eye."* (Matthew 7:3-5)

As with the former church history posts, I am deeply indebted to the giants of this field of study. For more information on Gregory of Nazianzus, I highly recommend:

Daley, Brian E. Gregory of Nazianzus (The Early Church Fathers). London, 2006.

Gregory of Nazianzus: Autobiographical Poems. trans. ed. Carolinne White. Cambridge, 1996.

Meredith, Anthony. The Cappadocians. New York, 1995.

Note: These sections on the Cappadocian Fathers were written by my friend, Aaron Moss.

GREGORY OF NYSSA

Today, droves of people flock to Cappadocia for many different reasons. Some come to see the distinct rock formations; some want to experience a new culture. Yet others, because of the early church history heritage in the region, come on a pilgrimage to better understand their spiritual ancestors.

One forerunner of the Christian faith and a so-called Cappadocian Father is Gregory of Nyssa (335-393? AD), the younger brother of the Great St. Basil of Caesarea.

Even though Gregory of Nyssa (present-day Nevşehir) had been appointed bishop of this area, he never would have qualified to be a faith tourism marketer.

This is what he had to say about pilgrimages in a letter he addressed to a colleague when asked about the profitability of a journey to Jerusalem to see the physical places where Jesus of Nazareth lived, as if they could get an extra dose of holiness by being there:

> *"[The pilgrim] cannot imagine that our Lord is living, in the body, there at the present day, but has gone away from us foreigners; or that the Holy Spirit is in abundance at Jerusalem, but unable to travel as far as us. Whereas, if it is really possible to infer God's presence from visible symbols, one might more justly consider that He dwelt in the Cappadocian nation than in any of the spots outside it. For how many Altars there are there, on which the name of our Lord is glorified! One could hardly count so many in all the rest of the world."* (On Pilgrimages)

The irony here is quite humorous: here is a man who is discouraging pilgrimages, but over time becoming the object of thousands of people's excursions over the centuries. It would be like a pre-famous Justin Bieber encouraging young girls to broaden their musical tastes only to become famous and have those same girls totally disregard his words!

Gregory had a vision of the imminence of God that pervaded all he did. He can say this about pilgrimages because he believed:

> *"Change of place does not effect any drawing nearer unto God, but wherever you may be, God will come to you, if the chambers of your soul be found of such a sort that He can dwell in you and walk in you."* (On Pilgrimages)

As with Basil, Gregory truly believed that God himself had visited humankind through the person of Jesus of Nazareth 300 years before his time, and that God continued to come to visit people through the work of the sent Holy Spirit.

EARLY LIFE

Gregory was greatly influenced by his elder brother Basil. When writing to his younger brother Peter, Gregory referred to Basil as being their "common father and teacher". (On the Making of Man) Even though he didn't have the extensive "secular" training that Basil did, he was far more influenced by his own reading of the classical Greek fathers, especially Plato, who came before him.

Gregory did not pursue the ascetic life, but rather is believed to have been married, which, sadly to say, maybe he came to regret later in life. In his work, On Virginity, he says this of marriage:

> *"[L]et us sketch a marriage in every way most happy; illustrious birth, competent means, suitable ages, the very flower of the prime of life, deep affection, the very best that each can think of the other, that sweet rivalry of each wishing to surpass the other in loving; in addition, popularity, power, wide reputation, and everything else. But observe that even beneath this array of blessings the fire of an inevitable pain is smouldering."*

What is this pain? It was the anxiety created by the certainty of death.

> *"This continued expectancy of death, realized by no sure tokens, but hanging over them the terrible uncertainty of the future, disturbs their present joy, clouding it over with the fear of what is coming...You would see there, if only you could do it without danger, many contraries uniting; smiles melting into tears, pain mingled with pleasure, death always hanging by expectation over the children that are born, and putting a finger upon each of the sweetest joys. Whenever the husband looks at the beloved face, that moment the fear of separation accompanies the look."* (chapter 3)

In light of this and other reasons Gregory puts forth a case for the virtue of living a chaste life. This way of life allows the person, male and female, to center themselves upon God and to live a "pure life" by thwarting the impulse of sexual desire. He looks upon the ascetic life as contributing to unleashing the life of God in people's hearts.

ENGAGING THE PHILOSOPHY OF THE DAY

Gregory shared the mantle, along with Basil and Gregory of Nazianzus, as being the defenders of the Nicene faith and responders to the attacks upon the Scriptural understanding of the Holy Spirit in the eastern Roman Empire. Whereas Basil defended the creed and the identity of the Holy Spirit through

Scriptural argumentation and ecclesiastical positioning, Gregory of Nyssa took more of a philosophical approach, greatly influenced by Plato and the earlier church father, Origen.

Gregory's use of Platonic forms and structures for understanding reality (classic Hellenistic thought) to showcase the Gospel and how it addresses the human soul was controversial. The early church father Tertullian (160-225 AD) asks,

> *"What have the philosopher and Christian in common, the disciple of Greece and the disciple of heaven?"* (Apology 46) He, and others, saw this friendship between philosophy and revelation as being a betrayal of St. Paul's words to the Corinthians: *"For since in the wisdom of God the world through its wisdom did not know him, God was pleased through the foolishness of what was preached to save those who believe."* (1 Corinthians 1:21)

But did this mean that there was nothing to learn from the classics?

What was their role within a Christian context? What was the relationship between culture and the Cross? (This question is as valid today as it was back then.) Basil came to the defense of Gregory by writing *To Young Men on the Value of Classical Literature*, addressing this issue. The ultimate criterion is 'usefulness', does it aid the reader toward a good, moral attitude?

Whether Gregory is intentionally contextualizing the Gospel to allow his contemporaries to "hear and understand" it through their worldviews, personally I do not know, but the fact that he is using cultural forms to do so has biblical precedence in St. Paul:

> *"To the Jews I became like a Jew, to win the Jews. To those under the law I became like one under the law (though I myself am not under the law), so as to win those under the law. I have become all things to all people so that by all possible means I might save some."* (1 Corinthians 9:20,22)

Gregory does not fall for Hellenistic thought hook, line and sinker. Of course, he is thoughtful in his approach. In a later work he lists a few of the areas where there is agreement and disagreement between philosophy and biblical revelation:

> *"Pagan philosophy says that the soul is immortal; this is a pious offspring. But it also says that souls pass from bodies to bodies and are changed from a rational to an irrational nature. This is a fleshly and alien foreskin. And there are many such examples. It says there is a god, but thinks of him as material. It acknowledges him as creator, but says he needed matter for creation."* (On the Life of Moses, 2.40)

CONTRIBUTOR TO MYSTICISM

In his defense of the Nicene Creed of 325 A.D., against a fellow Cappadocian, Eunomious of Cyzicus, who claimed that God's nature was capable of exact definition in words that could be understood by all (thus excluding the Son from the Deity), Gregory put forth the simple argument of divine incomprehensibility.

No one can find an adequate definition of his inner nature because he is infinite; he is the source of all and can be limited by none, thus, there is a sense of divine mysteriousness to his nature. Here Gregory departs from his fathers, Plato and Origen, who argued that lack of limit and form signal a defect in being.

This "mysticism" shows up later in his writings, primarily in the important and influential work called *On the Life of Moses.* In this treatise he builds upon the teaching of Matthew 5:8, "Blessed are the pure in heart, for they will see God" by using the events in the life of Moses to allegorically illustrate that religious virtue has to do with both right knowledge of God and right conduct. A mystical experience with God cannot be had without living a morally upright life.

> *"It is only when Moses has increased in knowledge that he confesses that he beholds God in the cloud, that is, that he knows that the Divine is by nature something above all knowledge and comprehension."* (2.164)

> *"Religious virtue may be distinguished in the following way. Part deals with the divine; part deals with moral behavior, for part of religion is purity of life. To begin with we must know how we are to think of God, and that knowledge entails entertaining none of the ideas which are derived from human understanding. The second part of virtue is taught by learning by what practices the life of virtue is realized."* (2.166)

Gregory claims that Moses, after receiving the Ten Commandments and "seeing" God as he passed by him (Exodus 33:18-23), was not a complete "knowing" or "experiencing" of God. Moses still had the duty to order his life around and practice the commands of God. Then, the knowledge that is above human understanding (i.e. "seeing God"), becomes something that has transpired in his life.

LATER PUBLIC LIFE

After Emperor Valens reduced the size of Cappadocia by changing its boundaries, in order to lessen Basil's Nicean influence in the region, Basil countered by creating a new bishopric see in Nyssa (371/372 AD) and appointed his younger brother Gregory. Gregory was not a skilled ecclesiastical authority figure, as Basil points out in this letter to a friend, "[I]f indeed my God-beloved brother Gregory consents to the voyage and to the commission concerning these matters.

For my own part, I do not know who can go with him, and am aware that he is quite inexperienced in ecclesiastical affairs." (Letter 215) And to Gregory himself, Basil writes: "Thus I write attacking your simplicity, which I see plainly to be neither what generally becomes a Christ man…I must speak to you with all freedom, and I tell you that you are an unworthy minister of things so great." (Letter 58) He was unable to hold up under the battle with the Arians (non-Nicene adherents) in his area and was eventually exiled in 375 AD, left to a life of wandering from town to town. He was allowed to return in 378 AD by imperial decree.

Maybe the public post wasn't his cup of tea, but after the death of Basil, he started to come into his own. By the time of the Council of Constantinople (381 AD), Gregory was selected to be one of the promoters of the orthodox teaching on the subject of the Holy Spirit in the Roman province of Pontus. He was also chosen to deliver three important funeral orations: one for Meletius, bishop of Antioch, who presided over the council; the second for Emperor Theodosius's daughter, Pulcheria; and finally, the death of the emperor's wife, Flaccilla.

The rest of his life, to our knowledge, was filled with much literary activity.

CONCLUSION

Gregory of Nyssa will probably forever live in the shadow of his big brother, Basil, but he by no means was inferior in intellect. Most scholars of this time in history testify to the fact that Gregory demonstrated his superior acumen through his extensive writings and his theological interaction with classical philosophy. However, becoming more famous was probably not what drove Gregory of Nyssa. Instead, his pursuit of the truth was propelled by the conviction that he had found the One who was limitless, infinite and good.

"And the true vision of God consists in this, in never reaching satiety of the desire. We ought always to look through the things that we can see and still be on fire with the desire to see more. So let there be no limit to curtail our growth in our journey upwards to God." (On the Life of Moses 2.239)

Note: These sections on the Cappadocian Fathers were written by my friend, Aaron Moss.

CHAPTER 25

GEOLOGY IN BRIEF

Turkey is interlaced with fault lines which have made themselves felt most recently in the 1999 Istanbul and 2011 Van earthquakes.

According to most geologists in time past (long past) the region of Cappadocia was covered with thousands of volcanoes. Only three remain today but are long dormant. However, the hot springs in the area bear witness to the geo-thermal activity going on under the surface.

When those volcanoes were active, their magma, lava, and ash covered the area. The ignimbrite rock worked together with these elements to cover the land giving us the strange landscape we enjoy today.

As gases were released from deep underground they hardened certain areas which became impervious to the water erosion that followed over the centuries. This meant that some places gave way while others remained, forming today's fairy chimneys and buttes.

At least these are the best theories available from geologists who have studied the region.

Regardless, we get to enjoy the beautiful benefit. Let's do our best to let all the coming generations enjoy it as well.

> **NOTE**: One WARNING to those of you who read this book before visiting Cappadocia. Turkish culture is shame-based which means that people do not like to lose face or be shown up (of course, nobody enjoys that but it is a much bigger deal here than in the West). Thus, I do not recommend correcting your guide in front of a group if they give a different explanation for the fairy chimneys..

** All of the information comes from Steve Eckert's Fairy Chimneys of Cappadocia: Evolution of a Landscape.*

CHAPTER 26

14 TOWNS IN CAPPADOCIA

Cappadocia is a vast region covering five Turkish states in inner Anatolia. However, the heart of the area centers around three towns, namely the Göreme-Ürgüp-Avanos triangle.

The vast majority of visitors spend their time within this domain. Included in this neighborhood are four other towns/villages: Uçhisar just above Göreme, Ibrahimpaşa and Ortahisar above Ürgüp, and Çavuşin between Avanos and Göreme.

Within 20 minutes of this triangle in different directions lie Nevşehir, the capital of the state by the same name; Mustafapaşa (aka Sinasos) an old Greek town beyond Ürgüp; Özkonak with its underground city; and rarely-visited but very friendly Gulşehir. Go a bit further (40 minutes from Avanos) and you will arrive at Hacı Bektaş. Go in the other direction and you will land in Kaymaklı and Derinkuyu with their fascinating underground cities.

Each town has a distinct personality and reputation. In this section I give a general picture of each. Each town also has historical sights, touristy shops selling the same "authentic Turkish" items, and friendly people. Do a little searching and you will find what sets them apart from their neighbors.

I have written this as if you were to get up one morning with the goal of seeing every town in one day. Following this route would get you there.

Uçhisar – Known for its towering rock "castle" that makes Swiss cheese look solid, Uçhisar sits on prime real estate with its view of the whole Göreme valley all the way to Avanos. And with the Argos, Museum, and CCR well placed on the hill, it boasts three of the nicest hotels in the region.

The tourist shops selling rugs and trinkets are worth visiting and the entrance to Pigeon Valley is located on the backside of the town. Step a few paces away from the center and the town looks like any normal Turkish village.

Head down the hill, stopping on the way to take in the view...

Göreme – With a population barely reaching 3000, unearthly Göreme sits amid giant rock cones like some elf village straight out of Lord of the Rings. People do live in this town, but their homes are hard to find as every rock is slowly being turned into a hotel or restaurant. I expect Göreme is close to being the world leader in overnight visitor to resident ratio with its close to 200 cave hotels.

Also, you will find the Open Air Museum, and within a few hundred meters every hot-air balloon ascends to the skies. This is important if you like to sleep but also want to ride the balloons. The rides usually begin before sunrise.

If you stay 15-20 minutes away in Ürgüp you must awake that much earlier. This may only be a big deal for the teenagers. In addition, the ATV/Quad rentals are based here and most of the popular valleys (except for Ihlara) are within walking distance.

Continue down the road for a few kilometers...

Çavuşin – This sleepy village has its two magnificent rock "churches" with a smattering of hotels and restaurants. The mesa above the village offers magnificent views (after a hefty climb) and the road leading out of the backside of the village runs into the beautiful Red and Rose Valleys heading towards the Panoramic View reached by the road from Ortahisar. Also, around the corner from Çavuşin you will find Paşabağ and the Zelve Open Air Museum (not to be confused with the more popular Göreme Open Air Museum mentioned above).

Just five more kilometers...

Avanos – Pottery. This quaint town of 14,000 souls sits on the Red River (Kızılırmak) and is home to countless potters offering their handmade wares. All of them will allow you to try your hand at the wheel. Do you have skills? This is your chance to shine. Of course you can find carpets and trinkets and get good food and a shave, but pottery is their bread and butter.

In the last couple of years they have renovated the river banks, making a nice park and beautiful walkways dotted with cafes. This is where you will find your opportunity to jet boat or float down the river on a gondola. The river development gives Avanos much potential for the future.

Now you need to make a side trip before rejoining the circle...

Özkonak - meaning "the essence of a house or mansion" or "the epitome of a place of lodging". The town is just 15 minutes by car or 25 minutes by bus from Avanos and boasts a great underground city, Ottoman-era bridge, and an amazing not-renovated church rumored to be from the 8th century. Be sure to head down to the center of town near the bridge and check out the valley lined with cave houses.

The people are quite gregarious, and don't be surprised to run into someone who speaks your language as the population of the town nearly doubles in the summer when all of its residents living outside the country return to visit.

Someone may even suggest you sample the wine from the "şarap evi" in the adjacent village of Göynük. Because the town is set on a hill you get great views of the fertile farm land below and Mt. Erciyes in the distance towards Kayseri.

Go back to Avanos and then head up the road out of town for 20 kilometers

Gulşehir– My guess is that 99% of visitors do not make it to Gulşehir, which is unfortunate as it is maybe the most friendly town in the region. With the Mushroom Rock (Mantar Kaya), the 800 year old St. Jean's Cave Church full of breathtaking paintings, the troglodytic hill at whose base the city sits, and the former Greek neighborhood with a renovated church building, this town of 10,000 hospitable people has much to offer.

Another half hour down the road…

Hacıbektaş – This 13th century Alevi spiritual leader allegedly settled in this area (not all accounts agree) and spread his teaching throughout the region. He was a man of peace and wisdom according to official historians and his followers had great influence in the Ottoman Empire.

The town centers around the excellent museum and cultural center which contains his grave and the graves of other leaders of the movement. Many rooms give a good picture of the life of the community when Hacı Bektaş was alive. Besides the museum we did not find much in the town, but honestly nothing else was needed.

In mid-August they have their annual festival, a weekend of music, dancing, and cultural events with visitors from all over the world. This is not a good time to visit the town unless you want to enjoy a chaotic time of Turkish Alevi cultural celebration.

Jump in your transport and return the way you came for about 45 minutes…

Nevşehir – This provincial capital with a population near 100,000 has a different feel from the smaller towns of the region. Although a number of significant sights are included within its boundaries, it does not have the touristy feel of the rest of the region. It is similar to any city that has a few historical attractions but does not define itself by them, more like Ankara than Istanbul in that regard.

However, this will be changing soon as an enormous underground city has been discovered under the hill in the center of town. This could open as early as 2017 which will greatly change the itinerary for visitors to the region.

Other attractions include the Seljuk fort which overlooks the city, the Ibrahim Paşa Mosque named after the Grand Vizier to the Sultan in the early 1700s along with the Madrassa and Hamam (Turkish Bath) and the museum which gives an excellent history of the region.

Catch the road to Ürgüp and exit before you arrive at the sign to…

Ibrahimpaşa – This little village between Üçhısar and Ortahısar is a hidden treasure in Cappadocia. Not because of its restaurants and not because of its hotels. No, simply the opposite is true. This village is so untouched by the tourist trappings of its neighboring towns that it warrants a visit.

But once you get here you will get a feel for what it was like to live in a Turkish village at the turn of the century. You will see how people built their new stone houses right out of the caves that were there before. You can take a walk down the narrow cobblestone streets passable only by foot or donkey.

Take a hike down one of the many valleys in the village and end up in Ortahısar. Or just drive into the village square, park your car, and have a cup of tea with the male* villagers who will enjoy your company.

* *Being a true Turkish village, no women would dare be seen with all the men in the village tea houses.*

Head back out to the main road and drive a few kilometers to…

Ortahisar – This town is mostly hidden from the main road except for its namesake rock "castle" which is visible from miles around. Not as strategically placed as Uçhisar, Ortahisar is better known for its cold storage.

Apparently, much of Turkey's produce is stored in the underground caves which have been renovated as storage rooms. With a constant cool temperature they make perfect low-cost cold containers. As you drive around be on the lookout for chimneys sticking out of the ground as well as for trucks from Mersin and other parts of southeastern Turkey.

Locally, Ortahisar is known for its barbers, and it boasts some excellent hotels, shops and restaurants. Besides the rock tower, however, they do not offer other historical sights.

Continue down the hill…

Ürgüp – The most developed and biggest town outside of Nevşehir with a population approaching 20,000, Ürgüp has much to offer the tourist with its spacious city center full of excellent restaurants and Turkish carpet/rug and gift shops. But Ürgüp's specialty is it wines sold in small shops and bigger wineries like Turasan. I highly recommend stopping in for a tasting when you visit.

In addition, the towering cliff overlooking the city houses the former fortress, and all around the outskirts of the town the explorer will find much with which to keep busy (especially on the road towards Mustafapaşa). I encourage you to visit the shops in the center of town and have tea with the owners. Due to the movement towards guided group tours, these shops are oft overlooked. Each has a story to tell and is worth a visit.

Head out of town past the open market and in a few minutes…

Mustafapaşa (Sinasos) – This unique town with its Greek church buildings and houses is worth a visit as well. Find an English speaker and learn about the history of the town including the massive people swap of the early 1920s. Be sure to eat at the Old Greek House if you are there at a meal time. Travel around the outskirts of the town and you will find some restored cave churches. *Take the winding backroads (an experience in itself) for 30 minutes or so to get to…*

Kaymaklı and Derinkuyu – These two underground cities are only a few kilometers apart and apparently have an underground tunnel connecting them. I think you only need to visit one of these cities. Kaymaklı is wider and Derinkuyu is deeper. The surrounding towns have little else to offer the tourist.

Return to Uçhisar and you are back where you started.

CHAPTER 27

40 RECOMMENDED BOOKS RELATED TO TURKEY

I do not think I am alone in enjoying a good book while traveling. At the same time, learning about the place I am visiting improves the experience. For these reasons I have compiled a book list for you to peruse. With each title I have written a short description to help. Also, I have included links to Amazon for each book that is available.

Note: I have only included books I have read.

The books are divided into the following categories:

- **History & Politics**
- **Cappadocia**
- **Culture/Anthropology**
- **Reflective/Personal or Travel Memoir**
- **Survival**
- **Fiction**

HISTORY & POLITICS

Turkey: What Everyone Needs to Know by Andrew Finkel

Finkel has been in Turkey for over 20 years and is well qualified to fulfill the challenging task the title of this book suggests.

Published in 2012, this 189 page book does an excellent job giving an introduction to all the key issues in modern Turkey. He covers history, economics, politics, the military as well as Ergenekon, Cyprus, the Kurds, Armenia, the EU bid, role of women, and on and on.

Crescent and Star: Turkey Between Two Worlds by Steven Kinzer

Kinzer was the NYT correspondent and spoke with "everyone" in Turkey. Excellent read if you want a basic understanding of Turkey's history, politics, and peoples. Kinzer clearly loved his time in Turkey and still keeps up with it today.

The New Turkey: The Quiet Revolution on the Edge of Europe by Chris Morris

Morris was a BBC correspondent who, much like Kinzer, connected the dots throughout the country and wrote an excellent and readable portrait of a country in transition. Although some of the book is necessarily a repeat of Kinzer and Mango, Morris adds his own flavor and includes much that is unique.

Overall, an excellent addition to this genre. At this point it is a bit outdated, but I have found that sometimes it is helpful to read something like that to catch a glimpse of just how much has changed in the last 10+ years.

Ataturk: The Biography of the founder of Modern Turkey by Andrew Mango

Long but a must read if you want to understand Turkey and the Turks, which is impossible without knowing the founder.

The Turks Today by Andrew Mango

Excellent resource and companion to Ataturk's biography. Very helpful in understanding what happened after Ataturk died. This book needs an update even from its 2004 publication date; but, among other good qualities, it has an excellent review of the different political parties in Turkey and how they have developed since Atatürk.

Ottoman Centuries by Lord Kinross

Invaluable resource for this history although seems to be a bit Britain biased. Regardless, I could not put it down- fascinating personalities and narrative.

Osman's Dream: The History of the Ottoman Empire by Caroline Finkel

Finkel uses the latest scholarship to paint a fascinating picture of the 600+ years of the Ottoman dynasty. Kinross does an excellent job with the material that was available at the time of his writing. However, the source material available to Ms. Finkel, especially in the Ottoman archives, means that she is able to paint a much fuller picture of the people and time.

She does an excellent job of giving the Ottoman perception of themselves and their world. This is a must-read for people who want to understand the Ottomans and, therefore, the Turks, but who are not able to read the Ottoman sources.

Sons of the Conquerors: The Rise of the Turkic World by Hugh Pope

This was an *Economist* "Best Book of the Year", and I can see why. Pope covers all of the Turkic peoples from western China through Central Asia into Europe and even to America. He deals with their place in history as well as the role they are playing in current events. Having lived among many of these people I found his account accurate and very helpful for understanding the ties between them and their importance in the unfolding events in the world today.

The Cyprus Problem: What Everyone Needs to Know by James Ker-Lindsay

If you are interested in Cyprus but are unclear on its history and why it is divided and why they can't "just all get along", then this is a great book for you to read. Ker-Lindsay does an excellent job of setting the context, detailing the history, describing the different interested parties, and explaining the complexities of the Cyprus Problem. I went from being ignorant on the subject to being able to engage with someone in a discussion about the sad state of affairs.

PODCASTS on iTUNES:

12 Byzantine Rulers: The History of the Byzantine Empire by Mr. Lars Brownworth

(Search it in the iTunes store; excellent and very entertaining history in audio format.) – I found these to be fascinating and cannot recommend them highly enough. If you have any kind of commute, these will make it speed by whether you are interested in Turkey or not. I wish my high school US history professor had been as interesting as Mr. Brownworth.

CAPPADOCIA

Fairy Chimneys of Cappadocia by Steve Eckert (also available in Cappadocia

Everything you thought you knew about Cappadocian geology is wrong! Fortunately, Mr. Eckert has written this short book to educate us. Although he is a brilliant scientist, he is able to use simple language that allows non-geologists to grasp very complex ideas. Geologists do not understand everything about Cappadocia, but Mr. Eckert gives us the latest theories on the formation of Cappadocia's unique landscape which was created by thousands of volcanoes.

Painting in Cappadocia: A Guide to the Sites and Byzantine Church Decoration by Cecily Hennessy

Hennessy has done a great service to Cappadocia visitors with this concise work. She adroitly covers more churches and paintings than any tourist could ever see in one visit. The book includes pictures, maps, and detailed descriptions. I recommend taking it on your trip and using it as a guide for the various churches you enter.

CULTURE/ANTHROPOLOGY

Once There Was, Twice There Wasn't: Fifty Turkish Folktales of Nasreddin Hodja by Michael Shelton

This may seem like a strange category for this book, but I think this is one of the best books on the market for understanding Turkish culture and how to survive within it. At the same time these are wonderfully entertaining folktales for adults and children. You will not be disappointed with this book, I promise!

Told in the Coffee House Turkish Tales by Allan Ramsay

This is an interesting set of tales that are similar to the Nasreddin Hodja stories mentioned above but have a clearly different spirit as they more firmly represent the time in which they were told. Ramsay sat in Ottoman Istanbul coffee houses at the end of the 19th century and listened to the stories told. He then translated them and put them in this book. As of this writing the Kindle edition is free, so what will it hurt to download it and give it a look.

Turkish Alevis Today by John Shindeldecker

Excellent resource for understanding this misunderstood segment of the Turkish population. I have Alevi friends and found this book very helpful in connecting with them on a deeper level. It provides many conversation topics. Plus this book is free as a PDF.

Tradition and Change in a Turkish Town (Schenkman Series on Socio-Economic Change) by Paul J. Magnarella

Quite academic and not an easy read (or easy to find for that matter) but well worth it for the nuggets contained within. He gives a useful picture of the change Turkey has undergone over the last 50 years.

Protestant Missionaries To The Middle East:: Ambassadors Of Christ Or Culture? by Peter Pikkert

For those who want to understand why Turks view Christian missionaries (and even Christians to some degree) as "dividers" and "enemies", this is the book for you. Pikkert gives a thorough picture of the work of missionaries during the late Ottoman empire and the repercussions today of the decisions they made over 100 years ago. This may seem like a strange one to include, but I found it invaluable for understanding societal issues that secular writers do not address.

Teach Yourself Turkish by David Pollard

I am still learning Turkish. This book is excellent for those who want to learn more than survival language. It comes with 16 excellent dialogues on CD as well.

REFLECTIVE/PERSONAL OR TRAVEL MEMOIR

Portrait of a Turkish Family by Irfan Orga

Irfan Orga was born in 1908 into an aristocratic Ottoman family that loved and cared for each other. Everything changed with the Ottoman entry into World War I. The book is written as a series of memories that give a fascinating picture of Ottoman culture, family life, and the tragic consequences of war on a family and a nation. This book is a must-read for those interested in Turkey as the experiences shared still impact and influence Turkey today.

A Fez of the Heart: Travels around Turkey in Search of a Hat by Jeremy Seal

Well-written memoir of one man's journey through Turkey tracing the history of the fez. This is maybe the perfect book to read for the tourist who is not interested in digging into Turkish politics but wants an interesting book that will give a memorable picture of the history and culture of this amazing land and people.

Meander by Jeremy Seal

Mr. Seal jumps in a canoe and heads down the legendary Meander river describing his experiences with modern Turks along the way while recounting the storied history of the river. All of this is done with expertise as he tries to make sense of Turkey's place between East and West. A must-read for those who love Turkey, adventure, and history.

Tales from the Expat Harem: Foreign Women in Modern Turkey (Seal Women's Travel) edited by Anastasia M. Ashman & Jennifer E. Gökmen

29 expat women from all over the globe but having lived in Turkey recount anecdotes from their experiences. Some are married to Turkish men, some single; some spent decades in Turkey, some only a couple of years; some had wonderful experiences, some not so good; but all of their lives were forever touched. One story would give a very skewed view of this land, but taken altogether you will get as well-rounded a picture of Turkey as you will find anywhere.

Tea and Bee's Milk: Our Year in a Turkish Village by Karen & Ray Gilden

The Gildens spent a year living in a seaside village in the late 1990's and retell their story in this small volume. The writing is decent and the stories are quaint. They give a good picture of Turkey at that time; it is almost unrecognizable today. I cannot recommend this book wholeheartedly, but I am sure it will be enjoyable to a certain crowd. I can see my grandmother really enjoying it, for instance.

They could have done more at comparing that Turkey to the present day country as well as the historical settings and making connections. Instead they give stories about trying to get their washing machine to work and going out on a friend's yacht and the difficulties of email with a 9600 dial up baud rate. They do have flashes of brilliance, but they are too few for me.

Turkish Reflections: A Biography of a Place by Mary Lee Settle

Ms. Settle was in Turkey in the late 1970s and then returned around 1990 and circumscribed the country in search of a hidden Seljuk history. The title fits the book. This is a great read for people who were not in Turkey before the turn of the millennium. The Turkey she describes is hard to find at this point but understanding it is helpful for understanding how the Turks arrived at their current state of affairs.

SURVIVAL

Turkey - Culture Smart!: The Essential Guide to Customs & Culture by Charlotte McPherson

Very helpful for the person who is planning on residing in Turkey. Note that this is written by an American who has lived in Turkey for over 30 years. The next book is written by a Turk. You can decide who would know better what foreigners need. I read them both and found them both helpful, although a bit repetitive. I think you only need to pick one.

Culture Shock! Turkey: A Survival Guide to Customs and Etiquette by Arın Bayraktaroğlu

See above. Although both of these are also helpful for the tourist, they cover much more than the average tourist will face. Also, their style makes the information quite forgettable if it is not being put to use on a regular basis.

A Handbook for Living in Turkey by Pat Yale

As the title states, this book is to be used more as a reference guide. I have used it to check on a number of issues I have faced while living here. I highly recommend it if you are living in Turkey or considering it. Pat Yale lives in Cappadocia and is a friend.

FICTION

Birds Without Wings by Louis de Bernieres

Wow! Great book. Set in a village in southwest Turkey during the 30 years covering the turn of the century, through WWI and the forming of the Republic of Turkey, this novel follows the lives of the villagers as told from their perspective.

Learn about their struggles and victories, their dreams, their sins and their love all while coming to a deeper understanding of the world that made Turkey what it is today. Interestingly woven within the narrative is a parallel story following the life of Ataturk during the same period. I cannot recommend this book highly enough.

Memed, My Hawk by Yashar Kemal

Great novel. Set in the mountain villages of the southeast, the reader gets an excellent picture of injustice and hope for the average peasant. I am reminded of the American wild west, a more melancholy version of Butch Cassidy and the Sundance Kid.

They Burn the Thistles (New York Review Books) by Yashar Kemal

An excellent follow-up to the above mentioned saga. I thought he went a bit overboard on the communist ideal, but the story was gripping.

The White Castle: A Novel by Orhan Pamuk

How different are the East and the West? Pamuk explores this idea through the lives of an Italian slave and his look-alike Ottoman master. This is probably my favorite Pamuk book.

Snow by Orhan Pamuk

Extremely dark and depressing. I gave this one to my dad and he did not finish it. However, for those who like Pamuk, he does not disappoint here. I found it helpful in understanding the complex issues surrounding Turkey, secularism, and Islam as embodied in the headscarf issue. A Turkish friend of mine from Van told me that the book is true to Van, Pamuk's birthplace. He said one needs to read Pamuk's books a few times to understand them.

My Name Is Red by Orhan Pamuk

Another look at East and West, this time through the eyes of Ottoman artists, with a love story thrown in for good measure. This one is a bit raunchy at times. I had not understood the issues about Islam and portraiture before reading this.

The Black Book by Orhan Pamuk

The search for identity in the Turkish mind. Galip's wife and journalist cousin have disappeared. He begins searching for them in classic detective style but the story quickly moves into a journey of the mind as he struggles with the idea of "being yourself". Is it possible? The story chapters seesaw between seemingly random newspaper columns (but the reader must assume they hold clues to the mystery) and continuing the account of Galip's journey.

The reader is reminded of Odysseus trying to return to Greece. Pamuk gives away his secular humanist leanings in all of his books as pessimism is the only outcome of that philosophy, and the overwhelming feeling words that describe his books are dark, depressing, heavy, and pessimistic. The translator's note in my edition was worth the price of the book. She gives excellent insight into the process of translating a novel.

The Janissary Tree: A Novel by Jason Goodwin

Yashim the eunuch serves the sultan as a detective in the Ottoman Empire in the 1830s. Reform is happening and not everyone is happy. The Janissaries were suppressed ten years ago. Four soldiers of the New Guard are missing and the Valide Sultan's (mother of Sultan) jewels are missing. What does it all mean? Who is behind it? Yashim only has 10 days to figure it out. Learn about the life, food, intrigue, and culture of the Ottomans through the eyes of this extraordinary eunuch who hobnobs with people from all walks of life.

The Forty Rules of Love: A Novel of Rumi by Elif Shafak

Follow the 13th century bromance between the wandering dervish, Shams of Tabriz, and the famous Konya preacher, Rumi, and the impact their story has on Ella, an unhappy and loveless, going-through-the-motions American-Jewish housewife. In the process we learn about the 40 Rules of Love which may or may not fit your notions of the concept. Regardless, both your heart and your mind will be engaged, and I expect that you will not be able to avoid the inevitable questions about the decisions you have made and the path of your own journey.

The Bastard of Istanbul by Elif Şafak

This novel was quite controversial upon its publication in the early 2000s, even landing Ms. Shafak in a Turkish court for "insulting Turkishness" (the case was thrown out). An American woman married an Armenian man and had a daughter. His family never accepted her, and they divorced. She then married a Turkish man studying in America.

The Turkish man's family of women (no men) is in Istanbul. His niece is the same age as his stepdaughter but the two girls live very different lives. What happens when this Turkish girl and this Armenian girl, connected by their stepdad/uncle, meet in Istanbul? Think about the Turkish – Armenian relationship through the lives of these two young women. The fact that this story was written by a Turk is what makes this book so important.

The Flea Palace by Elif Shafak

Have you ever driven by a big city apartment building and wondered about the residents? Shafak delves into the lives, relationships, identities, and history of an Istanbul building and its tenants. But this is not some docudrama. What is reality? In today's mega-cities what is real life? What have we become? Honestly, I still have no idea what the point of this novel is, and I cannot say I really enjoyed it, but I have greatly enjoyed thinking about it. I feel like the characters are still in my head asking me questions and forcing me to figure it out.

The Visitor: A Stranger, A Message, A Clash of Cultures by Peter Pikkert

The glum story of a Christian itinerant missionary trying to reach the Kurds of southeast Turkey. The chapters read like a ping-pong ball bouncing back and forth between a young Kurdish man opening up to new ideas and a middle-aged "missionary" seeking out those whom "God is calling". Overall, it is a very depressing read. The missionary is sort of "successful", but the reader is left with a dispirited notion.

Once There Was, Twice There Wasn't: Fifty Turkish Folktales of Nasreddin Hodja by Michael Shelton

See what I wrote in the Culture/Anthropology section above.

A Deceit to Die For by Luke Montgomery

An ancient Muslim conspiracy, a group trying to regain Ottoman glory, Islamic terrorists bent on breaking the West, an unsuspecting family caught in the middle- come along for a wild ride and deal with complex Muslim-Christian, East-West issues along the way.

CHAPTER 28

MY FAVORITE CAPPADOCIA PHOTOGRAPHS

I am not a professional photographer, but I do enjoy taking photographs and have captured a few nice ones of Cappadocia. I have not included a ton of photos in this guide, but I wanted to include some here to inspire and excite

Camel Rock in Devrent (Imagination) Valley

Lightning appears to strike Uçhisar

Balloons around Uçhisar

Over 250 days per year balloons fly in Cappadocia.

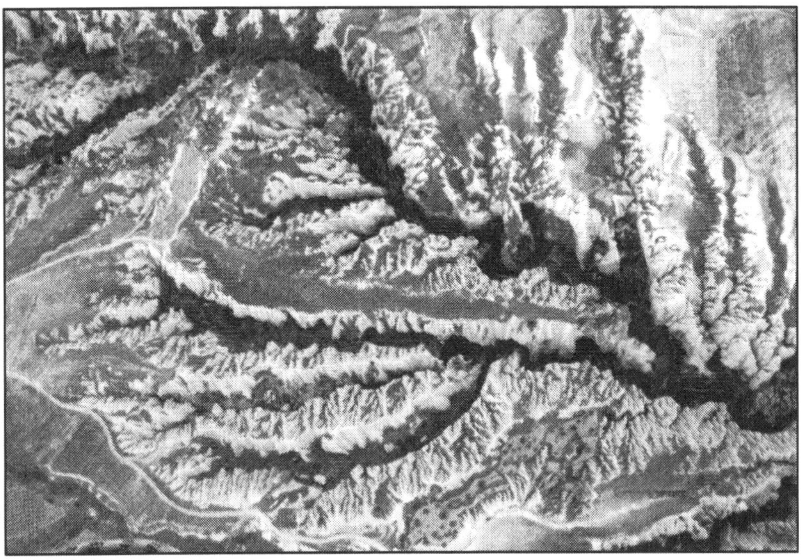

Cappadocia valleys viewed from a balloon

Erciyes Volcano as seen from near Göreme

Göreme Open Air Museum

Ever ride a camel? You can in Cappadocia.

Derinkuyu Underground City tunnel

Near Göreme

The apple blossoms are gorgeous in the late spring in Cappadocia.

Guzelyurt

Ortahisar

The Christian history of Cappadocia is hard to miss even in the courtyard of a mosque

Jandarma (police) office in Pasabag

Back side of Uçhisar

Vivew from our balloon.

Near Ürgüp

Çavuşin

Guzelyurt

Ortahisar

CHAPTER 29

HIKING CAPPADOCIA'S VALLEYS

NOTE: See the Maps in Appendix 7 to locate each valley in the region.

The central area of Cappadocia between Uçhısar and Çavuşin/Zelve has 8 main valleys with a plethora of tributaries running for miles in every direction.

Each valley has a well-worn path but no fences; the only thing determining your direction is your sense of adventure, your drinking water, and your next scheduled event (not necessarily in that order).

Each valley has breathtaking views and ancient caves, lush vegetation and varied wildlife, towering fairy chimneys and sheer cliffs.

And each valley has at least one Turk trying to make a living offering shade and selling freshly squeezed fruit juice, tea, and snacks as well as souvenirs in his ramshackle stand.

In this part I give a quick description to help you get a basic idea of each valley. In the following sections I go into more details about each valley and include some photos so you can make a more informed decision. I also include a section on Ihlara Valley which is not in the central Cappadocia area.

PREP NOTES

Before giving a brief description of each valley, let me add a few notes:

* All the valleys are great for mountain bikes.

* The paths make it possible for all ages to enjoy, however, 5-year-old-and-unders will probably find the hikes too long and spend much of the time expressing their desire to be carried.

* Be sure to wear sturdy shoes/boots (athletic shoes/sneakers are fine), carry some water, and don't forget your camera. You also may want to take a little money in case you want to buy fresh juice or a trinket from one of the stands. I recommend dressing in layers most of the year since the weather can change quickly. Also, use sunscreen and maybe a hat since there is little shade in many of the valleys.

* If it has rained in the day or two before you plan to hike, then expect to find some wet/muddy spots on the trail.

* Cappadocia is a safe place, but people are people and bad things can happen. Also, there are points on these trails that can be dangerous with a misstep and in some seasons other people may not pass your location for hours. For these reasons I strongly encourage you to hike with someone; don't go alone.

* Of course there are many other valleys in Cappadocia, but here I am only highlighting the valleys in the Göreme – Avanos area. There are a number worth exploring between Ürgüp and Mustafapaşa, but the vast majority of tourists do not go there. If you want more information about them, you can contact me at dukedillard@captivatingcappadocia.com.

PIGEON VALLEY

Google map coordinates (just put these in the search bar on maps.google.com):

Uçhısar long trail start: 38.621007, 34.804540
Uçhısar shorter trail start: 38.632229, 34.809004
Göreme trail start/finish: 38.640090, 34.822701

Starting at Uçhısar, this valley, named for the hundreds of pigeon houses carved out of the cliffs and fairy chimneys, winds down to Göreme. This is one of my favorite valleys in Cappadocia, and a great one for hiking with beautiful views and fascinating geological formations.

Regarding the route, you actually have two options as you can start on the backside near the Kaya Hotel for the long path or on the Göreme side of the rock tower for a shorter path (probably about 2-3 kilometers shorter). I recommend the shorter path because the trail for the longer path is a bit confusing and there are some angry dogs that hang out on it.

You can go the hard way uphill from Göreme or the more leisurely downhill walk from Uçhısar. Either way you will need to work out transportation as you end far from where you began. Starting in Göreme, I recommend taking the public bus up the hill to the start of the trail (get off the bus at the point where the road forks going into Uçhısar or around it), and then walking back to town.

Of course, if you are staying in Uçhısar and want to walk from Göreme back, then take the bus down and walk back to your hotel. The bus goes at least every hour.

Regardless, expect to spend 3-4 hours if you want to hike the whole thing, no need to rush through something so beautiful.

LOVE VALLEY

Google map coordinates (just put these in the search bar on maps.google.com):

Main lower entrance: 38.662767, 34.830555
Uçhisar upper entrance: 38.634479, 34.810069

This aptly named valley full of phallic fairy chimneys is most commonly entered from the west side of the Göreme – Avanos road between Göreme and Çavuşin.

The Turkish name is Bağıldere which does not mean love. The English name, Love Valley, was probably given because Porn Valley was inappropriate. Be prepared for lots of giggles from the less mature in your group.

This valley allows for more roundabout exploring and most hikes will begin and end at the same place. However, the actual valley does extend all the way up to the point on the Uçhısar - Göreme road where the road forks to go to Uçhisar. Very few visitors explore this section of the valley, but it does make for a great hike, one of our family favorites.

Expect 1 – 3 hours depending on your thirst for adventure.

ROSE/RED VALLEYS

Google map coordinates (just put these in the search bar on maps.google.com):

Entrance near Ortahisar: 38.652918, 34.863170
Entrance/Exit near Çavuşin: 38.662283, 34.841077

These two valleys wind out from the backside of Çavuşin and end up either at the overlook near Ortahısar or at Kaya Camping above the Göreme Open Air Museum (of course you can go the opposite route ending at Çavuşin).

I love both of these valleys (there are actually at least 3 trails in this area) as they provide some great views and include a few old cave churches.

One of our favorite experiences here is the full moon hike. If you happen to be in Cappadocia during a full moon with nice weather, a great adventure is to hike the valley in the dark. The full moon gives plenty of light for most of the hike although you will need a flashlight for some parts. I promise you won't forget it.

Expect to spend a few hours here. You may go for an hour without seeing another soul. How often can you say that?

ZEMI VALLEY

Google map coordinates (just put these in the search bar on maps.google.com):

Ürgüp – Nevşehir road entrance: 38.607922, 34.810466
Loop turn: 38.619513, 34.826211
Göreme entrance/exit: 38.643128, 34.837817

This breathtaking valley runs 5.6 kilometers from the Ürgüp – Nevşehir road to Göreme next to the Tourist Hotel. Another option is to start in Göreme and do a loop going through Görkündere. The distance is about the same. Beautiful rock formations, caves in cliffs, shady most of the way… This is my favorite valley hike.

Expect to spend 3-4 hours; wear good hiking boots or athletic shoes, and take some water and a snack. If you go in the late summer/fall, expect to enjoy plenty of fruit along the trail.

DEVRENT/IMAGINATION VALLEY

Google map coordinates (just put these in the search bar on maps.google.com):

Main observing point: 38.672529, 34.885353

Best known for the Camel Rock, this valley lies halfway between Avanos and Ürgüp. The tourist stop is situated right across from the Camel which gives visitors the opportunity to retake the same picture taken by millions who came before. For those who have more time, the valley is aptly named with its unique collection of eroded fairy chimneys allowing for infinite possibilities. For those of you who enjoy naming cloud shapes, allot a good chunk of time for this valley.

You need transportation to see this valley so if you are not with a tour, you will need to rent a car or scooter or hitchhike. But it is included in the Red Tour so you will not have to worry about transportation if you take that tour.

You can spend anywhere from 10 minutes (just take a picture of the camel) to a few hours exploring the hills and dales of this valley.

KILIÇLAR VADISI (SWORDS VALLEY)

Google map coordinates (just put these in the search bar on maps.google.com):

Entrance above Open Air Museum: 38.640532, 34.846540
Exit: 38.647111, 34.842601

This is the smallest valley with a name in central Cappadocia. It begins just up from the Göreme Open Air Museum and ends in the open area between Göreme and Çavuşin. There is a 300 meter tunnel, many interesting fairy chimneys and ruins, and part of the valley is very narrow, more like a ravine. Hiking the entire valley can be done in 1-2 hours easy making it a good option for those feeling a time crunch.

MONK'S VALLEY

Google map coordinates (just put these in the search bar on maps.google.com):

Entrance by Paşabağ: 38.677246, 34.858146

Zelve Open Air Museum: 38.669418, 34.863299

This is probably the least of the valleys as it winds from Paşabağ to the lesser known Zelve Open Air Museum. Start with Paşabağ's amazing Fairy Chimneys and go along the road with open space to your left and towering slopes to your right. Ending at the museum you can spend another couple of hours touring it, if you like. I don't include this one in the following section since there is not much more to say.

IHLARA VALLEY - See the section below.

Google map coordinates (just put these in the search bar on maps.google.com):

Ihlara village entrance: 38.239750, 34.307651
Main entrance for Green Tour: 38.253304, 34.302464
Green Tour exit (near Belisirma): 38.265000, 34.290519

With these 8 valley hikes you can spend many hours enjoying Cappadocia's unique brand of nature. The following sections provide even more details...

PIGEON VALLEY

Google map coordinates (just put these in the search bar on maps.google.com):

Uçhısar long trail start: 38.621007, 34.804540
Uçhısar shorter trail start: 38.632229, 34.809004
Göreme trail start/finish: 38.640090, 34.822701

As I have said in the past, one of the great things about Cappadocia is the absence of fences. The valleys have trails, but when you were in school, did you always color between the lines? When you see an area that catches your fancy, go for it.

Pigeon Valley offers many opportunities for this, especially if you take the long trail starting on the back side of Uçhısar.

NOW FOR THE DETAILS

How should you "do" Pigeon Valley?

TRANSPORTATION: The problem is that you begin and end at different points: Uçhısar to Göreme. You can go either direction but know that starting from Uçhısar is a bit easier as it is downhill the whole way.

Most people reading this will not have a car but this is not a problem since the bus, which goes either way at least every hour, is easy for this valley. This means you can either take the bus to one side and then hike back to your origin or hike and then take the bus back to your starting point.

The bus does not stop right at the entrance so be sure to be clear of your exit point before getting on. If you ask nicely, someone working at your hotel may agree to drive you one way. This is all much easier if you are staying in Uçhısar or Göreme

ACCESSORIES: Be sure to bring a bottle of water and a camera. You should wear sturdy hiking/walking shoes as the trail is a combination of rocks, dirt, grass, and sand with some water and steps thrown in for good measure.

STARTING POINTS: If you start in Uçhısar, be aware that there is a long trail and a short trail. The long trail starts at the Kaya Hotel on the back side of Uçhısar farthest from Göreme and is around 6km from start to finish with Hasan waiting for you at about the halfway point.

The so-called short trail (about 3km) starts at the bottom of the hill on the road to the CCR not far from the Göreme panoramic views. If you start here, Hasan's tea garden is just a few hundred meters away. And apart from what you spend at Hasan's, Pigeon Valley is free (no entrance fees).

THE PIGEONS (TURKISH: GÜVERCINLIK): The valley is named for the many pigeon houses or dovecotes carved into the rocks and cliffs. Years ago the pigeons were used as message carriers, and their droppings were used as fertilizer and maybe even for use in making explosives. Today very few, if any, pigeons are kept in the valley, although many locals keep them as pets in their own columbariums.

CONCLUSION

When you come to Cappadocia be sure to take half a day and hike Pigeon Valley and be sure to schedule in half an hour for refreshments with Hasan. If you want to make it a full day, plan on walking around Uçhısar and Göreme on each end of your hike. I promise you will sleep well that night!

Photo Tour of Pigeon Valley

Photo Tour: Now, here are a few more pictures of the valley to give you an idea of what to expect...

Pigeon Valley is a great hike from Uchisar to Goreme

Start the hike through Pigeon Valley at the lower part of Uchisar

What could this have been in its heyday?

Walking through Pigeon Valley often feels like being on another planet.

LOVE VALLEY

Google map coordinates (just put these in the search bar on maps.google.com):

Main entrance (northern side near Çavuşin): 38.662767, 34.830555
Uçhisar entrance (southern side): 38.634479, 34.810069

Most visitors to this valley (Bağıldere in Turkish and on Google maps) only see a small part of it and spend their time taking creative pictures and giggling a good bit. The fairy chimneys near the northern entrance/exit are the most phallic shaped formations in the region.

However, the few who hike the whole valley get a special treat. The total length is around 4.5 kilometers and the trail is not always easy to follow/find, but you can't get lost and the scenery is drop-dead gorgeous.

If a tour mentions Love Valley, it does not mean a hike but rather a few minutes in the northern part to look around and take pictures. If you want to hike it, you have 2 options. You can start at the northern end not far from Çavuşin and hike uphill towards Uçhisar. You will exit onto the Uçhisar - Göreme road where you can catch a bus to wherever you are staying. Or you can do the opposite. In the latter case you will exit onto the Göreme - Avanos road and again can catch a bus wherever you are staying or just walk back to Göreme which will be about a mile.

My family loves this hike. We did the whole valley starting from the Uçhisar side and finished it in around 3 hours which included the bus ride from Çavuşin to the southern entrance. This includes taking into account our 7 and 8 year olds who lagged behind at times.

One note to be aware of is that the northern entrance is much used and easy to find whereas the southern entrance below Uçhisar is not as well marked. The Google map coordinates should help pinpoint it.

Photo Tour of Love Valley

Majestic stems of asparagus?

Imagine these everywhere you look in Love Valley

All are pointing to the balloons

ROSE/RED VALLEYS

Google map coordinates (just put these in the search bar on maps.google.com):

> Entrance near Ortahisar: 38.652918, 34.863170
> Entrance/Exit near Çavuşin: 38.662283, 34.841077

These valleys make for great hikes and include the best cave churches of any of the valleys (don't compare to the open air museums but also do not cost anything to observe) as well as the steepest paths (in a few sections). The views are wonderful, and the variety of terrain is fun.

The picture opposite shows the different options. This sign sits at the entrance near Ortahisar. As you can see you have three valleys from which to choose. One note that is not clear from the sign is that the important distance is the length to Çavuşin which is somewhere between 4 and 5 kilometers. The differences show that the valley ends after the given distance but you still have to keep hiking to get to Çavuşin so you can get transportation to wherever you are staying.

Another option is to hike back to Göreme in which case you should add another 3 kilometers to the distance listed on the sign.

TRANSPORTATION: As with most of the valleys, you will need to work out transportation. The best/easiest route is the entrance near Ortahisar, however, this panoramic view is not easy to get to without a ride. You can either take a taxi or possibly talk someone at your hotel into giving you a ride.

Another option is to either hitchhike or take the bus heading to Ürgüp which will drop you off at the entrance to the road leading to the valley entrance which adds another 3 kilometers to the hike.

The other option is start near Çavuşin and either hike around in more of a loop fashion or hike all the way up to the overlook point and then out to the main road where you can catch the bus.

MOONLIGHT HIKE: One fun option that only presents itself a few times per year is the moonlight hike. You need a warm, clear night and a full moon (generally only works in the summer months). A few hotels know about this and can set it up for you.

You will do a loop from the Ortahisar entrance so you will need transportation. A flashlight helps for certain spots but you really don't need it for most of the hike. What makes it work well in this valley is that so much of the trail is treeless making for good visibility.

I know at least one guide who offers this to tourists and includes a stop in one of the cave churches to enjoy a glass of wine and hear some stories. Last time we did this with friends we came upon one of these groups sitting in a cave church with candles lit and wine glasses full.

Photo Tour of Rose/Red Valleys

The entrance to three valleys from this panoramic viewpoint

The glories of erosion in Red Valley

I picture an elf hiding in the bushes

You will find these open caves waiting to be explored all over Cappadocia

ZEMI VALLEY

Google map coordinates (just put these in the search bar on maps.google.com):

Ürgüp – Nevşehir road entrance: 38.607922, 34.810466

Loop turn: 38.619513, 34.826211

Göreme entrance/exit: 38.643128, 34.837817

This is my favorite valley to hike in central Cappadocia. The trail is nice, the natural diversity is wonderful, there is plenty of shade with probably the most trees of any valley in the area, lots of fresh fruit to eat off the trees (in season, of course), and it has a couple of options so hiking it more than once is not repetitive. The only negative is that you need transport to get to the start point, but a taxi will not be too expensive so it is doable.

In this section I will give details and some photos so you can make an informed decision as to whether you want to hike this valley or choose a different one.

Either hike the entire 5.6 km valley starting from the Ürgüp - Nevşehir road OR start at the road and do the red and blue lines OR start in Göreme and do the loop which is about the same distance.

DISTANCE: 5.6 kilometers (3.3 miles)

TIME: Expect it to take 3-4 hours. Do not be in a hurry; you will want to enjoy the beauty.

TERRAIN: Dirt trail most of the way; wet in some spots as it follows a stream part of the way; one area that is steep and requires holding onto a rope that is set in place; a couple of hills to climb or descend that are a 200-300 hundred meters total.

LOCATION: In Göreme on the road to the Open Air Museum right past the Tourist Hotel. The other end is off the Ürgüp – Nevşehir road not far from the turn off to Uçhisar. There is a sign and a souvenir stand making it is easy to find.

CLOTHING: Wear good shoes; hiking boots are probably best. There is plenty of shade but wear sunscreen if it is a sunny day. Wear clothes that fit the temperature. You do not need to worry about protection from thorns or similar hindrances.

NOURISHMENT: I would recommend a bottle of water and some kind of trail mix or other nutritious snack. Depending on the season you may find fruit on the trees to supplement but do not count on it.

PATHS: You have two options -

1. If you can get a ride, have them drop you off on the Ürgüp – Nevşehir road at the head of the trail and then follow the trail to Göreme. You can also take the Ürgüp – Nevşehir public bus and have them stop to let you off at the head of the trail.

2. Start in Göreme and do a loop. The distance is about the same. For this you go through both Zemi Valley and Görkündere, the ridge overlooking the valley. This option gives you wonderful panoramic views of the area.

WHAT TO LOOK FOR: Mainly this is a trail on which to enjoy the beauty of the nature you traverse; however you can expect to see a couple of churches, some caves, cool rock formations and fairy chimneys, and an array of fruit depending on the season. Do not expect to see wildlife except for birds.

If you enter from the Ürgüp-Nevşehir road (google coordinates above) this is the sign marking the beginning of the trail. Next to it sits these tables selling the same trinkets you will find at every stop in Cappadocia.

This is the one steep point on the trail but the rope makes it easy for all ages (our 4 year old managed it with no worries).

These markers are scattered along the trail but there are not very many of them so you will need to make some guesses at different points but you can't get lost.

This is where the trail forks. Go left (blue line) to Görkündere or right (red line) to stay on the Zemi Valley trail. They end up in the same place. If you are starting in Göreme and doing the loop, you will come out of the red line trail on the right (where the children are standing) and curve around to the blue line trail on the left rather than going straight (middle pink path) towards the camera which will take you up to the road eventually.

Watch your step on this initial part of the trail as it is a bit steep downhill, but it quickly flattens out. The rest of this section contains pictures I took when I hiked the trail. They give you a small taste of the beauty of this valley.

If you take the Görkündere trail you end up on this plateau for a bit and can enjoy captivating views of Uçhisar and the central valley towards Avanos.

These are some of the best fairy chimneys in the region hidden near Göreme.

Legend has it that one of St. Simeon's spots of solitude is located in this valley. St. Simeon's Cave is but a few minutes' hike from the head of the trail, which winds through these petrous formations. This valley supposedly helped him in his desire to attain a "closeness" with God, where other more urban areas only provided obstacles to this pursuit. You can search "St. Simeon Cappadocia" online to learn more about him.

Photo Tour of Zemi Valley

Perhaps a bunch of ancient garden gnomes?

These markers make it easy to navigate the trail. Here you must choose the upper or lower trail.

Zemi Valley is my favorite valley after Ihlara

Zemi Valley may have the most unique fairy chimneys

The entrance to Zemi Valley

The upper trail above Zemi Valley provides another great view of Uchisar

This is the only difficult section of Zemi Valley.

IMAGINATION (DEVRENT) VALLEY

Google map coordinates (just put these in the search bar on maps.google.com):

Main observing point: 38.672529, 34.885353

Imagination Valley (Devrent in Turkish) is a different kind of valley experience. The name comes from the challenge to name the odd-shaped fairy chimneys populating the hills. You will not be here for long without talking about what the different rocks look like. Everything you see is from natural erosion which for some is hard to believe.

Is the rock below a camel or a snail or something else? Below on the photo tour, I include a number of rocks and their popular look-alikes.

This valley is not for hiking as much as for looking and taking pictures. I have hiked around in it, but I would guess that 99% of tourists spend less than 30 minutes here and walk a total of 100 meters at most. It is worth seeing and is actually a fun place to hike around, but if you only have time to hike one valley, don't do this one. It is a stop on the Red Tour so no need to see it separately if you are planning on taking this tour.

DIRECTIONS: Imagination Valley is located about halfway down the old road from Avanos to Ürgüp. The public bus does not use this road so you will need to arrange your own transportation. A rental car or scooter will work or you can hire a taxi to take you there. Depending on where you are starting and how much time you have bicycles would be a lot of work and not recommended.

Below are some of the formations you will see when you visit this valley. Do you agree with the names? What would you call them?

Photo Tour of Imagination Valley

Camel Rock

Can you see the dancing couple?

Camel Rock is the most popular spot in Devrent (Imagination) Valley

Can you see the seal colony?

St. Simeon's cave in the cliffs is accessible if you want a closer look

SWORDS (KILIÇLAR) VALLEY

Google map coordinates (just put these in the search bar on maps.google.com):

Entrance above Open Air Museum: 38.640532, 34.846540
Exit: 38.647111, 34.842601

Let's say you are staying in Göreme and want to get out and do something but only have a couple of hours. Or maybe you finished touring the Open Air Museum and have a couple of hours to spare before heading to your next activity. If that describes your situation, then Kiliçlar Vadisi (Swords Valley) is calling your name.

The entrance to the valley is either right above or right below the Göreme Open Air Museum. I recommend the upper entrance; exit the museum, turn right, and head up the S-curvy road 100 meters or so. You will see the entrance on your left.

This valley is different from the others in that it is much shorter, has parts that are more like a narrow gorge, and has a lot more old church ruins. It also has a tunnel that is close to 300 meters long, but it is not so easy to find as it is not part of the main trail.

Photo Tour of Swords Valley

The entrance to Swords Valley is up from the Goreme Open Air Museum.

This next section of the trail becomes narrow and resembles a gorge more than a valley. The ladder is quite sturdy and safe. This makes doing this valley with a bicycle a bit problematic for most people.

This ladder is easy to navigate for young and old alike

These steep gorges are unique in Cappadocia

Swords Valley packs a lot of diversity in its short span

Once you exit the ravine the path opens up and allows for more exploring of the many fairy chimneys to the left and right.

Go through the small tunnel and enter an area of ruins on both sides. What must this community have been like once upon a time?

Did the people who used this cave church in Swords Valley think about what would remain 1000 years later?

Before you know it the end of the trail has come and you can head towards Rose Valley for more hiking or turn left and head back to Göreme.

Sights like this in Swords Valley make it worth hiking

IHLARA VALLEY

Google map coordinates (just put these in the search bar on maps.google.com):

Ihlara village entrance: 38.239750, 34.307651
Main entrance for Green Tour: 38.253304, 34.302464
Green Tour exit (near Belisirma): 38.265000, 34.290519

This is my favorite place in Cappadocia. The lush green valley surrounded by sheer cliffs pockmarked with ancient caves, the peaceful river flowing throughout, the gentle path, and the almost audible voices of history making themselves heard through the structures they have left behind.

DIRECTIONS: Ihlara is about an hour southwest of Göreme. Getting there is not easy so you will have to work out transportation. It is included in the Green Tour so that is the easiest way to experience it.

Another option is to rent a car but the problem there is that the valley hike is linear so you have to return the way you came to get back to your car. The easiest but most expensive option is to hire a car and driver and have him drop you off in one place and pick you up in another.

DETAILS: The valley is close to 12 kilometers total, but most tourists hike only 3-4 at most. You can enter at a few different places. The most common is a few kilometers outside of Ihlara village. This is where the Green Tour begins its hike with the many-staired descent. Another option is from the center of Ihlara village. This entrance requires less stairs.

Beginning at the village you hike around 3 kilometers to the point where the Green Tour begins. The first time my family did the hike we exited here. I then hitchhiked back to our car.

From this point it is another 3-4 kilometers to another exit/entrance. From here the valley goes for close to another 6 kilometers, but I have not hiked this section.

There are a few cafes along the trail so you should bring some money if you don't bring water and snacks or a picnic.

SUMMER FUN: One last note before the photo tour… If you happen to go in July or August on a hot day, be prepared to swim. My family was not prepared but had a great time nonetheless.

We started from Ihlara village and not long after entering the valley we came upon a bend in the river with a waterfall and small, deep pool before continuing on. There were some local boys swimming so we joined them in our clothes. We spent close to an hour jumping into the pool (see picture below) and then let the sun dry us as we continued our hike. It was a day we will remember for the rest of our lives.

Photo Tour of IhlaraValley

This entrance/exit boasts over 300 stairs with a nice river at the bottom.

Enjoy a nice swim if the weather is good.

Get a nice view of Uchisar from the end of Swords Valley

Definitely make time for an Ihlara Valley hike when you visit

Ihlara is my favorite place in Cappadocia

CHAPTER 30

OFF THE BEATEN PATH

Some of you are looking for the uncommon places, the diamonds in the rough. This section is for you. The reality is that the popular places are popular for a reason. However, there are so many cool sights in Cappadocia that some have escaped the notice of the masses. And for some people, going to a place that is relatively unexplored is part of what makes that place special.

Below you will find some ideas for escaping the common itineraries and seeing the "unseen". Actually, nothing is Cappadocia is common, but I think you know what I mean in the context. Maybe the best feature of Cappadocia is that almost no area is off-limits. You will not find fences and walls and "Private Property" signs; they are nonexistent.

This means the first option for getting off the path is to literally just go off the path. Stop on the side of the road at a place that looks interesting and start walking. See something from your balloon flight? Go find it on foot. Take a left halfway through a valley hike and see where you end up. Be careful of cliffs and the random stray dog, but otherwise you are good to go.

With that said, let's look at some actual places that are rarely visited by foreigners...

Guzelyurt - This is a great area to visit and even stay in if you are visiting Cappadocia for four or more days or if you are returning to Cappadocia for a second or third visit. There is enough to write that I have given it a separate section below.

Özkonak - This underground city is mentioned in the "Underground Cities" section so you can learn more there. I mention it here because it is rarely visited. It is a large underground city but only a relatively small portion is open to the public.

You will not have to worry about waiting on other tourist groups like you may in the more popular underground cities. The town also boasts the Bellha Greek Orthodox Church building which has not been renovated but is an interesting site especially if you can get a local resident to give you the historical information.

Gaziemir - This so-called underground city is mentioned in the "Underground Cities" section so you can learn more there. I mention it here because it is rarely visited. Don't be fooled by the sign on the main road claiming this as the "largest" underground city. It is not true. This was probably a large underground caravansary, not a city. It is interesting, and I guarantee you will not have to fight any crowds to see it.

Zelve Open Air Museum - Look below to see the fuller description of this sight. Very few visitors make it to this open air museum even though it is close to the main sights. The problem is that it does not have all the restored cave churches with frescoes. Those who take the time to explore are generally not disappointed, but if you are on a time budget, this is probably not going to be on your list. As with everything on this list, you will not have to fight the crowds here.

Bayramhaci - I am not sure how to write about these wonderful hot springs. They are for the truly adventurous, low-maintenance visitors. They are so nice in the winter. Sit in a steaming pool outside with snow or at least freezing cold air surrounding you (they have an indoor pool as well).

We love to go and spend a couple of hours relaxing. It is open in summer as well, but I'm personally not so eager to jump into really hot water in the summer. On the other hand the facilities are pretty rundown so it is just not as comfortable as most tourists like. If you are good with one star facilities and five star relaxation, then you'll enjoy this place.

The village is located about 15 minutes outside of Avanos so you will have to work out transportation both ways. A taxi there will not work unless the driver waits for you. Your hotel should be able to help you. Bring a bathing suit.

The fee is a few dollars per person for as long as you want to stay up to a whole day. Ask your hotel to call ahead to make sure the outdoor pool is full. They empty it and refill it every three or four days so there is a day or two each week when it is not available.

Area Between Ürgüp and Mustafapaşa - If you head out of Ürgüp on the road to Mustafapaşa, you will find a number of valleys with cave churches to explore on the right side of the road. Very few tourists ever enter this area. Just choose a place to stop and start exploring. I have only spent a little time in this area so am unable to say much more. For those who have the time and want to go to an area that is relatively untouched and yet not far away, this is the place for you.

Blue Tour & Soğanlı Valley - I cover this in the Tours section so go there to read more details. This tour covers a beautiful area but one that is rarely visited. I have a guide friend whom I have asked to let me know when a Blue Tour happens so I can join it. He never calls. This is one of those amazing regions in Cappadocia that is overshadowed by the rest of the area.

If it was the only valley, then it would get tons of visitors, but it is a bit further out and doesn't quite have the pizzaz. It is a good one again for those wanting to avoid crowds in the busy season. Also, in this area you will find Sobesos, Roman ruins from the 4th-9th centuries, and Keslik Monastery, an 8th century Christian cave community.

Incesu - This town is way off the beaten path and definitely not for everyone. However, if you are looking to go to a town that has some interesting attractions and absolutely no tourists, then this is a good option. The population is around 24,000 so just a little bigger than Ürgüp, but due to the lack of visitors there is almost no activity in the town outside of older men drinking tea and talking politics and normal citizens doing their shopping and errands. The town is blessed with a Caravansary-Mosque-Hamam complex (not open for inside tours except the mosque) built in the 1600s by Grand Vizier Kara Mustafa Paşa.

Apparently, he was traveling in central Anatolia with his army in the winter. They were cold and complaining they could not go on so he stopped here for 2 years and built this complex. He later became famous (or infamous?) for attacking Venice and losing badly. The biggest gain for the world in the defeat was that he left bags and bags of coffee which were taken by the Austrians and used to open coffee shops.

In a way you can thank Kara Mustafa Paşa for your coffee each morning. The least you can do is visit his buildings in Incesu. The town also has an old Greek Orthodox church building that has been closed since 1924. It is similar to the one in Gulşehir. There is no direct bus from Göreme/Avanos/Ürgüp to Incesu so you will have to rent a car or hire a ride.

Kozakli - About an hour away sits a hot springs resort that is rarely visited by non-Turks. The town has quite a few very affordable resort hotels built around the hot springs bubbling up from deep in the earth, signs of the volcanic activity that defined this region thousands of years ago.

This is a popular destination for Turks who are seeking healing for various ailments since the spring water is thought to have healing qualities. One note is that these resorts are run for more conservative, religious Turks so the pools are not coed; each hotel has pools, spas, hamams for women and separate ones for men.

Churches Near Göreme Open Air Museum - On the road to the Göreme Open Air Museum there are a number of stand-alone cave churches open to visitors. Directly past the Tourist Hotel take a right and go up aways to see the El Nazar Church. Right after the horses on the right you will find the Sakli Church. Then after the museum, further up the hill, you will find the Aynali and Firkatan Churches. Most of these require small entrance fees and are rarely visited.

Nar - I mention this because it is so unique. Across the main road from the Forum Mall in Nevşehir there is a valley and on the opposite hill of the valley sits one of the freakiest looking villages you will ever see. It is aptly named Nar, the Turkish word for pomegranate, and it fits because the town looks like the inside of a pomegranate. There is nothing to do except walk around but it may be one of the most interesting things you take home. Go to the main road in front of the mall and snap a few photos.

Rose/Red Valley Moonlight Hike - *I mentioned this in the valleys section but wanted to put it here as well since it is definitely a unique experience in Cappadocia.*

One fun option that only presents itself a few times per year is the moonlight hike. You need a warm, clear night and a full moon (generally only works in the summer months). A few hotels know about this and can set it up for you. You will do a loop from the Ortahisar entrance so you will need transportation. A flashlight helps for certain spots but you really don't need it for most of the hike. What makes it work well in this valley is that so much of the trail is treeless making for good visibility.

I know at least one guide who offers this to tourists and includes a stop in one of the cave churches to enjoy a glass of wine and hear some stories. Last time we did this with friends we came upon one of these groups sitting in a cave church with candles lit and wine glasses full.

> **NOTE**: I mentioned these next four towns in the "Towns" section but am also including them here since they are rarely visited.

Gulşehir - This town of 14,000 located on the Kizilirmak (Red River) about 25 kilometers west of Avanos has a number of sights worth visiting and is surprisingly hospitable for a town that does not see too many tourists. You can walk around and explore, but you should have transportation since the three main sights are quite spread out.

On the northwest end of town sits the Greek Orthodox Church of St. Demetrius. This is not a cave church but an actual building. It has not been used since 1924 and so all that remains is the building and a well.

The neighborhood leader whose office is across the street will loan you the key to enter the building. Then on the east side of town off the Nevşehir road you will find the beautifully renovated St. Jean's Cave church. Built out of two large fairy chimneys, this two story church from the 13 century is extraordinary, and you won't have to worry about fighting the crowds or being forced to leave after two minutes.

And lastly, further down the road you can enter a park and see the Mushroom Rock, a fairy chimney shaped like a giant mushroom, among other unusually shaped rock formations. Both St. Jeans and the Mushroom Rock require an entrance fee.

Hacıbektaş - This 13th century Alevi spiritual leader allegedly settled in this area (not all accounts agree) and spread his teaching throughout the region. He was a man of peace and wisdom according to official historians and his followers had great influence in the Ottoman Empire.

The town centers around the excellent museum and cultural center which contains his grave and the graves of other leaders of the movement. Many rooms give a good picture of the life of the community when Hacı Bektaş was alive. Besides the museum we did not find much in the town, but honestly nothing else was needed.

In mid-August they have their annual festival: a weekend of music, dancing, and cultural events with visitors from all over the world. This is not a good time to visit the town unless you want to enjoy a chaotic time of Turkish Alevi cultural celebration and a bunch of political speeches.

Ibrahimpaşa – This little village between Üçhisar and Ortahisar is a hidden treasure in Cappadocia. Not because of its restaurants and not because of its hotels. No, simply the opposite is true. This village is so untouched by the tourist trappings of its neighboring towns that it warrants a visit. But once you get here you will get a feel for what it was like to live in a Turkish village at the turn of the century.

You will see how people built their new stone houses right out of the caves that were there before. You can take a walk down the narrow cobblestone streets passable only by foot or donkey.

Take a hike down one of the many valleys in the village and end up in Ortahisar. Or just drive into the village square, park your car, and have a cup of tea with the male villagers who will enjoy your company.

Mustafapaşa - A few miles outside of Ürgüp, this old Greek town, also known as Sinasos, is worth a visit. The Greeks/Christians all left in the 1923-24 people swap after Turkey won its independence, but many of the buildings remain including a large church (not a cave) with a small museum inside.

This town is included in the Blue/Undiscovered Cappadocia Tour, but I mention it here as it is another Cappadocia sight that is not on most itineraries.

GUZELYURT

Guzelyurt sits about an hour from Göreme, close to Ihlara Valley. Lots of tourists pass it on the way to Ihlara but few stop or stay. I mention it here as an alternative to Göreme. This idea is not for everyone.

Let's say you have been to Cappadocia before and are planning a return trip. You saw the open air museum and an underground city, you took a balloon ride and hiked a valley and did some shopping.

This time you want to see something new and avoid the crowds. If this is you, then Guzelyurt may be the ideal place. Also, if you are staying in Cappadocia for five plus nights, you may want to spend a couple of the nights here.

Guzelyurt is a quaint little former Greek town with 1700 years of history and a beautiful view of Hasan Dağ, another volcano that helped form the region. Making this your headquarters means you can spend your time in Monastery and Ihlara Valleys, visit the lesser known Gaziemir Underground City, check out some Greek homes, and visit some fascinating historical churches.

ACCOMMODATIONS

There are not a ton of options, and I have not done much research in this area. My friend stayed at **Cappadocia Gelveri Cave Hotel.** They have 35 rooms total with 13 of those being cave rooms. The rooftop terrace offers a great view for sunsets and the surrounding valley.

You will definitely need your own transportation so plan on renting a car. This makes it easy to get here and back as well as to get around to the different attractions which are quite spread out.

Not far from the village you will find Ihlara Valley and Gaziemir Underground City which I have described in other sections of this book so will not go into detail here. There are a few more sights to enjoy in the area which I describe below...

On the next page you see a view of the lower section of Guzelyurt with the ancient St. Gregorios church, converted into a mosque after 1924, in the bottom left corner. It is named after one of the Cappadocian Fathers. This sits near the entrance to Monastery Valley.

MONASTERY VALLEY

Walking distance from your hotel is Monastery Valley, a lush green valley with a stream and cliff-face churches perfect for exploring on a nice day.

GREEK HOUSES

The name of the town before the Greeks left in 1924 was Gelveri and many of the Gelveri houses are still standing today. Walking around town down the different side roads provides you with an opportunity to see these antiques with their beautiful doors and epitaphs, many of which can still be read.

Lower section of Guzelyurt

HISTORICAL CHURCHES

Within a 10 km radius of Guzelyurt you will find a number of historic churches worth your time. Two that stand out are the Red Church which dates from the 6th century and the Yüksek Kilise (high church or Analipsis Church – pictured below) which sits on a lonely hill (a Bronze Age settlement according to the tourist literature) overlooking the valley with a view of Hasan Dağ.

Yüksek Kilise

In conclusion, if you want to avoid the crowds, get off the beaten path, and see another fascinating side of Cappadocia, then Guzelyurt and the surrounding region provide a great option.

ZELVE OPEN AIR MUSEUM

Zelve Open Air Museum was Zelve village just 60 years ago.

If you are coming to Cappadocia on your own (not part of a group tour) you might want to add Zelve Open Air Museum to your itinerary. It is unique and yet depending on what else you see, more historical caves may not interest you.

Once you enter the park you will see a map 50 meters ahead on the path.

COMPARE & CONTRAST

The natural question that most people ask is how it compares to Göreme's Open Air Museum. So, let's look at that.

First of all, save for one, there are no frescoes remaining in the caves. Secondly, there are no crowds. Thirdly, Zelve has a great mix of professional restoration while maintaining a natural feel.

Roughly four times as big an area as Göreme's Open Air Museum, Zelve Open Air Museum has four churches. However, only one of these churches has any of the classic paintings that you would find in Göreme. So if you are looking for the amazing frescoes of Byzantine history you will not find them at Zelve.

The fact that there are far fewer people who visit Zelve Open Air Museum should be a draw. Unlike the other open air museum, at Zelve it is possible for you to "have the place to yourself." Take as long as you like at one of the churches; there is no one behind you waiting to get in. Want to see the granary where they crushed the wheat into bulgar? No problem, there is no waiting in line for people to leave so you can have a space.

VALLEYS OF ZELVE OPEN AIR MUSEUM

The best thing that Zelve offers that Göreme does not is the valleys. Zelve consists of three valleys. Unlike Göreme, contained in a relatively small area, Zelve is a meandering 1.5 kilometers of sightseeing. You walk through the park on brick pathways and bridges the government has put in, along which you find historical markers explaining what you are seeing. But one does not need to stick to the paved path. There are plenty of roads-less-traveled to be explored. And for this reason alone many think Zelve is worth a visit.

It is not just a museum; it is a hike. The plethora of trails to innumerable caves will keep you discovering for hours. If you have kids they will enjoy climbing the

Yüksek Kilise

Yüksek Kilise

GÖREME OPEN AIR MUSEUM

IN SUMMARY

What: A collection of cave churches circa 900-1100AD with magnificent wall paintings

Location: 15 minute walk east of Göreme

Price: 30TL entrance fee, 10TL for audio guide (optional), plus another 10TL for the Dark Church (optional)

Note: Expect crowds and waiting in line during high season.

The Göreme Open Air Museum is perhaps the most popular non-hot air balloon attraction in Cappadocia. I would not be surprised if 90% of Cappadocia visitors view the ancient caves and beautiful paintings on the hill outside of Göreme. I have been a number of times and never grow tired of imagining what life must have been like for those early Christians, especially during the snowy winters!

St. Basil, who lived in the region during the 4th century, established monastic communities that fully participated in worship and service. This area is apparently a fruit of his labors, and it was mirrored in other parts of the region like Ihlara. Most of the open churches in the museum date from long after Basil, however.

The main parking lot is at the bottom of the hill so expect a nice uphill walk to the entrance unless you can get your driver to drop you off at the entrance before going to park.

Upon entering and buying your 20TL ticket (be sure to hold on to it as it allows you to enter the Buckle Church halfway up the hill outside the main entrance to the museum) you will see the Museum Shop. This relatively new addition to the park allows you to enjoy some Turkish tea or coffee while pondering the historical significance of the area.

WHAT YOU WILL SEE

The first piece of Swiss cheese you encounter is known as the Nunnery. Depending on the time of year and the ongoing renovations, you may or may not be able to enter the first two floors of this 6-7 story edifice. Inside you will find a dining hall, kitchen, some rooms, and a church all connected by tunnels which could easily be closed off in times of danger.

As you progress through the museum, moving from one cave church to the next, the details become more like a vegetable soup in your head so that by the time you leave, you have memories of seeing a bunch of fascinating paintings in random caves with names like Snake church and St. Basil church and Dark church.

You may remember that most of the churches date from the 10th-12th centuries and, depending on the time of year, you will have not so fond memories of standing in line waiting on the (English, Korean, Spanish, Japanese, fill-in-the-blank) tour group ahead of you over and over again. In the busy season the groups go throughout the day but your best bet is to go midday or towards the end of the day. I would definitely recommend against going in the morning during the summer as you will spend most of your time waiting in lines.

Expect to spend around 1.5 - 2 hours exploring and learning. You do not need a guide. There are detailed signs at each church. You can also rent the 5TL audio tour. They do not allow photos to be taken within the caves, and in busy seasons they only allow you to stay for a couple of minutes within each cave. I took the pictures below before these rules were implemented.

Later, when your friends back home ask about Cappadocia you will most likely say that the Göreme Open Air Museum was cool. You will have pictures in your head with few details other than the general facts, which is another reason why I do not recommend spending a lot of money on a guide for this area.

One church you will definitely remember is the Buckle Church which you enter after exiting the main entrance on the way down the hill to the parking lot. As mentioned earlier the entrance fee is included with your ticket. This breathtaking, massive cave church will leave a lasting impression. The other is the Dark church which requires an extra 10TL ticket purchased at the cave within the park. It is beautiful and worth the extra fee.

PHOTO TOUR

The museum shop offers souvenirs, helpful information, and a cafe.

Apparently the hole to the left was used as a grave in this church.

Each hole you see in the rocks is an entrance to a different church.

The more rudimentary drawings show this church was one of the older examples

Upon entering the museum this massive fairy chimney sits to your left but is closed to entry.

CHAPTER 31

MY EXPERIENCE AND A BRIEF HISTORY OF HOT AIR BALLOONING

Once in a lifetime. How often do you get to participate in a "once-in-a-lifetime" opportunity?

My guess is that for most of us, the answer is not very often. But in Cappadocia, Turkey these opportunities abound. One of them, in particular, is the hot-air balloon ride.

HOT AIR BALLOONING FIRSTS

Of course, this has not always been the case. The first flight in Cappadocia took place in 1987 by Hasan Ezel. But long before that, on November 21, 1783, the first manned balloon flight took place in Paris (actually a rooster, a duck, and sheep had flown 2 months earlier). Since then the popularity has ebbed and flowed with record-setting flights multiplying in the last 30 years (1987- First Atlantic Ocean crossing, 1988-Altitude 65,000 feet, & 1991- First Pacific Ocean crossing).

In Cappadocia, however, only since 2001 has ballooning as a tourist attraction really taken off (pun intended). More people fly hot-air balloons in Cappadocia than anywhere else in the world.

Thanks to Royal Balloons I joined the masses and had my first experience of silent flight over Cappadocia's uneven and exotic terrain in 2012.

The Cappadocia hot-air balloon's biggest enemy is wind. This moves every hot-air balloon customer into a state of Pope-like religiosity the night before and morning of their flight. I believe that the most common prayer God hears from Cappadocia these days has something to do with windless mornings.

But on those first flights in the late 1700s, the prayers were for safety. The early pioneers experimented with different gases and designs. Two years after his historic first flight, Pilatre De Rozier (whence the word Pilot originated) died in an attempt to cross the English Channel when his hot-air and hydrogen double balloon exploded 30 minutes after take-off.

Trying not to think about this, I roused myself out of bed at 5am thanks to my son's eager help. A bit later we were in the car heading to the Royal Balloon headquarters in Göreme. Suat Ulusoy, the chief pilot, greeted me as I exited my car in the cool darkness and laughingly blamed me for the windy conditions. Fortunately, he was optimistic that with sunrise the wind would die down, and we would be able to fly.

In the meantime Hudson and I made our way inside and enjoyed the delicious full buffet breakfast that Royal offers their passengers. After looking at Hudson's plate I was afraid the balloon was not going to be able to lift off the ground. Needless to say, he took full advantage of the all-he-could-eat Turkish breakfast!

THE FATHER OF MODERN BALLOONING

Of course I had nothing to worry about with these modern balloons. In the 1950s and 60s, Ed Yost, commonly known as the father of modern ballooning, implemented many of the developments that encompass today's hot-air ballooning experience. He made his balloons out of nylon and used a propane burner, which gave him significantly increased control.

Also, he made a deflation valve in the top of the balloon that was improved by Tracy Barnes, making it possible to partially deflate the balloon during flight. Without these advances balloon tourism in Cappadocia (or anywhere) would probably not be possible.

Thanks to Yost and Barnes our only worry was the wind and at 6:30 Suat gave the green light; we were good to go! We eagerly piled in Royal's comfy vans for the short ride to the take-off point; at least I expected a short ride. Next thing I knew we were heading past the Göreme Open Air Museum, through Ortahısar and into the hills approaching Ürgüp.

Suat later explained that given the peculiar wind conditions that morning, he felt the most scenic flight needed to start at that point. I had no trouble trusting a man who has been flying in this region since the late 1990s. Royal takes advantage of the flexibility their smaller fleet allows by changing starting points based on the wind conditions.

We arrived as they were blowing up the balloons which meant we did not have to stand in the cold waiting for the preparations to end. After a couple of minutes, 14 of us from all over the world climbed in the 16 person basket while other passengers did the same in the rest of Royal's fleet.

WE HAVE LIFT OFF!

Suat gave us a few instructions, and then we were in the air. The liftoff of a balloon is freaky in its uneventfulness, similar to a helium balloon leaving your hand. One second we were on the ground, the next second we were in the air; no sound, no buildup, just sudden weightlessness.

This must have been especially exhilarating for the first two balloon passengers as well as those who witnessed the historic event, including the King of France. Apparently George Washington was present to see one of the first flights in America and Benjamin Franklin observed an early flight as well while serving in France. But during take-off over 200 years later in Cappadocia, the leaders of the world are focused elsewhere. Much has changed since those early days.

One thing that has not changed is the vital role of the pilot. Suat's wisdom immediately became clear as we headed over scenic terrain towards Çavuşin. The silent flight, interrupted intermittently with blasts of flame as our pilot controlled the height and spin, was happily at the mercy of the wind's direction. We had a wonderful view of Ortahısar and the Uçhısar castles as our balloon headed towards Red Valley.

HIGHS & LOWS

After gaining initial altitude to give a wide panoramic view of the area, Suat masterfully guided us down into the valley past jutting fairy chimneys and through steep ravines. With the budding apricot trees showing off their popcorn-like flowers the scenery was breathtaking.

Exiting Red Valley, we passed over the Çavuşin cemetery, and I called Laurie to tell her to start looking for us from the kitchen balcony of our house on the far side of the village. A few minutes later, after seeing my home village from a completely new perspective, we were waving to each other.

TOUCHDOWN CAPPADOCIA

We crossed the Göreme – Avanos road and were descending towards earth again when the wind changed, and all of the sudden we were going the opposite direction. Suat adjusted accordingly, radioed his crew to change positions, and brought us safely down in a different field.

We were told to sit tight and give the balloon time to deflate a bit so that it would not ascend again once some of us climbed out. Apparently the vast majority of ballooning accidents happen during the landing- all of us were happily submissive and soon the 14 of us representing all four corners of the globe were safely standing in a Cappadocian field.

INTERNATIONAL FLAVOR

The global cross-section of passengers was fitting as the record-setting history of hot-air ballooning has quite an international flavor. From the first flights in France to subsequent rides originating in England, from surveillance flights in the American Civil War to Swiss Scientist Auguste Piccard's stratospheric rise

(52,000 feet), and even in rumored stories of early hot-air balloon flights in Russia, Portugal, Mexico, and Peru, the chronicles cover the world.

Our flight maintained this international tradition, including guests from Australia (Tasmania), Canada (Edmonton), the US (Connecticut), Brazil, Italy, and Turkey as well as Hudson and I. After landing, the crew got right to work taking care of the balloon while we were presented with silver medals and mimosas (currently alcohol licenses are expensive so only a few companies still serve champagne).

ARE YOU A TRADITIONALIST?

The tradition of champagne after the balloon flight dates back to the first flight in 1783, but the legends vary. Suat told us his favorite story is that upon landing, Pilatre and Francois said a prayer of gratitude to God for sparing their lives and, being French, drank a glass of champagne to celebrate. However, my personal favorite is that the locals attacked the first balloon as it was landing (aliens!) and to appease them Pilatre proffered a bottle of champagne.

Regardless of which tale is true, they all include champagne, showing that the first passengers planned on imbibing at some point. Everyone on our flight happily participated in the tradition (Hudson had orange juice) while Suat entertained us with comical anecdotes from his many years of floating.

By the time we had finished the makeshift ceremony, the crew had the balloon stuffed in its sack and were getting to the hard part of lifting the basket onto the trailer. Hudson walked home, and I returned to the Royal's headquarters to get my car. I arrived home ready for more flights with my other six kids and wife who want to fly. My prayer is that this will not have been a "once-in-a-lifetime" experience for me!

CHAPTER 32

UNDERGROUND CITIES

Can you picture the conversation?

Go back 1400 years. A man and his son are digging yet another tunnel in one of Cappadocia's underground cities. The boy is tired and ready to quit...

BOY: "Dad, why do we have to dig this tunnel? Don't we have enough space already?"

DAD: "I already told you. In 1300 years Turkey will be dependent on tourism for a healthy economy. People are not going to come from around the world to visit a large cellar. We have to get down at least 100 meters to make it a "Wow!" experience.

BOY: "Oh yeah, I forgot."

Maybe not!

But their blood, sweat, and tears are still helping the local residents. Only this time they are greeting the "invaders" and welcoming them into their underground cities.

Apparently, if you could cut a cross-section of Cappadocia, you would see tunnels everywhere like one of those ant farms you probably had as a kid. Hundreds of underground cities are quietly lying beneath the surface throughout the region. Unfortunately, only a few are open to the public.

IMPORTANT NOTES

* You only need to visit one "city". They are not all the same but they are similar enough to make multiple visits feel quite repetitive.
* For all of these underground cities you will be well-served to hire a guide as they have almost no signage or brochures to inform you. Usually local guides are waiting near the entrance. Be sure to haggle the price. They need you more than you need them. The going rate for guides comes to around 40TL per hour, and you will spend about an hour with the guide. I would not pay more than 50TL.
* Derinkuyu and Kaymaklı are the 2 most visited sites.
* Most of the tours go to these sites in the morning so during the busy season (April - October) I would recommend planning your visit between 12-4.

* Expect to spend about an hour underground.
* If you are claustrophobic, don't enter.
* The tunnels get small at points so expect to be bending over as you walk and don't forget to protect your head.

DERINKUYU: This is the deepest underground city going down 100 meters. It has a church, school, and dining room among its many rooms. The town also has an old Greek Orthodox Church but it is not open to the public.

KAYMAKLI: This is the most spread out underground city with a maze-like structure that will make you think you are in a honeycomb. It is not as deep as Derinkuyu but just as interesting. Again, there is nothing else in the town for tourists.

ÖZKONAK: This one might actually be the largest but most of it is closed to the public. This underground city is only 15 minutes from Avanos as opposed to 35+ minutes for the two listed above. Very few tourists visit this "city" so you can definitely avoid the crowds here. There is also an old Greek Orthodox Church (Belha) that is not renovated yet but is open.

GAZIEMIR: I doubt this was actually a city. My guess is that it was either a caravansary or a monastery of some sort. This site is located on the road to Ihlara near Güzelyurt. The signs claim it is the "Largest Underground City". Don't believe it. This is a good option for those who are more claustrophobic since there are very few, if any, tight spaces and no feelings of being trapped. It only goes down one or two floors.

DERINKUYU UNDERGROUND CITY

WHAT YOU NEED TO KNOW

* **Entrance Fee:** 25TL
* **Location:** 35km south of Göreme
* **Signage/information:** Very little. A guide is recommended.
* **Time:** Comfortably see it in an hour, 90 minutes at most.
* **Other sites:** A Greek church (St. Theodora) and a former Greek church converted into a mosque, but these are not really open to the public, just visible from the outside.
* **History:** Dates back to Hittites circa 1200BC and used by the local people until the 13th century AD at which point it was not needed

except for storage on the first couple of levels. Discovered in 1960s by German archaeologists.

* **Best way to see it:** Green Tour aka South Cappadocia Tour – day tour that also includes Ihlara Valley and Belisirma Monastery among other sites. OR "on your own" but hire a guide or it is just like any other cave.

* **Notes:** Deepest Cappadocia underground city open to the public (100 meters, 8 floors). Inside you will see a water well, ventilation shafts, meeting hall on 8th floor, stable, kitchen, living areas, round defensive stones, prisoner holding area.

* **Warnings:** You will go through small shafts that require you to hunch down but never crawl; lighting is good; if you get claustrophobic, you will be uncomfortable; watch your head with low ceilings.

DERINKUYU DETAILS

HISTORY: Cappadocia's geology is the result of many, many volcanic eruptions. Look around. How many trees do you see? Not many. This is not a land of fertile forests; fuel is in short supply. However, the volcanic rock and soil makes for easy digging and burrowing. During a cold winter with little fuel, the idea of underground living in which the temperature is always constant makes sense.

The Hittites must have figured this out and begun the process. One of the main reasons they get credit is the connection between the architecture at their capital, Hattusa, not far from Cappadocia, and similar designs in the troglodytic towns.

Over time as different empires replaced the Hittites, the need for the underground shelters ebbed and flowed. During Roman persecution of Christians in the 2nd and 3rd centuries AD and later during the era of Arab raids in the 8th-10th centuries, the need for a place to hide and stay safe was great. During these times the underground honeycombs were expanded and deepened. When no danger was on the horizon, they still served as natural cold storage facilities as well as barns for the animals.

After the 13th century as a relative peace (at least from outside invaders) took hold, the need for these subterranean labrynths diminished greatly, and they fell out of use. Residents only used the parts connected to their homes as storage cellars. Over time the lower floors were all but forgotten until German archaeologists discovered their vastness in the early 1960s.

Derinkuyu was officially opened to the public in 1965, one year after the other popular city, Kaymaklı, 9 kilometers away. Although it is not open to the public, a tunnel connects the two towns!

EXPECT TO SEE: Only about 20% of Derinkuyu underground city is open to the public but that is more than enough for the average tourist. The eight floors descend 100 meters vertically and provide access to storage rooms, ventilation shafts, water wells, a kitchen, a church, a classroom and meeting room, a place for prisoners, and many other miscellaneous rooms and tunnels.

HIRE A GUIDE: However, within the city you will find almost no signs or other information to indicate what you are observing. For this reason we recommend hiring a guide. The easiest way to do this is through the Green Tour, aka South Cappadocia Tour, but if you go on your own, you can expect to find a guide near the entrance waiting to be hired. You will probably need to haggle over price. I would not pay more than 50TL total.

Derinkuyu underground city is one of up to 200 Cappadocia underground cities according to some reports, but only a few are open to the public. You only need to see one in my opinion unless you have a special interest.

DERINKUYU: THE TOWN

Unfortunately, even though millions of people have descended into the depths under Derinkuyu, 99.9% of the visitors spend no time in the town itself. This is understandable given its distance from central Cappadocia and lack of other attractions, but the locals receive little benefit from their famous attraction as a quick drive through town reveals.

Derinkuyu residents are farmers or people who serve farmers. Potatoes and white beans are the main crops, and the prices of these commodities determine the prosperity (or lack thereof) of the town. Walk through town in October after a good harvest and everyone is smiling, pockets full of cash, debts paid off, and sporting new smartphones.

However, walk those same streets in May and see everyone's heads bowed praying for good crops as their debts mount. Each year sees more people moving to bigger cities. People with ambition send their kids to boarding schools in Kayseri or Nevşehir, hoping that they will be able to escape the toil and uncertainties of farming for a better life.

The town did not have running water until 1965 when the government finally connected it. Until that time the people drew their water from wells around town, thus the name Derinkuyu which translates Deep Well. At that time the wells were 80-90 meters deep according to a few town elders who reminisced about those halcyon days. Today, they told me, the farmers need to dig 200 meters to find water. Fears of a disappearing water table are real.

The Greek churches point to the Christians who lived here until the forced people swap of 1923-24. The exodus to Greece left the churches unused. The empty houses were filled with the Muslims arriving from Greece. These Muslims, called Muhacer, did not speak Turkish and were not readily accepted. However they are now fully integrated into the local culture while still maintaining some level of historical memory.

Aydin, an office supply store owner, explained that his wife's grandfather came from Greece in 1923. He had to steal his wife since the local residents would not give their daughters to the new immigrants. Aydin is happily married to a Muhacer and says it is not an issue anymore. I believe him, but it is interesting to note that after 90 years everyone in town still knows which families are Muhacer.

Ask around to find a key to the Greek church. The sellers you encounter around the entrance to the underground city are all local residents supporting families.

The people of this small town, a county seat in the province of Nevşehir, tend to be more conservative Muslims who are a bit suspicious of outsiders. However, I have found that as I spend more time in the town, they have warmed up to me. Speaking Turkish helps but the Turks cannot stop themselves from being hospitable.

While walking through town one afternoon a group of men stopped me and offered a cup of tea. Within a few minutes we were discussing everything from America's policies towards Israel and Iraq, topics I try unsuccessfully to avoid, to what happens after we die, surprisingly a much less hostile and more important subject.

All of this is to say that if you speak Turkish and are visiting Derinkuyu's underground city, plan an extra hour into your schedule to walk around town and connect with some locals. They will be quick to offer a cup of tea and good conversation. Ask for a key to the St. Theodora church and take a peek inside. You will not be sorry you did.

DERINKUYU PHOTO TOUR

Outside the entrance to Derinkuyu's underground city you will find no lack of souvenirs and cafes as the locals try to benefit from the curiosity generated by their history.

Thankfully they have added electricity to make it easier for visitors to enjoy the deep underground rooms.

Close the tunnel knowing your enemies would not be able to move this massive rock from the other side once it was locked in place.

The upper floors were mainly used for animals.

If you are claustrophobic, I don't recommend a visit to any of the underground cities

KAYMAKLI UNDERGROUND CITY

WHAT YOU NEED TO KNOW

* **Entrance Fee:** 25TL
* **Location:** 26 km south of Göreme in the town of Kaymaklı
* **Signage/information:** Very little. If you go on your own (without a tour), be sure to hire a guide or you will just be looking at a bunch of rocks underground. The guides really bring the place to life. You can expect to find guides waiting to be hired at the entrance. Definitely negotiate the price.
* **Time:** Comfortably see it in a hour, 90 minutes at most. (Plus the 30 minute drive each way.)
* **Other sites:** None to speak of although there are signs of the Greeks that lived in the town until 1923 but none of them have been restored.
* **History:** Dates back to Hittites circa 1200BC and used by the local people until the 13th century AD at which point it was not needed except for storage on the first couple of levels. Opened to the public in 1964.

* **Notes:** This is the most spread out underground city although it does not go as deep as Derinkuyu. It feels more like a honeycomb or maze than Derinkuyu's straightforward layout. You will see ventilation shafts, a winery, the massive stone doors, a food storage room, and various other large rooms and small tunnels. The lighting is good.
* **Warnings:** You will go through narrow tunnels that require you to hunch down but never crawl; lighting is good; if you get claustrophobic, you will be uncomfortable; watch your head as the low rocky roofs can be painful.

KAYMAKLI DETAILS

Except for the Bible, the Hittite people are absent from history and until their capital, Hattusa, was discovered in central Turkey, many historians did not believe they existed. But exist they did and apparently they were diggers. Architectural similarities between arches at Hattusa and in Cappadocia's underground cities have led archaeologists to believe that they were the first people to dig out these underground areas. Most likely they did not dig down more than the first two levels.

Cappadocia's volcanic earth makes it ideal for digging, and the lack of fuel makes underground storage and dwelling a good idea (temperature does not change underground). Every people that has lived in this region since the Hittites has added to what the Hittites started.

In certain eras the need to develop these lairs was greater than others. During the Roman persecution of Christians in the 2nd and 3rd centuries AD the need to hide was great. During this time the subterranean areas were expanded. Again, in the 8th-10th centuries, when Arab raiders roamed at will, the desire to become invisible quickly was at a peak.

Apparently, thousands of people could live in these rock rooms for months at a time. Archaeologists have found a 9 kilometer tunnel connecting Kaymaklı to Derinkuyu. This makes it clear how desperate these people were. They could descend into the underground city from each of their homes and close off the tunnels, and then if their oppressors did not leave, they could make the 5 mile trek and come up in another town. Pretty amazing.

Upon descending into Kaymaklı Underground City and imagining yourself being there a thousand years ago, a few things become apparent. It must have stunk like no other, vitamin D supplements would have been helpful, it had to be really smokey, and conflict- resolution skills would be a must!

Kaymaklı's tunnels are passable for the most part and it really is an architectural masterpiece, especially considering they did it with hand tools and no electricity. There is a winery, ventilation shafts that reach beyond sight, storage rooms, bedrooms, and meeting rooms all in a labyrinthine structure begging for Ariadne's thread. Fortunately, they have placed red (in) and blue (out) arrows to let you know which direction to go.

Of course, the guides have done it a thousand times and have no problems leading their charges through the maze. Although I did hear that a European group was exploring on their own and lost track of time. The staff made a final sweep, closed the gates, and left for the night. The next morning this group was waiting at the gate on the inside!

Kaymaklı was opened to the public in 1964 but did not get lighting until 1968. Our guide, who grew up in Kaymaklı, spoke of playing in the tunnels as a child. He remembered fondly those early days before electric lighting had been installed when he led people around in the dark with a flashlight. I was thankful for technology myself.

Even though they have lights now, within the city you will find almost no signs or other information to indicate what you are observing. For this reason I recommend hiring a guide. The easiest way to do this is through the Blue Tour which your hotel should be able to arrange for you.

If you go on your own, you can expect to find a guide near the entrance waiting to be hired. Be sure to bargain over the price as they will expect that and, therefore, start high. I would not pay more than 50TL total for the one-hour tour.

Kaymaklı underground city is one of maybe 200 Cappadocia underground cities, but only a few are open to the public. You only need to see one in my opinion unless you have a special interest.

KAYMAKLI: THE TOWN

As you drive into Kaymaklı, the underground city would be invisible if not for the big parking lot which explains why it went for so long undiscovered. But most tourists never step out of the park area. They only see the run-down small town from their bus and car windows. Unfortunately, it is clear that very little money from the tourism stays in the town.

All the sellers are local Kaymaklı residents trying to make a living and care for their families. The people are farmers, growing potatoes and beans, and, due to poor crops, many of the residents have gone bankrupt and moved to bigger cities to try to find work. I spoke with a few of the sellers in the shops close to the entrance to learn about their lives which are inextricably connected to this historic site.

Ismail grew up near the entrance. He showed us where his house used to stand next to the ruins of an old Greek church. "My bedroom was right here and this was the tandir oven in which we cooked our bread, and our animals stayed in this room," he said as he pointed to plots of dirt near the entrance.

As a boy the government bought the land and he had to move. Now he sells tea and juice and these really tasty potatoes-on-a-stick snacks with a partner. He is worried about making it through the winter and whether he will be able to pay rent in the spring. As we sat talking many tourists passed by but none stopped to buy anything.

The farmers pray for good weather and a bountiful harvest while Ismail and his peers in the trinket shops pray that foreign visitors will find something they like among the stacks of hats, bags, scarves, and bric-a-brac.

As I walked around the town I was greeted with friendly smiles but, for the most part, the people did not seem too interested in me and my friend . They do not expect foreigners to venture outside the parking lot and do not expect those that do to speak Turkish. The town seems to be low on hope these days. Time will tell how that will change.

Regardless, the underground city is evidence that people have lived in this town through numerous empires and have survived through much worse times than these. Surely they will find a way to flourish again. That is my prayer for them.

With little written record archaeologists must guess how these large rooms were used

Get a feel for the size of the rooms with 12 of us tucked into the alcoves.

When enemies approached the residents could close the tunnels with these massive stone discs.

Upon entering Kaymaklı our guide gave us a quick introduction before leading us deep underground.

Watch your head as you descend the updated stairwell.

The underground cities have very little signage so I recommend hiring a guide to get a better understanding of what you are experiencing.

ÖKONAK UNDERGROUND CITY

WHAT YOU NEED TO KNOW

* **Entrance Fee:** 10₺
* **Location:** Özkonak
* **Signage/information:** Not much
* **Time:** 1 hour at most
* **Other sites:** Belha Church, Old oak tree, Ottoman bridge, the town
* **Notes:** This is sort of like the stepsister of the other underground cities. It is not as big and interesting as the Derinkuyu and Kaymaklı ones but it gives a good feel of what an underground city is like, and you will not find any crowds here.
* **Warnings:** None

ÖZKONAK DETAILS

The next time I went to Özkonak I visited the underground city. It has everything you are looking for in a subterranean dwelling: a winery, tunnels, air shafts, and giant stone door closures. It has two levels and allowed my 6' 1" frame to move about easily unlike some of the other cramped cities.

The 8TL entrance fee was also inviting. The fact that Özkonak is just 15 minutes from Avanos is another draw. You don't have to drive an hour and pay twice as much (20TL for Kaymaklı and Derinkuyu) to have a great experience in an underground city.

ÖZKONAK: THE TOWN

The town is like many small Turkish towns which means the people are hospitable but generally not open to outsiders; very few speak English. The residents do a lot of farming and one of the biggest butchers in the region hails from Özkonak. There are a number of sights to see in the town.

BELHA CHURCH, OAK TREE, & OTTOMAN BRIDGE: Belha church is a five minute drive from the Underground City. This place is really a well kept secret. First of all, it is not an official museum and therefore has no entrance fee. It differs from other churches in the area by its large size. It is rumored to be an 8th century church. To me it had a more medieval feel to it because of its size. Enter through a pitch black 15 meter tunnel and into a large room.

You'll need a flashlight to see the holes carved out of the walls and floor. Apparently, it was where they tied up invaders/persecutors or those in rebellion to the church, and made them stand in the darkness. The church has long since been pillaged and there are no surviving frescoes but the grounds themselves are worth exploring.

You can also visit the ancient Oak that looked like one of the Trees in "Lord of the Rings." Supposedly some researchers from Europe and Istanbul confirmed that the tree was 520 years old (but no one remembers when the sign was put there so it may be older!). From there go down to the bridge built by the Ottoman Sultan Selim in 1514. Under Sultan Selim the Ottoman Empire spread and it was on a military campaign to Iran that the Sultan built the bridge in Özkonak.

TRANSPORTATION: The other great thing about Özkonak is that you can take public transportation. The bus leaves Avanos every hour. And except for a trip to Belha church, you can do everything on foot. You can also rent a scooter if you're up for the mild adventure. If you wanted to rent a car then you could get to Belha church on your own. You could always ask for a tour guide and book your own Özkonak tour, but that will be significantly more costly, of course.

If you are in the heart of Cappadocia (Avanos, Göreme, Ürgüp) and are looking for a great way to see Turkish village life while taking in some sights, I highly recommend a stop in Özkonak.

GAZIEMIR UNDERGROUND CITY

WHAT YOU NEED TO KNOW

* **Entrance Fee:** 10₺
* **Location:** On the road to Ihlara after Derinkuyu (about halfway)
* **Signage/information:** Not much
* **Time:** 30-45 minutes
* **Other sites:** None (just a village)
* **Notes:** This would be amazing if it was in some other place but in Cappadocia it does not really compare with the other underground cities. Not worth a special trip for the average tourist.
* **Warnings:** None

GAZIEMIR DETAILS

On the way to the Ihlara Valley, my family and I saw signs for "Gaziemir Underground City, the largest underground city in Cappadocia". We decided to check it out. A bit of false advertising should not deter you from a visit.

Actually, I think it was probably a large caravansary, but they call it a city for marketing purposes. With huge wine containers, a jail, a church, places for animals to sleep, ceilings tall enough for camels, and a Turkish bath (hamam) as well as large areas for food storage it has enough to give you an impression of ancient times.

Also, some of the roofs have caved in leaving the rooms open to the sky so there is much more light than in the other underground sites. If you are going to Ihlara and want to avoid the crowds at the other underground cities or you want to see an underground location without feeling claustrophobic, you may want to consider Gaziemir as a viable alternative.

Gaziemir's large rooms are unique but it doesn't go nearly as deep underground as the other "cities".

CHAPTER 33

HORSEBACK RIDING TOUR OPTIONS

Here you will find a brief overview of the companies offering horseback riding tours. This should give you enough information to be able to pursue the Cappadocia horseback riding options that fit your preferences and budget.

> **Note**: There is a 90 kilo weight limit for riders. And children under 14 cannot do hour tours. They can ride the horse around the corral for a minimal fee for 10-15 minutes.

There are at least 13 ranches in Cappadocia. The ranches in Göreme/Çavuşin have formed a cooperative so that they are not competing against each other. The other ranches are on their own.

Göreme/Çavuşin Ranches

Cappadocia Ranch
Dalton Bros.
Doğa Binicilik Merkezi
Göreme Ranch
Kadost Ranch
Lucky Horse Ranch
Moonlight Ranch
Museum Ranch

Avanos Ranches

Akhal Teke
Kirkit Ranch
Körükçü Ranch

Ortahisar Ranches

Cemal Ranch

Uçhisar Ranches

Melissa's Secretive Ranch

CAPPADOCIA HORSEBACK RIDING AKHAL TEKE

WHEN DID THEY OPEN?	1985
NUMBER OF HORSES?	20 - all Arabian
HOW MANY GUIDES?	4; speak English
GUIDE EXPERIENCE?	The owner is professional with years of experience... two others have 6-10 years

Available Tours: Whatever you like - 1 hour, 2 hours, half-day, all day, multi-day, sunrise, sunset... Happy to work with you. (You can request multiple day custom tours as well... 3 day, 6 day, 2 weeks, they will work with you)

Unique Feature: Located on the river in Avanos and on the grounds of a fine restaurant for before or after riding dining. Evliya Çelebi was a Turkish explorer who traveled the world and Turkey. Akhal Teke has a 45 day expedition from Cappadocia to Istanbul following the route that this famous explorer took!

* Aydin Alti Mahallesi Gesteric sokak No:21 50500/AVANOS

* Telephone - +90 384 511 5171, +90 506 022 0648 Erdem Özçekiç

* Website: www.akhal-tekehorsecenter.com

CAPPADOCIA HORSEBACK RIDING CAPPADOCIA

WHEN DID THEY OPEN?	2015
NUMBER OF HORSES?	28
HOW MANY GUIDES?	5; speak English
GUIDE EXPERIENCE?	20+ years

Available Tours: Whatever you like - 1 hour, 2 hours, half-day, all day, multi-day, sunrise, sunset... Happy to work with you.

Unique Feature: They have the most horses of any ranch and are able to handle larger and more tours.

* Behind the Göreme cemetery

* Telephone - +90 535 681 0568

* Website: www.cappadociaranch.com

CAPPADOCIA HORSEBACK RIDING CEMAL RANCH

WHEN DID THEY OPEN?	2012
NUMBER OF HORSES?	26
HOW MANY GUIDES?	3; speaks English
GUIDE EXPERIENCE?	Cemal has ridden horses his whole life

Available Tours: Whatever you like - 1 hour, 2 hours, half-day, all day, multi-day, sunrise, sunset... Happy to work with you.

Unique Feature: Tours include transportation and tea/coffee at the ranch. Organic garden. Family run. Beautiful outdoor cafe with breathtaking views. Insured in case of fall.

* Two Locations: (1). İsak Kalesi Bayır Arası Mevkii. Ortahisar Village / Cappadocia. (2). Outside Ortahisar on the road to the head of Rose/Red Valley and Panoramic Viewpoint.
* Telephone - +90 532 291 0211 – Cemal Köksal
* Website: www.cemalranch.com

CAPPADOCIA HORSEBACK RIDING DALTON BROS

WHEN DID THEY OPEN?	2000
NUMBER OF HORSES?	25
HOW MANY GUIDES?	3; speak English
GUIDE EXPERIENCE?	Ekrem and his son Omer 15 years, other 5+ years

Available Tours: Whatever you like - 1 hour, 2 hours, half-day, all day, multi-day, sunrise, sunset… Happy to work with you.

Unique Feature: He gets his horses from a wild pack on the mountains of Erciyes and trains them himself. Insured in case of fall.

* On the way to Open Air Museum; left side of the road after Tourist Hotel Göreme
* Telephone - +90 384 271 28 40 – Ekrem Ilhan
* Website: www.cappadociahorseriding.com

CAPPADOCIA HORSEBACK RIDING DOĞA BINICILIK MERKEZI

WHEN DID THEY OPEN?	2018
NUMBER OF HORSES?	9
HOW MANY GUIDES?	1; speaks a little English
GUIDE EXPERIENCE?	Grown up with horses.

Available Tours: Whatever you like - 1 hour, 2 hours, half-day, all day, multi-day, sunrise, sunset… Happy to work with you.

Unique Feature: Based in Cavusin Village. Happy to customize a wedding proposal (engagement) tour.

* Çavuşin right off the main road on the Göreme side.
* Telephone - +90 530 656 6840, +90 545 314 4828
* Website: None
* Instagram: doga_binicilik_merkezi

CAPPADOCIA HORSEBACK RIDING GÖREME RANCH

NUMBER OF HORSES?	13
HOW MANY GUIDES?	3; speak English
GUIDE EXPERIENCE?	15 years

Available Tours: Whatever you like - 1 hour, 2 hours, half-day, all day, multi-day, sunrise, sunset… Happy to work with you.

Unique Feature: Along with Kirkit and Akhal Teke they have been doing horseback tours for close to 30 years.

* Open Air Museum Road, Göreme

* Telephone - +90 507 575 2470 – Ali Özcan

CAPPADOCIA HORSEBACK RIDING KADOST

WHEN DID THEY OPEN?	2012
NUMBER OF HORSES?	9
HOW MANY GUIDES?	2; speaks a little English
GUIDE EXPERIENCE?	10+ years

Available Tours: Whatever you like - 1 hour, 2 hours, half-day, all day, multi-day, sunrise, sunset… Happy to work with you.

Unique Feature: If you are looking for more adventure in your trip, they offer canoeing, trekking, biking, ATV, jeep safaris and even scuba diving in Mersin, as well as mountaineering on Hasan and Erciyes, in addition to horseback riding.

* Göreme Aktivite Tesisleri: Göreme-Çavuşin yolu 1.km Kapadokya/Türkiye

* Telephone - +90 (384) 271 30 27 – Mehmet Üçman

CAPPADOCIA HORSEBACK RIDING KIRKIT

WHEN DID THEY OPEN?	1980 but current location since 2005
NUMBER OF HORSES?	15
HOW MANY GUIDES?	3; speak French and English
GUIDE EXPERIENCE?	15+ years

Available Tours: Whatever you like - 1 hour, 2 hours, half-day, all day, multi-day, sunrise, sunset… Happy to work with you.

Unique Feature: Give 3 day lessons then 3 day tour. Also, their name, nobody's been doing horse tours in Cappadocia longer than Kirkit. Horses are mixed breed from Sürüç near the Syrian border. Their youngest horse is 12 years old and they have a 25 year old and a 35 year old horse which are very gentle for beginners and children.

* Ataturk Caddesi 50 Avanos

* Telephone - +(90) 384 511 3259 – Ibrahim Çalışkan

* Website: www.horseridingcappadocia.com/

* Instagram: kirkithorsecenter

CAPPADOCIA HORSEBACK RIDING KÖRÜKÇÜ

WHEN DID THEY OPEN?	2017
NUMBER OF HORSES?	9
HOW MANY GUIDES?	Hires as needed, very little English
GUIDE EXPERIENCE?	Over 35 years

Available Tours: Whatever you like - 1 hour, 2 hours, half-day, all day, multi-day, sunrise, sunset... Happy to work with you.

Unique Feature: Also serves breakfast if you want (costs extra). He is a third generation horse man. His grandfather delivered the mail on horseback in the region.

* Avanos Bahçelievler Mah- Between Mado and the Nevşehir road.

* Telephone - +(90) 537 958 2456 - Yücel Körükçü

* Website: none

* Instagram: korukcuatlisporkulubu

* Facebook: Körükcü At Çiftliği

CAPPADOCIA HORSEBACK RIDING LUCKY HORSE

WHEN DID THEY OPEN?	2015
NUMBER OF HORSES?	11
HOW MANY GUIDES?	1; speaks English
GUIDE EXPERIENCE?	Over 20 years

Available Tours: Whatever you like - 1 hour, 2 hours, half-day, all day, multi-day, sunrise, sunset... Happy to work with you.

Unique Feature: Customizes tours based on you. What do you want to see and not see (or have already seen)?

* Behind the Tourist Hotel in Göreme

* Telephone - +(90) 537 319 4455 - Irfan

* Website: www.luckyhorsecappadocia.com

* Instagram: luckyhorseranch

CAPPADOCIA HORSEBACK RIDING MELISSA'S SECRETIVE RANCH

WHEN DID THEY OPEN?	2016
NUMBER OF HORSES?	19
HOW MANY GUIDES?	2; speaks a little English
GUIDE EXPERIENCE?	3 years

Available Tours: Whatever you like - 1 hour, 2 hours, half-day, all day, multi-day, sunrise, sunset... Happy to work with you.

Unique Feature: Only ranch in Uçhisar with a great view of the entire region.

* On the Göreme – Uçhisar road right before Uçhisar on the left.
* Telephone - +(90) 539 731 0650 - Bilal
* Website: none
* Instagram: melissassecretivera

CAPPADOCIA HORSEBACK RIDING MOONLIGHT RANCH

WHEN DID THEY OPEN?	2012
NUMBER OF HORSES?	29
HOW MANY GUIDES?	2; speaks little English, Farsi
GUIDE EXPERIENCE?	Over 10 years

Available Tours: Whatever you like - 1 hour, 2 hours, half-day, all day, multi-day, sunrise, sunset... Happy to work with you.

Unique Feature: Great facility with fairy chimneys and restaurant

* Aydınlı Orta Mah., Adnan Menderes Cadd., Karşı Bucak Mevki
* Telephone - +(90) 384 271 2423, +90 535 088 8575
* Website: www.moonlighthorseranch.com
* Instagram: moonlighthorsefarm

CAPPADOCIA HORSEBACK RIDING MUSEUM RANCH

WHEN DID THEY OPEN?	2015
NUMBER OF HORSES?	12
HOW MANY GUIDES?	2; speaks English
GUIDE EXPERIENCE?	Over 15 years

Available Tours: Whatever you like - 1 hour, 2 hours, half-day, all day, multi-day, sunrise, sunset... Happy to work with you.

Unique Feature: Like a couple of other ranches in the area, they only have registered Arabian horses.

* Open Air Museum road, on the left before the big fairy chimney, Göreme
* Telephone - +(90) 543 319 8709
* Website: www.museumranch.com
* Instagram: museumranchcappadocia

CHAPTER 34

JEEP SAFARI TOURS

Jeep Safari Tours are a relatively new activity in Cappadocia. As of this writing they are still unregulated and evolving. There is no standard tour or pricing so each company does their own thing and the differences are vast. In my research I was able to find 6 companies offering many different tours. You have the option of a 2-hour tour, a half-day tour and a full-day tour depending on the company you choose. Below you will find a list of the alternatives to help you decide what is best for you. The company contact information is included to help you book what you want.

TO THINK ABOUT

1. **OFF-LIMITS:** The local authorities have limited where the jeeps can explore, making some valleys off-limits. This means that the companies are only able to customize the trips to a certain degree. There may be some places you want to explore that are not allowed in a jeep. Be sure to check this before you book a tour if it is important to you.

2. **MINIMUM**: Another important feature to understand is that each "jeep" holds up to 4 passengers (except the Capp-Off jeeps which are open-backed and hold up to 8 people). Some companies will take one person whereas others will take one but charge as if 3 or 4 are going.

3. **TIME OF DAY:** The companies give you the option of choosing when you want to go. None of the tours go in the early morning because of the balloons. This is mainly important because of the photography options. After the sun rises, taking nice pictures becomes more difficult. For this reason going later in the day near sunset may be better because it will provide better photo opportunities.

4. **PRICE:** The prices vary significantly between the companies. I encourage you to try different companies and negotiate.

5. **VIEWS:** Most of the companies put you in trucks that fit 4 people. If you are with 3 other people someone is going to have to sit in the back middle seat which means their view will be quite limited. This may be a reason to choose a company like Capp-Off that has open-backed jeeps. The companies are regularly buying new trucks so ask about their jeeps when you write or talk to them.

And with that said, let's get to the company details...

CAPPADOCIA JEEP SAFARI COMPANIES

- * **Capp-Off Jeep Safari**
- * **Istanbul Balloons Jeep Safari**
- * **Kapadokya Jet Jeep Safari**
- * **Tempest Jeep Safari**
- * **Fairyland Jeep Safari**

CAPP-OFF JEEP SAFARI

TOUR LENGTH?	3 hours
TIMES?	10am-1pm (includes lunch) and 4-7pm (includes wine)
PRICE?	40 euros/person (minimum 1 person)
JEEPS?	Open back for easy viewing

PROGRAM: Göreme Görçeli Valley, Ibrahimpaşa Village, Gamirasu Valley, Goligoli Caves & Monastery, Damsa Dam, Gomeda Valley & Ruins, Pancarlik Valley, and Ortahisar Panorama.

EXTRAS: Note that they include lunch in their morning tour. Also, their open-backed jeeps make for easier viewing. They also do a special tour for professional photographers. They will do custom tours as well.

* Email: info@cappoff.com

* Website: www.cappoff.com

ISTANBUL BALLOONS JEEP SAFARI

TOUR LENGTH?	1.5 - 2 hours
TIMES?	Whenever you want to go
PRICE?	90 euros/person (minimum of 2 people)
JEEPS?	Toyota Hilux

PROGRAM: Ortahisar, Pigeon Houses and Grape Vines, Red Valley, and Uçhisar Panoramic View with stops at each place for photographing the views.

EXTRAS: None.

* Email: fly@istanbulballoons.com

* Website: www.istanbulballoons.com/111-JEEP_Safari_Tours.html

KAPADOKYA JET JEEP SAFARI

TOUR LENGTH?	1.5 or 2 hours
TIMES?	Whenever you wish
PRICE?	Ask the company
JEEPS?	Land Rover

PROGRAM: 4-5 Valleys included

EXTRAS: They can customize the tour to your liking up to a point.

* Website: www.kapadokyajet.com/en/index.html

TEMPEST JEEP SAFARI

TOUR LENGTH?	2 - 2.5 hours
TIMES?	Any time after 10am
PRICE?	Ask the company
JEEPS?	Toyota Hilux

PROGRAM: Mount Gemili, Uzengi Panorama, Gomeda Valley & Ruins, Ortahisar Panorama, and Red Valley (stops at each place for photographs)

EXTRAS: A certificate at the end of the tour and a glass of alcohol-free champagne

* Email: tempest@uluergroup.com

* Twitter: www.twitter.com/cappadociajeep?lang=en

FAIRYLAND JEEP SAFARI

TOUR LENGTH?	2.5 - 3 hours
TIMES?	Whenever you wish to go
PRICE?	25 Euros
JEEPS?	Land Rovers with open backs that hold up to 7 people (minimum 2 people)

PROGRAM: Varies as they try to customize to what you want. They can include Rose, Love, Gomeda, Devrent, Görçeli, and Pigeon Valleys, as well as Damsa Lake, Ortahisar, and Çavuşin.

EXTRAS: If your tour is during midday, then lunch will be included, otherwise you will enjoy a glass of champagne.

* Email: info@goremefairyland.com

* Website: www.goremefairyland.com/fairyland-jeep-safari/

CHAPTER 35

TURKISH NIGHT CULTURAL SHOW

Generally I try and stay away from these types of shows as they come across to me as a "Tourist Trap".

But having attended one and really enjoying it, I highly recommend you take in a "Türk Gecesi" (Turkish Night) while you're here.

There are five options to choose from: two in Avanos and three in Uçhisar.

The dinners and shows vary slightly from place to place but for the most part this is what you can expect.

ITINERARY

8:00pm - arrival

8:15 - 8:30 Whirling Dervish dance (some places do not have this performance)

8:30-10:30 Dinner and show including Romali music, Bitlis, Girls' Folk, Black Sea, Spoon, Central Anatolian Bride and Groom, Zebek and the Belly dancer

Dinner: Cold and hot appetizers, main dish (lamb, chicken, or fish), fruit and dessert

Drinks: All you can drink wine, beer, raki, mixed drinks, soft drinks, and fruit juice

And with that said, here are the five options:

EVRANOS - AVANOS

* Orta Mahalle No. 88 Taşköprü Karşısı Avanos
* Telephone - +(90) 384 271 2423, +90 535 088 8575
* Email: info@evranos.net
* Website: www.cappadociarestaurants.com
* Price: Check with you hotel or travel agent

Only at Evranos, and very cool!- the Egyptian Light Dance

URANOS - AVANOS

* Akbel mevkii Köprü Başı 50500 Avanos
* Price: Check with you hotel or travel agent

Uranos is also open for set menu lunch

YAŞAR BABA - ÜÇHISAR

* Haci Ibey Cd. West, Uçhisar, Turkey
* Telephone: +(90) 384-219-28-70-71
* Email: info@yasarbaba.com
* Website: www.yasarbaba.com
* Price: Check with you hotel or travel agent

The FIRST to do Turkish Night in Cappadocia and longest running…36 YEARS! Dancers come in on horseback and Belly Dancer descends from the ceiling!

HARMANDALI - UÇHISAR

* Kavak köyü yolu, 50210, Uçhisar
* +(90) 384-219-2364
* Price: Check with you hotel or travel agent

CHAPTER 36

WHIRLING DERVISH SHOWS

They have been performing this ritual for close to 800 years. It has since become a cultural symbol of this incredibly diverse land of Turkey and now you can witness this spiritual dance on your trip: The Whirling Dervish in Cappadocia.

Mevlana Celaleddin (or Rumi as he's known in the West) was the 13th century religious leader behind the Whirling Dervishes. His philosophy of "come as you are" was attractive to many people searching for true meaning in life.

As people began to follow Mevlana they came to love the Creator and his creation. This love is expressed in the dance of the Dervish. With one hand raised to the Creator, the dancer receives, and with the other hand turned down toward the earth, he passes on the blessing to the creation.

There are three venues for seeing this inspirational performance in Cappadocia:

Saruhan Caravansarai outside of Avanos,

Motif Culture Center in Avanos, and the

Dervish Evi in Ortahisar.

SARUHAN CARAVANSARAI

* 1 hour exhibition
* **Website:** www.sarihan1249.com
* **Telephone:** +(90) 384-511-3795
* **Price:** Ask hotel or travel agent

DERVISH EVI

* 1 hour exhibition
* **Website:** www.dervisevi.com
* **Telephone:** +(90) 384-343-2080, 0532-486-3254
* **Price:** Ask hotel or travel agent

MOTIF CULTURE CENTER

* 45 minute exhibition
* **Website:** www.kapadokya-motif.com
* **Telephone:** +(90) 384-511-4859
* **Price:** Ask hotel or travel agent

SECTION V:

APPENDICES

CHAPTER 37

APPENDICES INTRODUCTION

In this last section of the book we have included 7 appendices.

1. PRONUNCIATION GUIDE

The Turkish alphabet has 29 letters (six letters English does not use; three English letters are not in their alphabet). This guide explains the details.

2. TURKISH LANGUAGE HELP

Many people in Turkey speak English so the need for short term visitors to speak Turkish is minimal. Regardless, you may be surprised at how much it blesses your new Turkish acquaintances that you make an effort to speak their language. In this appendix we list a few words and phrases you can use in the various circumstances you will find yourself.

3. PRICE LIST

The purpose of this list is to give you one place to go for all the prices you will need. It also makes updating the book easier.

4. UPDATE WEBSITE

I will update this website with changes to the book before the next edition comes out.

5. CAPTIVATINGCAPPADOCIA.COM LOGO

Use this for the discounts.

6. DISCOUNT OFFERS

All the stores, restaurants, balloon companies, hotels, and rental places that offer discounts to you who purchased this book.

7. CAPPADOCIA MAPS

6 different maps of Cappadocia to help you with walking and hiking routes, the different tours, and to get a better perspective on where Cappadocia is and where the sites are in Cappadocia.

APPENDIX 1

PRONUNCIATION GUIDE

The Turks use a Latin based alphabet similar to English except for a few extra letters.

They do not use Q, or W or TH or X, so if your name uses the "w" or "th" sounds, do not expect people to pronounce it properly.

Turkish is phonetic meaning that each letter only has one sound. English vowels have a few sounds each, but Turkish vowels are stuck in one place.

A - is always **ah** as in **body**

E - is always **ae** as in **air**

I - is always **ee** as in **feet**

O - is always **oh** as in **boat**

U - is always **oo** as in **hoot**

Here are the extra letters:

Many of these have sounds that English speakers do not normally make (thus the need for different letters). I will give some help but expect to not be able to pronounce these letters perfectly. As my teacher said, if your mouth does not feel wrong when you say them, then you probably are not saying them correctly.

Ö - similar to **oo**

Ü - similar to **oo**

Both of these are unique but sound very similar for English speakers.

Ç - **ch** as in **church**

Ğ - silent but adds a slight pause to the word when you say it. English yogurt is Turkish yoğurt pronounced "yo-urt".

Ş - **sh** as in **shout**

I - a very short I as in the **I** in **halibut**

Also,

J - **zh** as in **regime**

C - **j** as in **jump**

H - is like a soft **k** as in **Ahmet**

The rest of the consonants are the same.

APPENDIX 2

TURKISH LANGUAGE HELP

You can easily find help on the internet so we will just give a few helpful words and phrases here that will get you in the door with those who do not speak English.

GREETINGS/FAREWELLS:

Hello = **Merhaba** or **Assalamualaikum**

Goodbye = **Görüşürüz** or **Hoşça kalın**

HELPFUL WORDS/PHRASES

Thank you = **Teşekkür ederim** OR **Sağol**

You're welcome = **Rica ederim** OR **Bir şey değil**

How are you? = **Nasılsınız?**

Good = **Iyim**

Great/beautiful = **Gözel**

So-so = **Şöyle böyle**

Lost = **Kayboldum**

I do not understand. = **Anlamadım.**

I do not speak Turkish. = **Türkçe bilmiyorum.**

Do you speak English? = **Inglizce biliyormusunuz?**

Is there an English speaker? = **İngilizce konuşan var mı?**

Please repeat slowly. = **Lütfen tekrar yavaş.**

Can you please help me. = **Bakarmısınız**.

Welcome = **Hoşgeldiniz***

* The Turks have a response to this. When you arrive at a place the host will welcome you with the phrase above (hoşgeldiniz). You respond with: **Hoş bulduk**

When you give a cashier money or when someone gives you change or your food or anything, the word that is used is **Buyurun**.

You will hear this a good bit.

POWER QUESTIONS:

How much?	When?	Where?
Ne kadar?	**Ne zaman?**	**Nerede?**

NUMBERS:

1 **bir**	3 **üç**	5 **beş**	7 **yedi**	9 **dokuz**
2 **iki**	4 **dort**	6 **altı**	8 **sekiz**	10 **on**

Numbers can easily be written down so this is plenty.

PRICE LIST

In an attempt to make planning easier I am including a quick list of entrance fees for Cappadocia attractions.

Prices updated winter 2019 (Listed in alphabetical order by Category)

TURKISH GOVERNMENT TOURISM WEBSITE

I do my best to keep the prices up to date, but if you want to double-check, please go to the Turkish government's tourism website by clicking on the link above or right here: https://www.muze.gov.tr/en/museums

You will find all the latest prices on every government run museum in Turkey.

For Cappadocia you will want to click on Nevsehir, Aksaray, and Kayseri.

HISARS

Prices are for entrance fee to the rock tower.

* Uçhisar-Adults 7₺, Students 3.50₺
* Ortahisar-5₺

NIGHT SHOWS

* **Turkish Night:** Around 120₺ per person (includes all you can eat and drink and the show) Best to ask your hotel or travel agent and/or go straight to the location and make the reservation yourself.
* **Whirling Dervish Ceremony:** Around 25 euros per person for one hour

OPEN AIR MUSEUMS

* **Göreme Open Air Museum:** 30₺ (Dark Church is additional 10₺, Audio Tour is 15₺, Parking 5₺)
    * High Season Hours: 8am - 7pm (ticket booth closes at 6:15pm) (April 15 - October 3)
    * Low Season Hours: 8:30 - 5pm (ticket booth closes at 4:15pm)
* **Zelve Open Air Museum:** 10₺ + 5₺ for parking
* **Zelve and Göreme Open Air Museums Special Deal:** 35₺

RIDES- BALLOON, MOTORS, ANIMALS, WATER

* **ATV/Quad Approximate prices:** 1 hour = 80₺ (Buggy 100₺), 2 hours = 130₺ (Buggy 150₺), 3 hours = 150₺ (Buggy 180₺)
* **Bicycle Approximate prices:** 1 hour = 10₺, 24 hours = 50₺ (You can rent for any number of hours you like. Prices will be within this range.)
* **Camel Ride:** 10₺ (sit on camel for picture for 5₺)
* **Car Rental:** Prices start around 42 euros per day and go up. Gas is not included. Silk Road Rentals in Goreme should give you a good discount if you mention the book and/or my name, Duke.
* **Hot Air Balloon Ride:** Advertised prices range from 150-175 euros
* **Scooter Approximate prices:** 1-3 hours = 50₺, 24 hours = 80₺
* **Jet Boat:** 30 euros per person (minimum of 7 people – this means if you have 6 people but are willing to pay an extra 30 euros you can ride)
* **Gondola:** 10 euros per person (minimum of 4 people – this means if you have less than 4 people you must pay 40 euros total if you want to ride)
* **Swimming pool day price** (at campgrounds and Konak Event Center): 20₺

TRANSPORTATION

* **Gasoline:** around 6+₺ per liter
* **Van with Driver:** Unlimited mileage for a day is 300₺ plus gas. If you stay in the Urgup-Goreme-Avanos area it will be 180₺.
* **Taxi Rate:** *(The taxis use meters so the price will vary based on where you start and finish. Here are the prices I was given when I asked a taxi driver for approximate rates.)*
    * Avanos to Göreme 25₺
    * Avanos to Ürgüp 35₺
    * Göreme to Ürgüp 30₺
* **Public Buses:** Avanos to Nevşehir 4₺ (stops in-between are less); Avanos to Ürgüp 4₺ (stops in-between are less); Longer distances like Haci Bektas and Derinkuyu are around 7₺
* **Airport Shuttle:** 30₺ to Kayseri and 25₺ to Nevsehir

TOURS

* **Green Tour:** 33 euros
* **Red Tour:** 28 euros
* **Blue Tour:** 120₺ (Blue Tour is often hard to book, but this tour happens regularly only with Heritage)
* **Undiscovered Cappadocia Tour (Heritage Travel):** 55 euros (credit card) or 45 euros (cash).

  NOTE: This tour requires a minimum of four people so you will need to pay extra if nobody else signs up.

* **Jeep Tour:** There are lots of different options depending on the company and tour, but we found 35 euros per person for a 3+ hour tour including lunch.
* **Tour Guide:** Day price- 400₺

UNDERGROUND CITIES

* **Derinkuyu:** 25₺
* **Özkonak:** 10₺
* **Kaymaklı:** 25₺
* **Gaziemir:** 10₺

VALLEYS & CHURCHES

* **Ihlara Valley:** 20₺ Summer 7am-7pm, Winter 8am-5pm
* **Selime Monastery:** Use Ihlara ticket for Selime - you only need one ticket for both
* **Çavuşin Lower Church (Nicephorus Phocas Church):** Closed for repairs

APPENDIX 4

BOOK UPDATE WEBSITE

One guarantee with travel guides is that changes will occur and updates will be necessary. We are not able to publish a new book every couple of months so we have created a website on which we will put updates as they occur. Thus, we recommend checking it before making plans.

The page address is:

www.captivatingcappadocia.com/cappadocia-guidebook-update-page/

APPENDIX 5

CAPTIVATINGCAPPADOCIA.COM LOGO

Just show this logo to the hotels, balloon companies, restaurants, rental places, and shops listed in this book to get your discount.

To see a list of the available discounts, see Appendix 6.

APPENDIX 6

DISCOUNT OFFERS

One of the great benefits of buying this book is that it is virtually free. The information contained herein is worth much more than the price of the book, but even so the discounts given by hotels, balloon companies, and restaurants mean that you actually make money!

If you stay at a hotel listed in the book for 2-3 nights, fly with one of the balloon companies, and eat at even one of the restaurants, you will save around $50. Subtract the price of the book, and you come away well in the black.

But I thought it would be helpful to list out the discounts available rather than making you read through the whole book to find them.

> **PLEASE!** I want to ask you one more time to respect the work put into this book and not give away this information. I have spent over four years building relationships and gathering the information for this book. I get nothing from any of these businesses when you use their services. I recommend them (these represent a small percentage of the total options in the region) because I know them, and know they will take good care of you.
>
> If they don't, I'll do my best to make it right. So, use them and take advantage of the discounts, but please DO NOT share this information with others who have not bought this book. Tell them to buy the book then all the discounts will be available to them as well. I greatly appreciate your consideration in this matter.

And with that, here we go...

HOTELS:

These are divided by city but cover a wide range of quality and pricing. To get more details either follow the link to the website or check out the Hotels section of this book.

GÖREME

Kismet Cave House - www.kismetcavehouse.com/

UÇHISAR

Taşkonaklar - www.taskonaklar.com/

ÜRGÜP

Kayakapı Premium Caves - www.kayakapi.com/

Selçuklu Evi Cave Hotel - www.selcukluevi.com/

AVANOS

Hikmet's House - www.hikmetshouse.com/

Duru Hotel - duruhotel.com/

ÇAVUŞIN

Azure Cave Suites - www.azurecavesuites.com/ - *Special gift upon arrival.*

BALLOON COMPANIES:

Royal Balloons - http://www.royalballoon.com/#

Turkiye Balloons - http://www.turkiyeballoons.com/

RESTAURANTS:

Seten Anatolian Cusine - Göreme - www.setenrestaurant.com/

Pumpkin - Göreme

Fat Boys - Göreme

ATV/MTN BIKE/SCOOTER/RENTAL CAR:

Silk Road Rentals - Göreme - www.silkroadrentacar.com/

Öz Cappadocia - Göreme - www.ozcappadocia.com/en/

CAPPADOCIA MAPS

MAP 1: CAPPADOCIA WITHIN TURKEY

This map includes a few of the most popular sites/cities in Turkey as well as the surrounding countries. Many people want a better understanding of where Cappadocia is within Turkey. We hope this map helps with that. Note that a bus ride from Istanbul to Nevsehir takes 10-12 hours depending on how many stops are made and where you begin in Istanbul.

MAP 2: GREATER CAPPADOCIA

This is another homemade map that hopefully gives a good perspective on the main touristy part of the region. This map covers the area that 99% of visitors will see.

> Note that regarding scale the drive from Kayseri Airport to Göreme takes about an hour and from Kapadokya (Nevşehir) Airport the drive is about 40 minutes. From Göreme to Ihlara is also about an hour and to Derinkuyu is about 35 minutes.

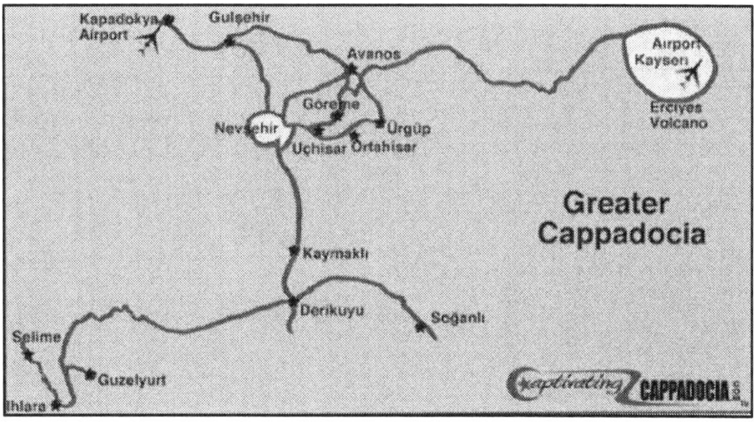

MAP 3: CAPPADOCIA TOURS

Now for a more professional looking map! This shows the main sites and routes of the three most popular Cappadocia tours.

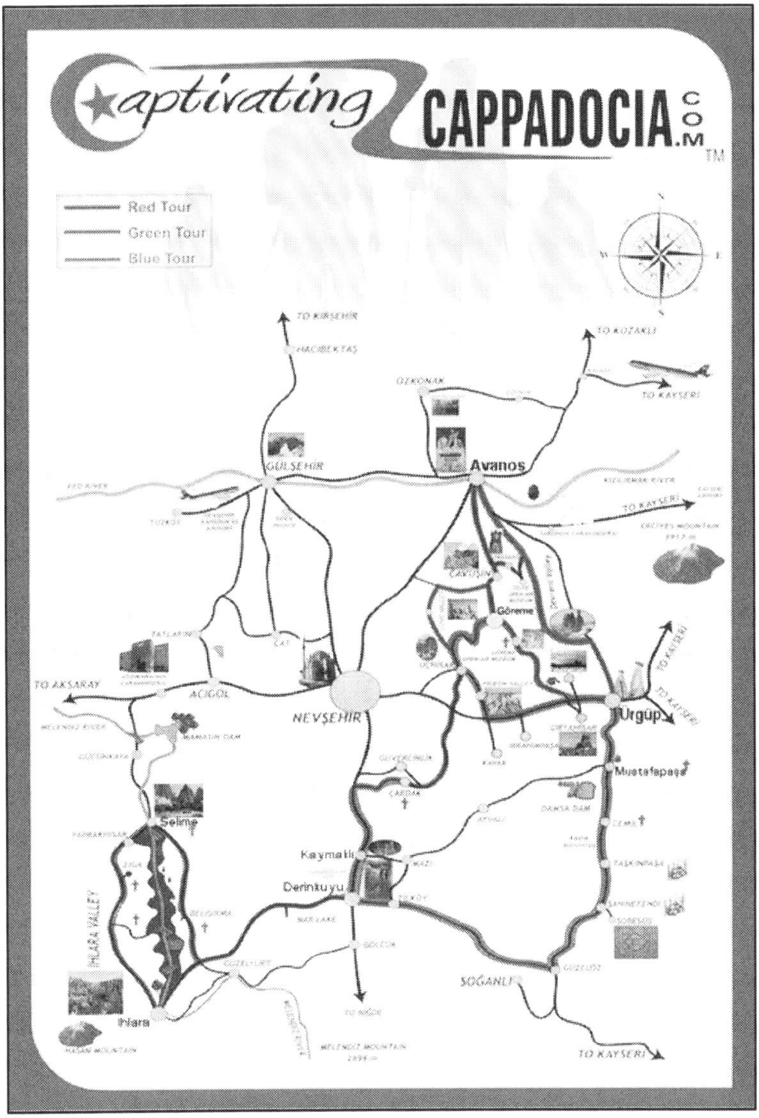

MAP 4: CAPPADOCIA TOURS 2

My wife thought this homemade map does a better job of capturing the big picture of the different tours. It is not so helpful for specific sites but does give you a quick sense of what parts of the region are covered by each tour.

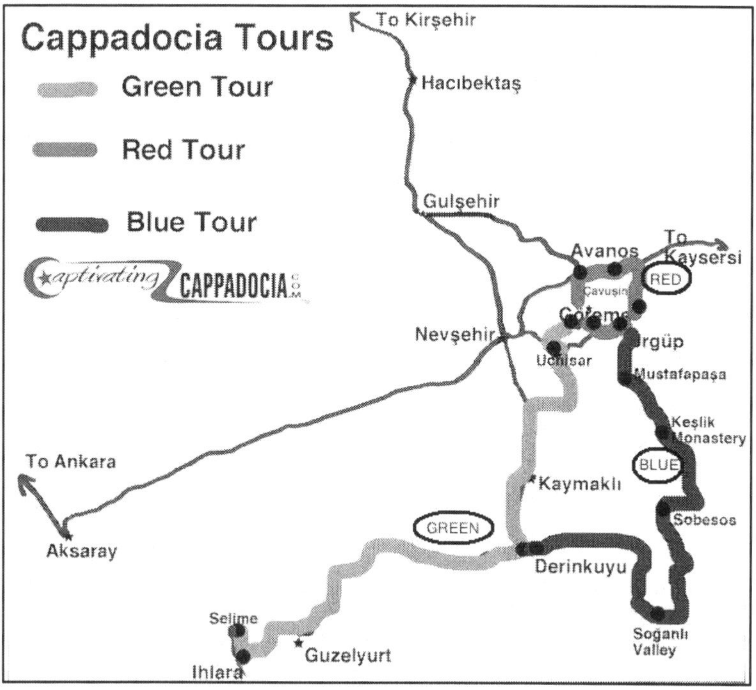

MAP 5: CAPPADOCIA WALKING MAP

This map highlights the main valleys of Cappadocia as well as the key sites around Göreme.

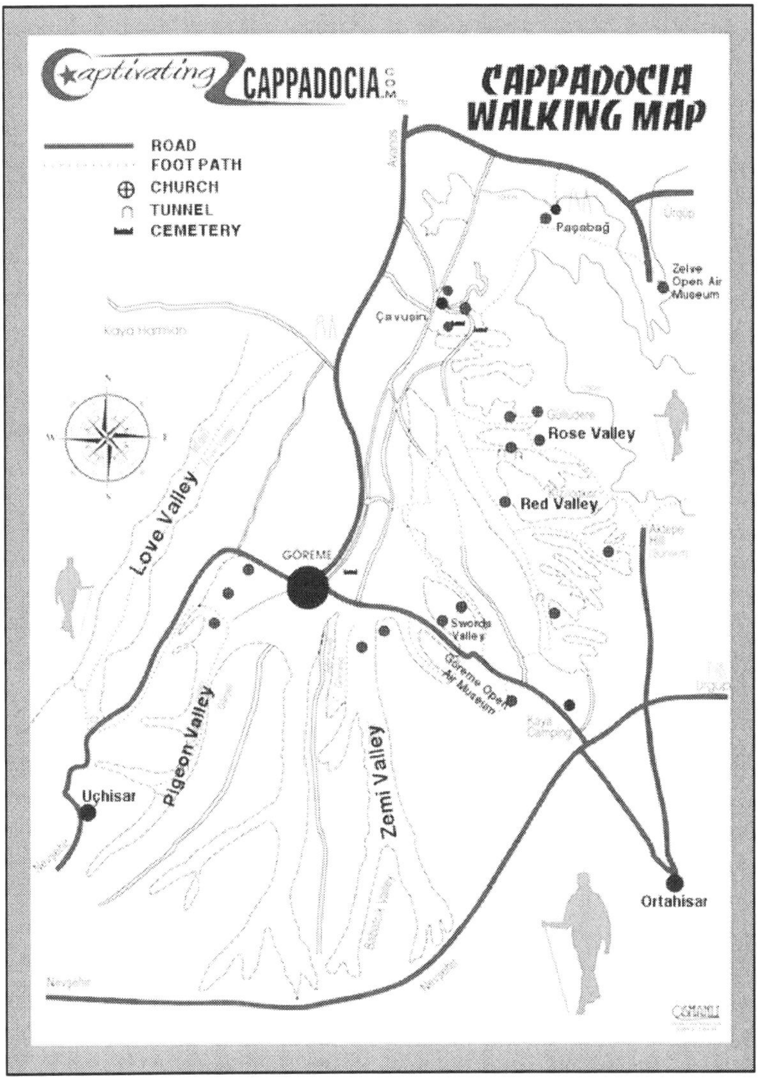

MAP 6: CAPPADOCIA HIKING MAP

This map provides another view of the valleys and hiking trails delineating the degree of difficulty of the different options.

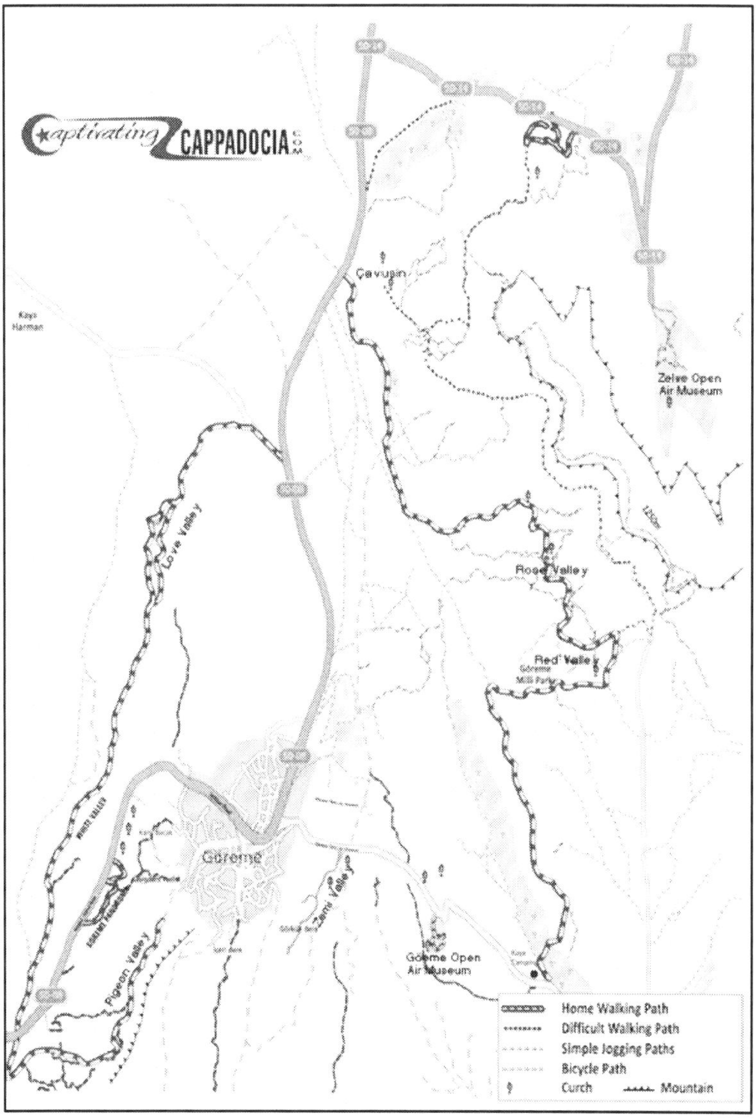

ACKNOWLEDGEMENTS

I know it is cliche but having finished this process I can wholeheartedly say that although I am the writer of this book, it would never have come into being without the help/work of many precious people.

Thank you to **Richard and Diane Dillard** who adopted me at birth and raised me with as much love as any natural-born child has ever received. They worked hard to give me the best life possible. Of the many things I have received from them, a life of faith, a heart of generosity, and a love of reading probably played the most into inspiring this book.

Also, my brother, **Duffy Dillard**, played a significant role in making me the man I am today. I am glad we both lived long enough for me to see the light and apologize for terrorizing him so much when we were kids. I am grateful he accepted and forgave me.

I am thankful for my amazing children, **Emily, Hudson, Hayden, Keaton, Colton, Kaylie,** and **Weston**, who were constantly encouraging and with whom I explored most of the places described in this book. You are each a gift from God to me, and I love you.

I dedicated this book to my wife, **Laurie**, but want to also thank you here for your expertise in editing the manuscript. This book has over 80,000 words but that is very few compared to what I would need to describe how wonderful you are and how much I love you.

Christian Dedrick has been a close friend since 1993. We have worked together in four different countries, participated in each other's weddings, been there when our kids were born, supported each other during very difficult times, shared the depths of our hearts, and together watched God do amazing things in and around us.

I would not not be who I am if not for Christian. Your work on the website has been invaluable. I cannot imagine a better blessing to give my readers than that they may have a friend like Christian.

Aaron Moss played a significant role early on, welcoming us to Cappadocia, introducing us to his many friends, and helping with the blog. I have never met anyone with as strong a gift at making a community a safe place for people to really know and trust each other.

The **people of Cappadocia** have been wonderful hosts since we moved here in 2011. There is no way I can list all of them here, but I will point out a few who have been especially helpful to us and to the creation of this book.

Faruk Keles, the owner of Kismet Cave House, welcomed us upon arriving and helped us find our house. He has always been ready to lend a helping hand in whatever need we had. Every winter he helps me find needed wood for heating our house. You have been a good friend. Thank you.

Oktay and **Rabia Parlak**, our landlords, have been like grandparents to our children. Their house, the top two floors of which we are inhabiting, has been a haven of rest for many people living in and visiting Cappadocia.

Çavuşin village has been a great place to live, and the people here have been very open to having crazy foreigners living among them. Especially the **Başyiğit family**, our next door neighbors, have been wonderful. The saying goes that you don't rent a house, you rent neighbors.

We would need to spend a million dollars to equal the value these neighbors have been to us. They have been patient and gracious, have taught us Turkish and how to cook Turkish food, welcomed us into their garden and home for tea, and have never hesitated to make us feel like family.

Yakup and **Mehmet Dinler**, owners of a few hotels including Kayakapi Premium Caves as well as Royal Balloons, have been incredibly generous to me and our family. They took us on our first balloon ride and invited us to their hotels. I stop by their offices every so often for a cup of tea and to catch up, and they have always dropped what they were doing and made me feel welcome. Thank you.

Tolga Akarcalı, owner of Taşkonaklar Boutique Cave Hotel, found me on Twitter shortly after I arrived in Cappadocia and invited me up for a cup of tea. Over the next few years we connected when he was in town. He was very generous towards me, and I am grateful. Thank you.

In addition, a number of expats living in Cappadocia have provided a grace-filled community for my family without which our time in this unique region would have been much less meaningful. **Mikey and Stacey, Mike and Joann, Chris and Kai, Alison, Aimee, Marcie, Lynn, Matt, Sara,** and **Jayson and Angie** have each been a gift to us. Thank you for loving us and our kids and the people of this region and making our time full.

And lastly, of course, I thank **Jesus,** the author of my life and purpose. All I am and have flows from Him. Thank You.

Duke Dillard

January 11, 2016

ABOUT THE AUTHOR

DUKE DILLARD

Born in 1969 in Munich, West Germany and adopted at four days old by an American couple serving in the US Army, I seemed destined for overseas travel and residence. My dad finished his military service, we moved back to the states, and I grew up in Chattanooga, TN, USA with one brother. At nine years old I had an encounter with Jesus Christ that forever altered my life as my desire has been to follow Him with everything in me ever since.

In 1987 I went to Washington & Lee University in large part because I wanted to play soccer and thought I could make the team, which I did. Four years later I graduated with degrees in Economics and German having spent six weeks in Germany during my sophomore year.

After graduating I moved to Los Angeles, CA to begin working with Teach For America as a middle school math and science teacher in the Long Beach Unified School District. Working in the "hood" was no problem; dealing with middle schoolers everyday nearly drove me to my grave! During my 3.5 years teaching in Long Beach Unified School District I met the love of my life (also a teacher) and in 1995 we married.

At that point I had quit teaching and started working for Crystal Cruises in their retail department (actually worked at a warehouse in San Pedro, CA).

After those years teaching middle school I put price tags on shirts and shorts for six months before I found it boring. I kept working for another year and a half so my wife and I could go on an amazing Alaska cruise.

In 1997 we moved to Kazakstan with our four-month-old daughter. Among other things we taught English and made some of the dearest friends anyone could meet. If you are looking for somewhere else to visit, the Kazaks are beyond compare.

In 2003 we moved to Uzbekistan with four children (two born while in Kazakstan and one while we were back in the USA). While there we directed an NGO office that built a soccer field for the people of the city, distributed clothes to poor villages, taught English and computer classes, partnered with the government to help the villages get clean water, all while trying to be a blessing to an amazing community. We received far more than we gave.

In 2007 we moved once again, this time with six children, to Ankara, Turkey where I got my MBA at Bilkent University. Child number seven was born in Ankara. After graduation we decided to settle in Cappadocia.

As mentioned earlier I have always enjoyed travel and adventure. This includes canoe trips down the Buffalo river in Arkansas as well as the Rio Grande river, hiking to the bottom of the Grand Canyon, riding my bicycle from Seattle to Boston, and trips to Mexico, Canada, Russia, Europe, Thailand, Singapore, and the Philippines. But with all of that I can honestly say that there is no place I would rather be than in the arms of my gorgeous wife surrounded by our seven precious kids.

Our Family

WEBSITE: **www.captivatingcappadocia.com**

EMAIL: **dukedillard@captivatingcappadocia.com**

FACEBOOK: **@CaptivatingCappadocia**

TWITTER: **@CaptCappadocia**

OTHER BOOKS BY DUKE DILLARD

Captivating Cappadocia ebook series

The Comprehensive Guidebook to the Heart of Turkey

This first book in the Captivating Cappadocia series is also available as an ebook.

Up to 3 Days in the Heart of Turkey

The second book in the Captivating Cappadocia series was written specifically for visitors looking to make the most of the limited time available.

1, 2, & 3 Day Itineraries for the Heart of Turkey

The third book in the Captivating Cappadocia series provides detailed itineraries for one, two and three days.

OTHER BOOKS BY BIRDS OF A FEATHER PRESS

The Bodrum Peninsula Travel Guide: Turkey's Aegean Delight

The Gümüslük Travel Guide: Bodrum's Silver Lining

INDEX

Symbols

10% discount, 12
24 hour, 149–150, 152

A

activities, 6, 21, 37, 55, 83, 88, 90, 95–96, 99, 149, 155–156, 159, 161
Adana, 11, 39, 122
airlines, 9–10
  Atlas Global, 10
  Onur Air, 10
  Pegasus Airlines, 10
  Turkish Airlines, 9–10
airport, 5, 9–10, 12, 82, 150, 152, 324; *see also Argeus Travel Airport Shuttle; Kayseri Airport; shuttle*
Aksaray, 3, 91, 169
Ankara, 9, 11, 13, 332
Antalya, 9, 11, 13, 35, 82
anthropology, 199, 202, 207
Archangel Michael Church, 47
Argeus Travel Airport Shuttle, 10
Ariarathes I, 169
ATS Fly Transport, 10
attractions, 6, 27, 36–37, 41, 45, 83–84, 88, 94, 105, 156, 161, 170, 195, 260, 276
authentic, 15–18, 114, 193
autumn, 6
Avanos, 15–17, 19, 22, 27, 41, 43, 69, 79, 85–87, 90–97, 105–106, 113–114, 122, 137, 143, 151, 193–195, 222–224, 229, 237, 242, 256–258, 271, 274, 287–288, 291–292, 294–295, 301–303, 322

B

balloon, 5–6, 21, 31, 41, 46, 51–57, 59–63, 65–79, 83, 88, 95, 112, 139, 149–150, 153, 155, 159–161, 163, 194, 210–211, 217, 231, 255, 264, 269–272, 297–298, 307, 319, 321–322, 330
books, 167, 173, 199–200, 202, 204–206, 208, 333
breathtaking, 17, 22, 25, 40, 87, 151, 195, 221, 224, 265, 271, 292
budget, 9, 13, 17, 22, 24, 35–36, 60, 90, 107–108, 115, 131, 138, 147, 256, 291
bus, 11, 13, 16–18, 26, 85–86, 89, 96, 98, 103, 105–106, 111–112, 150, 152, 155, 159, 222, 226, 229–230, 232, 236, 242, 257, 282, 287, 323
  bus companies, 11
  bus station, 16–17, 89, 96, 98, 105, 111–112, 150, 152
Byzantines, 169

C

camping, 29–33, 92, 97, 223
Cappadocia, 3, 5–7, 9–13, 15–19, 21–26, 29–30, 32, 35–42, 44–46, 48–49, 51–57, 59, 61, 65, 67, 73–74, 76, 81–85, 88–90, 93, 95–99, 101, 103, 105–111, 113–115, 119, 121–123, 125, 127, 129–131, 133–141, 143–144, 147, 149, 152–154, 156, 159–162, 165, 167, 169–189, 191, 193–197, 199, 201, 203, 205, 207, 209–219, 221–227, 234–253, 255–265, 267, 269–271, 273, 275–277, 279, 281–283, 285, 287–289, 291–299, 302–303, 307, 322–330, 332–333
Cappadocia Maps, 307, 323–324, 326, 328
car rental, 314
  Avis, 12

Enterprise, 12
Hertz, 12
cave church, 16, 39, 42, 48, 83–84, 86, 150, 162, 170, 195, 197, 223, 232–233, 248, 256–258, 264–265
cave hotel, 16–19, 23–27, 109, 134, 194, 322, 330
christian, 47–48, 170–175, 177–178, 183, 185, 187, 202, 207–208, 216, 257, 259, 264, 275–276, 281, 329
church, 16–17, 39–40, 42, 46–48, 83–86, 150–151, 162, 170–175, 177–179, 182–185, 187, 194–195, 197, 201, 223, 232–233, 236, 245, 248, 255–262, 264–267, 274, 276–277, 283, 286–288, 309
cultural show, 160, 167, 301–302; *see also Turkish night cultural show; Whirling Dervish Shows*
culture, 134, 152, 162, 172–173, 185, 187, 191, 199, 202–204, 206–207, 277, 303–304

D

Damat Ibrahim Pasha, 171
Derinkuyu Underground City, 37–38, 45, 48, 152, 213, 274, 276
Devrent Valley, 41
discount, 12, 21–25, 51–52, 65, 81, 88–89, 96, 103, 107, 109, 111, 159, 307, 319, 321–322
discount offers, 307, 321–322
DIY tours, 36
drinks, 37, 39, 41, 43, 45–46, 66, 112, 117–118, 120, 122, 124, 126–128, 301

E

emergencies, 103

F

fairy chimney, 16–18, 37, 40–41, 44, 53, 60–61, 84, 87, 139, 151, 162, 176, 191, 201, 221–225, 229, 236–237, 239, 241, 248, 258–259, 268, 271, 296
fall, 5–6, 36–37, 41, 45, 52, 92, 117, 125, 154, 169–170, 175, 187, 224, 292–293; *see also seasons*
fiction, 199, 205
fly, 6, 9–10, 13, 51–53, 55–57, 59–60, 69–71, 74–75, 78–79, 83, 211, 269–270, 272, 298, 321

G

Gaziemir Underground City, 17, 260, 288
geology, 46, 167, 191, 201
gifts, 84, 103, 129, 138–140, 151, 174
Göreme, 12, 15–19, 23–24, 26, 29–33, 37–38, 40–43, 46, 48, 53, 67–68, 70–79, 81, 84–87, 89–94, 96, 105, 108–112, 129, 132, 134, 140, 149–153, 155–156, 160–162, 167, 176, 193–194, 212, 214, 222–227, 229, 235–237, 245, 248, 250, 257, 260, 262, 264, 269, 271, 274, 280, 288, 291–296, 321–322, 324, 327
Göreme Open Air Museum, 37, 41–42, 75, 96, 149–152, 155, 161, 167, 212, 223, 225, 264
green tour, 37–38, 44, 46, 84–85, 87, 152, 161, 225, 249–250, 276
Gregory of Nazianzus, 170, 172, 174–175, 177–180, 182–184, 186
Gregory of Nyssa, 172, 175, 180, 185, 187, 189
Guzelyurt, 15, 17, 24, 215, 219, 255, 260–262

H

Helios Transfer, 10
hiking, 16, 18, 37, 48, 86, 90–91, 95, 107, 150–151, 155, 161, 167, 221–222, 224–226, 232, 234–236, 238, 240, 242, 244, 246, 248–250, 252, 307, 328, 332
Hisar, 18, 25, 87
historical, 17–19, 25, 48, 160, 169, 178, 193, 195–196, 204, 255, 260–262, 264, 277
history, 18, 38, 42–43, 46–48, 52, 134, 167, 169–172, 174, 176–178, 180, 182–186, 188–189, 195, 197, 199–201,

203–204, 207, 216, 249, 260, 262, 269–272, 274–275, 278, 280–281
Hittites, 39, 43, 48, 170, 274–275, 280–281
horseback riding, 162, 167, 291–296
Hot Air Balloon, 5–6, 41, 51–52, 54–57, 59–60, 62, 65–68, 70, 72–74, 76, 78, 88, 139, 149–150, 159, 264
hotels, 6, 15–19, 21–27, 29, 38, 41, 46, 49, 63, 71, 77, 84–85, 92, 99, 117, 134, 136, 167, 193–194, 196, 232, 257–259, 307, 321, 330

I

Ibrahimpaşa, 17, 94, 114, 193, 196, 259
Ihlara Valley, 37, 39, 87, 97, 152, 156, 161, 221, 225, 249, 252, 260, 275, 288
Imagination Valley, 224, 241–242
intercity bus, 16–17, 98
internet, 29–33, 63, 70–71, 73, 76, 78–79, 88, 172, 311
Islam, 170, 205–206
Istanbul, 9–13, 59–60, 67, 71, 74, 79, 114–115, 130, 182, 191, 195, 202, 207, 287, 292, 298, 323
itinerary, 54, 87, 145, 147, 151–152, 155, 157, 161–163, 195, 255, 259, 262, 301, 333
Izmir, 9–10, 13, 135

J

jeep safari tours, 167, 297–298

K

Kamil Koç, 11
Kaymaklı Underground City, 281–282
Kayseri, 3, 10, 13, 15, 19, 91–92, 98–99, 123, 169, 172, 174–175, 179, 195, 276, 324
Kayseri Airport, 324
keepsake, 103, 138
Keslik Monastery, 45–47, 257
kids, 95–99, 122, 124–125, 138–139, 262, 272, 276, 329–330, 332
Kirşehir, 3

L

language, 57, 59, 66–79, 84, 151, 172–173, 194, 201, 203, 307, 311–312
Love Valley, 17, 53–54, 96, 223, 229–231
lunch, 35–37, 39, 41, 43, 45–46, 48, 90, 94, 108, 112, 122, 150, 152–153, 298–299, 302

M

Map, 108–115, 171, 201, 222–225, 229–230, 232, 235, 241, 245, 249, 262, 307, 323–328
market, 29–33, 91, 123, 125, 197
Metro, 11
meze, 48, 117, 119, 127

N

Narligöl crater lake, 17
Nevşehir Seyahat, 11
Nigde, 169

O

off the beaten path, 22, 27, 95, 108, 161, 167, 255–258, 260, 262, 264, 266, 268
Ökonak Underground City, 286
Ottoman Empire, 170, 195, 200, 202, 259

P

packaged tours, 35–36
panoramic, 17, 37, 59, 115, 194, 232–233, 236, 271, 293, 298
Paşabağ, 16, 43, 87, 96, 162, 194, 225
Persians, 169
Personal anecdote, 22–26, 81–82
photo tour, 227, 230, 233, 237, 242, 245, 251, 266, 278
Pigeon Valley, 18, 37, 40, 115, 135, 193, 222, 225–229, 299
politics, 172, 199, 203, 257
pottery, 16, 37, 41, 43, 85, 93–95, 129, 136–138, 140, 151–152, 162, 194

price list, 12, 89–90, 92–93, 95–96, 98, 106, 307
prices, 9, 12, 21–22, 24, 30–33, 43, 52, 65, 96–98, 106, 110–111, 130–131, 137, 139–140, 143, 307

R

Red River, 16, 136, 194, 258
restaurants, 6, 16–19, 24, 43, 84, 103, 107–108, 110–111, 113–115, 117–124, 126–127, 134, 136, 162, 167, 194, 196, 259, 307, 319, 321–322
ripped off, 85, 129–130, 134
rock fortress, 18
Rose/Red Valleys, 223, 232–233
Red Valley, 42, 54, 150, 223, 232–234, 258, 271, 293, 298–299
Rose Valley, 16, 194
RVs, 29–33

S

safety, 51, 53–55, 57, 62, 65, 171, 269
seasons, 5, 36, 52, 92, 222, 265,; *see also fall,; spring,; summer,; winter*
Seljuks, 169–170
shopping, 36–37, 41–42, 45, 84–85, 94, 98, 103, 129–130, 132, 134, 136–138, 140, 149, 151, 153, 160, 162–163, 167, 257, 260
shuttle, 10–11, 23, 26, 82
Silk Road, 12, 89, 96, 322
Sinasos, 18, 110, 162, 193, 197, 259
ski slopes, 19
Sobesos, 45–47, 88, 257
souvenirs, 37, 40–41, 45, 140, 162, 221, 266, 278
special treats, 117, 126
spring, 6, 37, 41, 92, 97, 124, 191, 214, 256–257, 283,; *see also seasons*
St. Basil of Caesarea, 172, 174, 185
St. Stephanos Church, 47
Süha, 11
summer, 6, 37, 70, 91–92, 121, 149, 194, 224, 232, 256, 258, 265,; *see also seasons*
Sun Express, 10, 13
sunset, 17, 24, 84, 150–154, 156,

T

taxi, 11, 18, 26, 98, 115, 144, 150, 232, 235, 242, 256
tents, 29–33
things to do with kids, 95
three day, 159–163, 333
touristy, 15–18, 91, 95, 108, 122, 193, 195, 324
tours, 3, 5, 16, 18, 21, 35–36, 38, 40–46, 48, 75, 81–84, 89–91, 94, 134, 147, 153, 159, 167, 170, 197, 256–257, 273, 291–295, 297–298, 307, 325–326
blue tour, 35, 45, 88, 90, 149, 153, 256, 282
private tours, 36
red tour, 35, 41, 44, 84, 87, 152, 224, 242
train, 293
transfer, 9–10, 105, 183
transport, 10, 16, 19, 61–62, 66–79, 149, 155, 195, 235,; *see also ATS Fly Transport,; bus,; bus companies,; bus station,; intercity bus,; public transportation,; train*
travel memoir, 199, 203
Turkish carpet, 129, 131, 133, 139, 196
turkish food, 98, 103, 112–113, 117–118, 120, 122, 124–126, 128
Turkish language, 307, 311–312
Turkish night, 92–93, 150, 152, 154, 156, 160, 163, 167, 301–302
Turkish night cultural show, 167, 301–302,; *see also cultural show*
Turkish village, 16–17, 193, 196, 204, 259, 288
Turks, 47, 85, 91, 107, 118, 120–121,

123, 126–127, 143, 170, 200, 202–204, 257, 277, 309, 311
two day, 153–154, 156, 161

U

underground cities, 48, 84, 95, 167, 170, 193, 197, 255, 273–274, 276, 278, 280–282, 284, 286, 288
undiscovered Cappadocia tour, 36, 85, 88
Ürgüp, 12, 15–19, 25–26, 31, 41, 44, 68, 72–73, 75–78, 82, 85, 87, 90–91, 93–94, 96, 105–106, 108–109, 125, 127, 129, 135, 140, 151, 161, 193–194, 196, 218, 224, 232, 235–236, 242, 256–257, 259, 270, 288, 322

W

weather, 5–7, 25, 37, 52, 83, 89, 92, 98–99, 111–112, 150–151, 153–154, 156, 160, 221, 251, 283
what to do, 83–84, 86, 88, 90, 92, 94, 96, 98, 103, 121, 155, 162
what to see, 15, 83
Whirling Dervish Shows, 303–304; *see also cultural show*
wine, 19, 49, 93–94, 108, 127, 129, 134–137, 140, 151, 162, 195–196, 233, 258, 288
wineries, 18, 127, 134–136, 196
winter, 5, 16, 29, 36–37, 39, 53, 91–92, 97–99, 115, 174, 256, 264, 275, 283; *see also seasons*

Z

Zelve, 87, 90, 105, 161–162, 194, 221, 225, 262
Zelve Open Air Museum, 90, 162, 194, 225, 262
Zemi Valley, 151, 155, 224, 235–237, 239–241